The Way Back

RESTORING *the* PROMISE *of* AMERICA

F.H. Buckley

ENCOUNTER BOOKS  NEW YORK · LONDON

First American edition published in 2016 by Encounter Books,
an activity of Encounter for Culture and Education, Inc.,
a nonprofit, tax-exempt corporation.
Encounter Books website address: www.encounterbooks.com

Manufactured in the United States and printed on
acid-free paper. The paper used in this publication meets
the minimum requirements of ANSI/NISO Z39.48—1992
(R 1997) (*Permanence of Paper*).

FIRST AMERICAN EDITION

LIBRARY OF CONGRESS CATALOGING-IN-PUBLICATION DATA
Names: Buckley, F. H. (Francis H.), 1948– author.
Title: The Way Back : Restoring the Promise of America / F.H. Buckley.
Description: New York : Encounter Books, 2016. | Includes bibliographical
references and index.
Identifiers: LCCN 2015028091| ISBN 9781594038570 (hardcover : alk. paper) |
ISBN 9781594038587 (ebook)
Subjects: LCSH: Social mobility—United States. | American Dream. | Elites
Social sciences)—United States. | United States—Economic conditions. |
United States—Social conditions. | United States—Politics and government.
Classification: LCC HN90.S65 B83 2016 | DDC 305.5/130973—dc23
LC record available at http://lccn.loc.gov/2015028091

For Esther, Sarah, and Nick

Contents

PART III

Things We (Mostly) Can't Change: Technology, Taxes, Welfare, Culture, Genes

Acknowledgments

A GOOD MANY PEOPLE HELPED ME WITH THIS BOOK, AND I am very grateful. For his comments, and for our long conversations about Abraham Lincoln, I am greatly indebted to Allen Guelzo, the leading scholar on the sixteenth president, and who if pressed can provide a very credible imitation of Lincoln's accent.

Jonathan Clark, the eminent historian of the long British eighteenth century, gave this book a close reading and his wise advice on British constitutional history was most helpful. Jeff Broadwater has written the best biography of the never-too-much-to-be-praised George Mason, and kindly helped me with questions I had about my school's namesake.

My colleague, David Levy, was extremely helpful on regression analysis and for tips on where I might find bluegrass music. Dartmouth's Jason Soren's also gave very useful advice on the empirical portions of the book.

For their comments and help on questions of income inequality and immobility, I am indebted to Sarah Buckley, Miles Corak, Tyler Cowen, Chris DeMuth, Frank Fukuyama, Robin Hanson, Glenn Hubbard, Bob Levy, Tom Lindsay, Tom and Lorraine Pangle, and

John Samples. Brian Lee Crowley and the Macdonald-Laurier Institute brought me to Ottawa to debate Chrystia Freeland, now the Candian Minister of International Trade, on the subject of income inequality, and we also debated on CBC. She and I gave it as good as we could, as proxies for Laurier and Macdonald, respectively.

For his advice on U.S. tax law I am indebted to my colleague, Terry Chorvat.

Academic lawyers are quick to pick up on whatever is trendy in other disciplines, and twenty years ago there was a spurt of interest in evolutionary biology. We're due for a revival. As we age, and the "me" generation becomes the "them" generation, we'll be taking a greater interest in who comes after us, especially our children. Evolutionary biology is not my field, but I was lucky enough to be able to meet Robert Trivers at a program I organized. Five hundred years from now, when everyone else around today is quite forgotten, he'll be remembered.

Long talks with Tom Lindsay helped inform the chapter on education, and George Borjas has for many years been the person to whom I turned on questions about immigration policy. Ron Maxwell, the director of *Gettysburg* and *Gods and Generals,* is an astute student of politics and I enjoyed many helpful discussions with him on immigration matters. On criminal law matters, I was happy to rely on Jeff Parker and Ewan Watt, as well as Norm Reimer, the very able Executive Director of the National Center for Criminal Defense Attorneys.

On the rule of law, I owe a huge debt to George Priest, Michael Trebilcock, and Kip Viscusi for their help on our civil liability regime. Over bowls of pho, my friend Jim Wooton led me to understand how state courts treat out-of-state defendants unfairly, and what might be done to correct this. Stephen Magee's work was particularly useful, and from friends such as Eric O'Keefe and Wallace Hall I learned that we can't readily solve problems of corruption simply by passing more anti-corruption legislation.

Other friends, including Lord Black, Tom Pangle, Wlady Pleszczinski, Al Regnery, Jeff Sandefer, Roger Scruton, and Bob Tyrrell, heard me out and sharpened my ideas greatly. I owe a debt to Barre Seid, who gave me useful comments on the book, which I shall never be able to repay.

I also thank participants at workshops at the University of Texas, as well as the Texas Public Policy Foundation and the Heartland Institute for sponsoring book talks.

Sadly, two friends and colleagues from whom I learned so much about economics, Henry Manne and Gordon Tullock, passed away in the last year: Five other friends who strongly believed in the promise of America, Walter Berns, Jim Buchanan, Harry Jaffa, Leonard Liggio, and Douglass North, also died over the last two years. *Les chênes qu'on abat…*

The first injunction in the Hippocratic Oath is to hold one's teachers dear to one, and as I myself have taught for more years than I care to remember this increasingly seems like wise advice. And so I acknowledge my debt and gratitude to Saul Schwartz, who taught me of the common law's intrinsic excellence; and to Charlie Goetz, from whom I learned that economics can be fun, at least for its teachers.

George Mason law student Dan Schneider provided excellent research assistance, and if you're a judge or lawyer you'd do very well to hire him. For regressions and graphs I employed STATA software.

I also thank George Mason School of Law and George Mason's Mercatus Institute for their generous support. Cattelya Concepcion at the George Mason Law Library was extremely helpful in getting interlibrary loans and finding online materials for me.

My thanks as always go to Roger Kimball and to the superb editorial and marketing departments at Encounter Books, to Heather Ohle, Katherine Wong, Sam Schneider, and Lauren Miklos. For his very professional help editing the book I also thank James Hallman at WriteWorks. Dean Draznin and Anna Walsh were indefatigable publicists, from whom I could not have asked for more.

This book would not have been possible without the encouragement and invaluable organizational and editorial assistance offered from the very beginning by my wife, Esther Goldberg, whose help I cannot ever adequately acknowledge.

—F.H. BUCKLEY
Alexandria VA
October 14, 2015

The Way Back

Socialist Ends, Capitalist Means

IN 1977 THE UNITED STATES LAUNCHED THE VOYAGER SPACE probe with the goal of explaining planet Earth to the residents of other galaxies. Aboard was a gold-plated phonograph record, bearing greetings from UN Secretary-General (and former Nazi officer) Kurt Waldheim, as well as a sample of our music: Chuck Berry's *Johnny B. Goode* and three pieces by Bach. We don't know what the space aliens might have made of this. *Saturday Night Live* reported that we received a message back: Send more Chuck Berry. For his part, William F. Buckley thought that three selections from Bach was rather like boasting, but if so this was remedied by Jimmy Carter's lugubrious message: "This is a present from a small, distant world... We are attempting to survive our time so we may live into yours."

Notwithstanding its provenance, there wasn't anything particularly American about what was on the record. Suppose, then, that you were charged with selecting a single text (this time on a flash drive) to explain America to Kurt Vonnegut's Tralfamadorians. Would it be the Constitution? The Declaration of Independence? The Gettysburg Address? Very reasonable suggestions, all of them, but I'd choose a much-derided children's novel by Horatio

Alger, *Ragged Dick*. The book is never read today, which is a shame, since it is as witty as anything by Mark Twain and Alger's street-sharp urchin provides a fascinating look at the streets and slang of nineteenth century New York. Dick has the wiles to escape the con man's snares, but he isn't a thief and has a personal code of honor. He's also ambitious and smart enough to profit from the book's simple messages: that all labor is respectable, that poverty is no bar to advancement, that getting ahead requires education and saving one's money.

Those unfashionable messages, and not a lack of literary merit, explain why the book is scorned today. It celebrates, unabashedly, the traditional American virtues of open-handedness, pluck, and optimism. Mostly, it's a book about mobility, about making it in a country that welcomed those who wished to get ahead; and that message, not the Constitution or the Declaration, is at the heart of the idea of America. A boy with Dick's drive, intelligence and honesty would make his way where others lagged behind, for mobility wasn't the same thing as equality of outcome.

Ragged Dick is very much an American hero. Other cultures don't celebrate the rags-to-riches *arriviste* as Americans do. In France, Molière's *Le bourgeois gentilhomme* mocked middle class pretentions, and Honoré de Balzac told us that great fortunes which came out of nowhere were built on crime. The English gave us "ill-bred" and "bounder," words never heard in America. For the lowly born Pip, the dream of advancement was a cruel snare in Charles Dickens' *Great Expectations*. Not surprisingly, things were worse still in Russia, and in Dostoyevsky's Raskolnikov the desire to rise bred a murderous resentment.

Even in America, twentieth century writers lost faith in economic mobility. F. Scott Fitzgerald seemed to agree with Balzac about the criminal origins of new money, since the Great Gatsby's wealth came from illegal bootlegging. As for the promise of

economic success, Arthur Miller lectured audiences on its hollow-
ness. But America was a mobile society for most of the twentieth
century, and during Horatio Alger's time—the late nineteenth
century—a good many people followed Ragged Dick's path up the
ladder. More recently, however, the ladder has been rolled up, and
Alger's America is another country. The level of income inequality today is higher than at any time in the last 90 years. There's
even less mobility in America than in most First World countries.
That's new, and it will transform American politics.

We've already seen this, in the 2012 presidential election, and
even more so in the 2016 presidential campaign. The anger expressed by the voters, their support for candidates from far outside
the traditional political class, has little parallel in American history. From the Left there have been protest movements in the past,
but what we've seen on the Right is new and amounts to an entire
repudiation of complacent establishment Republicans. Presidential candidates who in years past might have seemed shoo-ins have
faltered, their places taken by a more rambunctious set of outsid-
ers who communicate through their brashness, their rudeness,
their belief that we are in crisis. To their more polite critics they
say: We are not so nice as you!

The Republican establishment seeks to persuade voters of its es-
sential niceness, but niceness has not closed the deal. On measures
of freedom provided by respected conservative and libertarian think
tanks, the United States has fallen like a rock (down to twelfth for
the Heritage Foundation, sixteenth for the Cato Institute). Once
the country of promise, America now lags behind many of its First
World rivals on measures of economic mobility and has spawned
an aristocracy. A broken education system, a dysfunctional immigration law, a decline in the rule of law, and a supercharged regulatory state have rolled up the ladder on which the Ragged Dicks of
years gone by climbed. Voters across the spectrum demand radical

change, and yet the Republican establishment seems content with minimal goals at a time of maximal crisis. Rejecting the Party establishment, the Republican insurgent might hope for less conservative heart, more conservative spleen.

The Republican insurgent has a vision of the good society that is not so different from that of the old-fashioned liberal of fifty years ago. For both, the goal is a society of opportunity, where all may rise, where we're judged by the content of our character, where class distinctions were something we left behind in the countries we came from. Unlike the modern liberal or progressive, however, the Republican insurgent believes that the best way to get there is through free markets, open competition, the removal of wasteful government barriers. The Republican insurgent pursues socialist ends through capitalist means.

The Left has complained of inequality. What rankles the Republican insurgent, however, is immobility, and in particular the idea that it might result from a set of unjust rules that advantage a new class of aristocrats. We might be prepared to accept the fact of deep income inequality if we thought that everyone stood the same chance of getting ahead, and that people were sorted out by their abilities. Ragged Dick is a desperately poor, orphaned bootblack, but he's accepted as an equal by his wealthy friend, Frank Whitney, and we're led to believe that they'll end up in the same place. Henry Fosdick, honest and intelligent but lacking Dick's ambition, will find himself a rung down on the scale. The Hibernian Johnny Nolan, honest but lacking in both intelligence and ambition, will end up yet another rung down. Those at the very bottom are not even honest, and an unpleasant end is prophesized for them. But what if we're not like that anymore? What if today's Ragged Dick lags behind, his place at the top taken by those who have gamed the system, whose wealth is founded upon illicit advantages? If that's the case, if America offers no better opportunities for advancement than other countries, then the core understanding of American Exceptionalism will have been lost.

This would be a tragedy, for income inequality and immobility are serious problems, and we'd all want to return to the levels of income equality and mobility of 50 years ago, if we could leave everything else the same, if we could do so without cost. That might seem impossible, for most of the things which have been proffered—free trade barriers, massive tax hikes and the like—would be enormously costly. But then there are other solutions which would give us an economy both wealthier and more just, an entrepreneurial society in which people would have a better chance of getting ahead. We'd all want to go there—unless we were one of America's aristocrats.

Things We Can't Change

As an ideal, income mobility wasn't there at the country's formation, but emerged later when Lincoln and the Civil War gave America a new birth of freedom, in which the opportunity to rise above one's station came to define the country's promise. If one had to pick the crucial moment it would be a little-known speech by Abraham Lincoln at an agricultural fair in 1859, when he worked out the implications of the Declaration of Independence in a country that was still half slave. From this everything else followed, the Civil War, the land grant colleges, the open door policy for immigrants, Ragged Dick's America.

Today, however, the United States is a highly unequal society and, what is far worse, a highly immobile society as well. Jobs have expanded at the very top and bottom of the economy, while middle class jobs have cratered. That's regrettable, for countries with greater economic equality have higher levels of civic participation and personal trust. People feel better about each other when the game doesn't seem to be rigged against them. They're also happier and less likely to support demagogues who promise greater equality but would restrict political freedom and threaten the rule of law to attain it. Finally, inequality and immobility are unjust when they result from special favors the government grants to its political friends and cronies.

So we'd want more income equality and mobility. Easier said than done, however. People on the Left have argued that inequality might go away if we could only raise taxes on the rich. However, the top U.S. marginal rates for individuals and corporations are amongst the steepest in the world, and capital gains taxes here are much higher than the First World average. Attacks on greed aren't going to do very much either. The acquisitive instinct (to give it a less emotionally charged name) is coded in the DNA of the species, and I haven't heard of plans to rewire our brains to eliminate it. In any event, as greed is ubiquitous, it can't explain why there's more immobility in America than elsewhere.

Nor are there any magic fixes in our welfare system, which is one of the most generous in the world. Not only is this a pretty good country to be poor in, but people at the bottom rung in America are amongst the richest people in the world. Moreover, the kinds of welfare improvements that get proposed are often self-defeating. For example, increasing the minimum wage would benefit some workers at the margin, but would also hasten the trend to automation, with store clerks replaced by check-out kiosks. Between 2007 and 2009 a Democratic Congress raised the minimum wage from $5.15 to $7.25 an hour, this as the economy plummeted and unemployment skyrocketed. There's no persuasive evidence that the higher minimum wage did workers any good.

Then there's the move to an information economy, free trade, and globalization. In the recent past, good jobs awaited high school grads on the assembly lines and in the factories of America, jobs that gave people a solid and secure footing in the middle class. Those jobs, however, are increasingly a casualty of an economy that requires higher levels of skill. High-tech jobs have increased in number, while low-skilled jobs are disappearing. In addition, free trade has moved low-tech jobs to countries with lower labor costs, while at the same time increasing the number of high-skilled jobs in America. Globalization brings Third World people into the middle class, but shrinks the First World's middle class.

We might not like what this has done to income equality and mobility, but there's not a lot we'd want to do about it. Or could do. We can't smash our computers, the way that 19th century Luddites smashed cotton looms, and expect we'd be doing anything other than shipping more jobs offshore. The same goes for free trade. Lower trade barriers have greatly strengthened the economy and increased the number of jobs overall, as American companies became better able to meet the challenge of foreign competition. A retreat from free trade would also encourage firms to incur the deadweight losses of lobbying for sweetheart trade barriers from politicians, in order to protect the firms from foreign competition.

There are also several reasons why we'd never expect to see perfect income mobility between generations. First, it always helps to have the head start that wealthy parents give one: better schools, better networks, better first jobs. That's why countries with high levels of income inequality are also countries with low levels of income mobility. From rich parents, rich kids. Second, and relatedly, the environment in which children are raised matters. Children raised by wealthy parents are less likely to come from broken homes, and will learn by example to value education. Compared to poor children, they're exposed to a much higher social and cultural environment. In addition, there's a developing empirical literature suggesting that the personal qualities ("phenotypes," for the geneticist) that are correlated with economic success are heritable. That is, we'd expect to see some correlation between the personal (phenotypic) attributes of parents and children.[1] A lot of things we thought to be random or a product of our environment seem now to be inherited, and this might also be true of the things which make people wealthy. If Lady Gaga was born that way, why not the rich?

Legacy Nation

A degree of aristocracy is thus to be expected in any society, and not merely expected but also natural. We are apt to think that economic inequalities are self-correcting, self-arighting, but it's not so; and the natural rights lawyer who said that all men are equal lied to us. Instead, equality cuts against the grain, and what is natural are differences, the differences between rich and poor, high and low. What is natural is aristocracy, the natural default position of any society, and not just aristocracy but a hereditary aristocracy. What is unnatural, unexpected, anomalous, the briefest of interludes in the world's long history of class distinctions, is Ragged Dick's America.

For a hereditary aristocracy to arise, only two things are needed, common to all of us: a bequest motive and relative preferences. The *bequest motive* is simply the desire to see our children do well, a sentiment that does not require an evolutionary explanation, but one which I nevertheless provide in Chapter 13. We are hard-wired to seek to pass on our genes, and this means that, like Deuteronomy, we distinguish between strangers and brothers.[2] We'll be willing to incur enormous sacrifices for children and near relatives, but for strangers to whom we are not related we have only a constrained sympathy. What that will leave us with is a world of family ties and the thick nepotism where sons succeed fathers in politics, business, Hollywood, art, and music.

The bequest motive is one of the strongest human impulses,

stronger even than the instinct for self-preservation. We read of parents who give up their lives to save their children, and marvel at this. But would we have done anything else? We were told we were members of a "me" generation, but it's not so. Instead, we sacrifice for our children, only dimly aware of the costs we incur in doing so, unless perhaps we recall how our parents sacrificed for us. If we should then want to see our children end up on top, in an aristocratic society, is that so very surprising?

The second needed thing, for an aristocracy, is *relative prefer-ences*. We have absolute preferences when we want something, and relative preferences when we also want more of it than the other fellow. And as we wish well for out children, given the bequest motive, we would want them to fare better than other people's children, given relative preferences. We would be willing to accept a poorer world, so long as our children end up on top. We might even prefer a world that leaves our children worse off, so long as everyone else fares worse still.

That's enough to kick-start an aristocracy. But for an aristoc-racy to persist over time, its members must be able to identify each other and form an alliance against the new men who wish to rise. Through their schools, their neighborhoods, their politics, they must be able to recognize each other. And of course the members of America's elite can do so. They'll have gone to Harvard, not Podunk U. They'll live in Wesley Heights D.C., and not Manassas VA. They'll subscribe to liberal politics and abhor the Tea Party. In all of this they'll recognize each other as members of a New Class that constitutes the country's elite and frames its policies, and in this way a society of peers and peasants has replaced Hora-tio Alger's country of equal opportunity.

Rising inequality in American has been blamed on the "one percent," the people in the top income centile making more than $400,000 a year. For those making less than that, bumper stickers on cars proclaim their drivers to be members of the 99 percent. The distinction between the two groups is useful, since income tax data permits us to identify the one percent. We know what they earn, what their jobs are and how they came by their money. They can serve as proxies for inequality generally. In truth, however, the one percent includes a very disparate group of people, the entrepreneurial gazillionaire and the car dealer making just a bit more than $400,000 a year. But it also includes members of the New Class whose unearned privileges are more questionable, who were given an unjust head start.

What I would do, then, is direct attention away from the super-rich whose wealth is derived from their entrepreneurship, their energy, their ideas, their basketball skills, their Hollywood films. As members of the one percent, they were the villains of the Occupy Wall Street movement of several years back. Yet there is nothing intrinsically objectionable about a one percent. By definition, every society has one. Let us turn, then, from the risk-taking entrepreneurs who constitute the very wealthiest of Americans, the 0.1 or the 0.01 percent, to the risk-averse members of the New Class, the one, two or three percent, the professionals, academics, opinion leaders and politically connected executives who float above the storm and constitute an American aristocracy. They oppose reforms that would make America more mobile, and have become the enemies of promise.

Every society has its upper classes, richer and more powerful than the common herd. In America, however, they form a tighter group, with their distinctive set of jobs, neighborhoods and beliefs. By comparison, the House of Lords and *Académie Française* are more democratic. In our personal habits, there's also a widening chasm between America's New Class and those below it on the scale. Charles Murray and Robert Putnam tell us that America's middle class increasingly mimics the underclass in its destructive vices, such as its high unwed birth and divorce rates, that are apt to condemn one to poverty.[3] Crucially, America's New Class wields a vastly disproportionate political power, almost unmatched in the First World, and supports policies that burden the Ragged Dicks. If we're less mobile than we used to be, that's importantly the reason. Technological change, globalization, genetic advantages, even greed, are to be found everywhere, and can't explain why we are more immobile than the rest of the First World. What those countries lack, however, is an elite with the clout of America's New Class.

The New Class is apt to think it has earned its privileges through its merits, that America is still the kind of meritocracy that it was in Ragged Dick's day, where anyone could rise from the very bottom through his talents and efforts. Today's meritocracy is very different, however. Meritocratic parents raise meritocratic children in a highly immobile country, and the Ragged Dicks are going to stay where they are. We are meritocratic in name only. What we've become is Legacy Nation, a society of inherited privilege and frozen classes.

I do not say that America's aristocrats consciously seek to live in an immobile society, but only that they act so as to bring it about. Between our desires and our actions a curtain is demurely drawn, and to know ourselves requires what Alain Finkielkraut calls La Rochefoucauld's pitiless *ne ques*.[4] What we take for virtue is frequently *nothing else but* the concurrence of several actions which our own industry or fortune contrives to bring together. Humility is often *nothing else but* a false submission that we employ to dominate others. What men call friendship is often *nothing else but* a prudent reciprocity of interests. While he loudly decries immobility, the self-satisfied member of the New Class nevertheless supports policies that make us less mobile. That's bad enough, but his self-deception only makes it worse.

Things We Can Change

With greater self-awareness, the American aristocrat might recognize that the barriers we have erected to income mobility are often unjust. The most obvious of these is a broken educational system. Our K–12 public schools perform poorly, relative to the rest of the First World. As for our universities, they're great fun for the kids, but many students emerge on graduation no better educated than when they first walked in the classroom door. What should be an elevator to the upper class is stalled on the ground floor. Part of the fault for this may be laid at the feet of the system's entrenched interests: the teachers' unions and the professoriate of higher education. Our schools and universities are like the old Soviet department stores whose mission was to serve the interests of the sales clerks and not the customers. Why the sales clerks should want to keep things that way is perfectly understandable. The question, however, is why this is permitted to continue, why reform efforts meet with such opposition, especially from America's elites. The answer is that aristocracy is society's default position. For those who stand at America's commanding heights, social and income mobility is precisely what must be opposed, and a broken educational system wonderfully serves the purpose.

America prides itself on being the country of immigrants. There's a bit of puffery in this, since there's a higher percent of foreign-born residents in Australia and Canada, and America ranks only a little ahead of Great Britain and France. Still, the country historically has been the principal haven for waves of immigrants (not to mention the 15 percent of people who were here already here as Native Americans or who were brought here as slaves). Before the Immigration Reform Act of 1965, the new arrivals added immeasurably to the country's economy, culture, and well-being.

Since then, however, the quality of the America's immigrant intake has declined. We're still admitting the stellar scientists of years gone by, but on average immigrants are less educated than they were in the past, or even than Americans are today (not the highest of bars). We're also incurring the opportunity cost of a broken immigration system, in the high quality immigrants we don't admit, and who either stay home or move to more immigrant-friendly countries. That burdens the country, but it's very Heaven for an American aristocracy, which can hire cheap household labor without worrying about competition from high-skilled immigrants.

For the Ragged Dicks who seek to rise, nothing is more important than the rule of law, the security of property rights, and sanctity of contract provided by a mature and efficient legal system. The alternative, contract law in the state of nature, is the old boy network composed of America's aristocrats. They know each other, and their personal bonds supply the trust that is needed before deals can be done and promises can be relied on. We're all made worse off when the rule of law is weak, when promises meant to be legally binding are imperfectly enforced by the courts, but then the costs of inefficient departures from the rule of law are borne disproportionately by the Ragged Dicks who begin without the benefit of an old boy network.

For all these barriers to mobility we can thank the members of the New Class, which dominates America's politics and constrains our policy choices. It is they who can be blamed for the recent run-up in American income inequality, more than anything else. The economy has become sclerotic, and the path to advancement over the last 40 and 50 years has been blocked by a profusion of new legal and regulatory barriers, all of which they have supported. The terrible schools, the broken immigration system, the decline in the rule of law—all of that is recent, and the member of the

New Class who professes to be surprised by the rise in inequality seems a wee bit hypocritical.

Of the New Class, I can write with some authority, since as a lawyer and a tenured academic I am one of its members. But then I aspire to be, like Franklin Roosevelt, a traitor to my class, and will seek to explain how the land of opportunity became class-ridden. How did it happen that, while this country became immobile, the American Dream is alive and well in Denmark? In particular, why is there such an enormous difference in mobility rates between the United States and the country it most resembles, Canada?

One can't account for the rise of an American aristocracy without answering these questions, and the reasons most often given aren't up to the task. Did the move to a high-tech world make the difference? But then it's not as though the rest of the First World is living in the Stone Age. As for globalization, that's by definition a worldwide phenomenon. America's growing inequality has been blamed on the disappearance of manufacturing jobs, lost to automation and globalization, but the manufacturing sector is larger in the U.S. (one in six jobs) than in, say, Canada (one in ten jobs).

We need to pay attention to cross-border differences. Those who tell us that inequality and immobility are our most pressing problems seem not to care overmuch why the rest of the world fares better. And that's taking American Exceptionalism a bit too far. If we seek to return to Ragged Dick's America, we need to know precisely why other countries are more mobile, and how we might follow their example.

That's where I am headed. To begin, however, let's examine how America became the land of opportunity, how the promise of income mobility came to define the very idea of America.

PART I

The Idea of America

A city ought to be composed, as far as possible, of equals and similars; and these are generally the middle classes. This is the class of citizens which is most secure in a state, for they do not, like the poor, covet their neighbors' goods; nor do others covet theirs, as the poor covet the goods of the rich; and as they neither plot against others, nor are themselves plotted against, they pass through life safely.

—ARISTOTLE, *Politics*

Up from Aristocracy

PHILADELPHIA WAS NOT UNUSUALLY HOT IN THE SUMMER of 1787, as is often supposed. The weather was cooler than normal and it often rained, as it did on the morning of Monday, June 18 when Alexander Hamilton stepped out from Miss Daley's boardinghouse. His walk would take him the three blocks to the Pennsylvania State House, where the delegates to the Constitutional Convention were meeting (the name Independence Hall came later), and where he served as a representative from New York.

Hamilton strode into the Assembly Room, past the guards, and took his seat at the table on the left, at the back of the room. Was he a little nervous? He was young, only 32—or possibly only 30, for his birth to a single mother on the West Indian island of Nevis was so obscure that historians cannot agree when it happened. Before him, on the dais, stood George Washington, the Convention's president, for whom Hamilton had served as aide-de-camp during the Revolution. The other delegates included Benjamin Franklin, James Madison, George Mason, John Dickinson, Gouverneur

Morris, and James Wilson. When he learned their names, Jefferson described them as "demigods" in a letter to John Adams.[1] It was an audience that might intimidate a person with more age and experience than Hamilton, who was about to deliver one of the most remarkable speeches in American history.

Alexander Hamilton Stumbles

The Convention was then at a standstill. On May 29, Edmund Randolph, Virginia's Governor, had presented what came to be called the Virginia Plan, which would have replaced the decentralized government of the Articles of Confederation with a strongly national constitution. The plan, drafted principally by James Madison, was supported by the large states of Virginia and Pennsylvania. On June 15 the small-states delegates responded with the rival New Jersey plan, which was much more decentralized. Until that point Hamilton had been silent. Now, on June 18, he would rise to speak.

Neither the Virginia nor the New Jersey plan would do, he said. He was particularly opposed to the New Jersey plan, but even the Virginia plan left too much power to the states. It was, "pork still, with a little change of the sauce."[2] In principle, said Hamilton, we might as well abolish the states, and in any event the national government should be given the power to veto their laws. By this point, the small state delegates were likely apoplectic, but Hamilton hadn't finished (he went on for five or six hours in all). In what followed he gave the most ringing endorsement for aristocratic government by any major American politician, then or now.

He began by praising the British constitution. Many of the delegates had good things to say about it, but Hamilton went further and doubted whether anything short of a constitutional monarchy would do for America. A republic could serve up nothing suitable for the man who would be president, and "the English model was the only good one on this subject."

> The Hereditary interest of the King was so interwoven with that of the Nation, and his personal emoluments so great, that he was placed above the danger of being corrupted from abroad.[3]

Perhaps we shouldn't be surprised by this. Monarchy prevailed everywhere else, and historian Gordon Wood has observed that, "we shall never understand events of the 1790s until we take seriously, as contemporaries did, the possibility of some sort of monarchy developing in America."[4] Still, this was much further than any of the other delegates would go, and Hamilton knew an American king wouldn't do. What he suggested instead was a lifetime appointment for the president during good behavior, a republican government but one as close to monarchism as republican principles would permit. Call the president an elective monarch, if you want, said Hamilton. That's just what the country needs. He would also have given senators lifetime appointment, during good behavior, which was his way of engrafting a British House of Lords onto a republican constitution. "Having nothing to hope for by a change," the senators would then form a barrier against the "pernicious innovations" of democracy.[5]

Hamilton wasn't the only delegate who was fearful of democracy. Many thought that the defects of the Articles of Confederation could be traced to an "excess of democracy,"[6] with its "turbulence and follies."[7] Nor was Hamilton without friends. Washington relied on him,[8] and Gouverneur Morris might silently have agreed with much of what he said. For the rest of delegates, however, Hamilton's aristocratic government was anathema, even when adorned in republican robes. Hamilton, they thought, would be quite prepared to accept the corruption they thought endemic to monarchies, with the fawning courtiers that surround a prince and the kings who trade off favors for support. That was what they had seen of colonial government, and they meant to have something better with a republic, a form of government in which they thought that private interests would be trumped by the public good.[9] What the delegates would have hated is the crony nation America has become, where ambassadorships are bought and sold in return for campaign contributions, and pay-for-play is the order of the day as much as ever it was in eighteenth century Britain.

Hamilton was so far outside the mainstream that when he finished his speech no one seconded it or even thought it necessary to speak against it. A few days later a delegate reviewed the various plans that had been presented, and of Hamilton said that, "though he has been praised by every body, he had been supported by none."[10] Hamilton recognized that he had marginalized himself, and chose to absent himself for much of the rest of the debate. He left on June 29, popped in on August 13, and returned to Philadelphia only on September 6, at the Convention's close. What the delegates adopted became our Constitution, but no one who reads their debates would ever think of consulting Hamilton on how to interpret it.

An Aristocratic Colony

Hamilton had come from the humblest of backgrounds, and it was ironic that of all the delegates he should defend aristocratic rule. It was equally ironic that the Virginia delegates should have objected to this, for their state had created a minor aristocracy in the Old Dominion, and the myth of a Cavalier Virginia was not entirely without foundation. The second generation of arrivals to the colony in the mid-seventeenth century included the younger sons of well-born Englishmen, who over the next century elbowed their way into social and financial eminence. The proudly self-assertive Tidewater planters along the James, the Rappahannock, and the Potomac, the slave-owning members of the Established Church, the Carters, Byrds, Lees, Fitzhughs, Beverleys, and Washingtons, aspired to the condition of English gentility in their homes, offices and manners.[11] There were no Blenheim Palaces in Virginia, but the Carter's Grove, Sabine Hall and Shirley plantations of the Carters, the Westover of the Byrds, the Stratford of the Lees, and the Mount Vernons left no doubt that their owners were masters of large fortunes.

Some concessions were made for local conditions, to be sure. The colonial Tidewater gentry dispensed with their periwigs and lace-ruffled cuffs in the hot Virginia summers, but at other times dressed like English gentry. Venturing forth, their carriages carried them down the sandy streets of Williamsburg, with postilions, drivers, and footmen dressed in the distinctive livery of their respective houses. Sword on hip, the planters bandied jests just short of the point where a duel was required, and sometimes past that point, as where someone was called a lout or a Scot. Or perhaps, for those more concerned to insist upon their honor, when they quarreled over the pronunciation of a word.[12] Their sons idled away the time in dancing, gambling, and horse-racing. Until 1784 Virginia asserted a claim over all the lands westward to the Mississippi, from Memphis to Manitoba. Had it not abandoned its territorial ambitions, the national pastime today might be riding to hounds and not baseball.

Great families augmented their wealth through profitable marriages, producing the thickest of family connections amongst them. The Byrds intermarried with the Carters and Culpeppers, and the Washingtons were connected to the Lees, Beverleys, Randolphs, and Jeffersons. By the nineteenth century, the Virginian's love of family had turned into ancestor worship. John Randolph of Roanoke, Thomas Jefferson's cousin and a descendant of Pocahontas, lovingly recorded the names of all his ancestors and relatives in a book. "I am an aristocrat," he said. "I love liberty. I hate equality."[13] Even today one can while away an idle afternoon by asking a Virginia docent if Robert E. Lee was a fifth as well as a double-third cousin of George Washington.

Virginia lacked banks, and great landowners became a source of capital in an economy fueled by the promissory notes they gave to the younger men they sponsored. Those a notch down on the financial or social order would look up to wealthy patrons, for open-handed liberality was prized as an aristocratic virtue; and in this way networks of interest were created throughout what was an essentially hierarchical society.[14] Rising men, such as George Washington and Thomas Jefferson, looked for "friends" amongst the great planters, people such as Lord Fairfax to whom they could turn for credit, advice, and advancement. For the planters who mentored them, the relationship offered the prestige and power that came from an entourage of dependents. In this way, the Tidewater planters became what Gordon Wood describes as the strongest aristocracy that America has ever known.[15]

Children of the gentry were taught to be conscious of their position and to respect their superiors. The sixteen-year-old George Washington dutifully copied out *110 Rules of Civility & Decent Behavior in Company and Conversation*, to remind him of what was expected of a Virginia gentleman.

> 1. Every Action done in Company, ought to be with Some Sign of Respect, to those that are Present.
>
> 19. Let your Countenance be pleasant but in Serious Matters Somewhat grave.
>
> 25. Superfluous Complements and all Affectation of Ceremony are to be avoided, yet where due they are not to be Neglected.

26. In Pulling off your Hat to Persons of Distinction, as Noblemen, Justices, Churchmen &c make a Reverence, bowing more or less according to the Custom of the Better Bred, and Quality of the Person.

29. When you meet with one of Greater Quality than yourself, Stop, and retire especially if it be at a Door or any Straight place to give way for him to Pass.

36. Artificers & Persons of low Degree ought not to use many ceremonies to Lords, or Others of high Degree but Respect and highly Honor them, and those of high Degree ought to treat them with affability & Courtesy, without Arrogance.[16]

People so self-conscious of their dignity are not given to familiarity or levity, and Washington was no exception. During the Convention Hamilton dared Gouverneur Morris to greet Washington and pat him on the shoulder. Morris accepted the challenge, and at a reception walked up to Washington, bowed and, laying his hand on Washington's shoulder, said, "My dear General, I am very happy to see you looking so well." Washington withdrew the offending hand, stepped back and glared at Morris until he retreated. Perhaps Washington had remembered the sixty-fourth of his Rules of Civility:

> Break not a Jest where none take pleasure in mirth. Laugh not aloud, nor at all without Occasion, deride no mans Misfortune, though there Seem to be Some cause.

Later Morris told Hamilton that, though he had won a bet, he would never repeat the attempt at familiarity.[17]

While their plantations kept the Virginia gentry busy, they aspired to an aristocratic idleness.[18] They were forced to deal with the merchants and tradesmen who lived in their towns, but had little love for them. "Let your Discourse with Men of Business be Short and Comprehensive," was Washington's Rule 35. To finance their purchase of Hepplewhite chairs and all the latest clothing from London, the planters sold future interests in their tobacco crops to the Scottish factors of Norfolk and Alexandria, and after a financial crisis in the early 1770s found themselves indebted to the hilt to a set of creditors increasingly anxious about the direction American politics was taking. Their impudent demands for payment dismayed the planters, who had been accustomed to easy credit, and for whom the Revolution amounted to a welcome bankruptcy petition in which debts to British creditors were effectively discharged. No one profited from this more than the planters, for Virginians accounted for nearly half (£1.4 million) of all American debts owed to British creditors at the Revolution, and it has even been argued that this helps explain why the most aristocratic of all the colonies rebelled.[19] The debt crisis is only a part of the story, however, and perhaps a small part. Something else had happened to the way the Virginians understood the relation between man and the state.

A Revolution of Ideas

George Mason was there first. In June 1776, as the delegates to the Continental Congress in Philadelphia debated whether to declare independence, back in Richmond Mason provided the justification for the break from Britain in the Virginia Declaration of Rights:

> Section 3—Government is, or ought to be, instituted for the common benefit, protection, and security of the people, nation, or community;...And...when any government shall be found inadequate or contrary to these purposes, a majority of the community has an indubitable, inalienable, and

indefeasible right to reform, alter, or abolish it, in such manner as shall be judged most conducive to the public weal.[20]

These ideas had been expressed before, by Algernon Sidney and
John Locke, amongst others. The Declaration of Rights was a legislative act, however, and that was new.[21]

Word of Mason's Declaration spread quickly throughout the
state. Thomas Jefferson, at the Philadelphia Congress, learned
of it and employed its theory of a right to self-determination in
drafting the Declaration of Independence. Jefferson would also
have noted the statement of individual rights in section 1 of the
Virginia Declaration.

> All men are by nature equally free and independent and
> have certain inherent rights, of which, when they enter into
> a state of society, they cannot, by any compact, deprive or
> divest their posterity; namely, the enjoyment of life and lib-
> erty, with the means of acquiring and possessing property,
> and pursuing and obtaining happiness and safety.

Jefferson's draft dropped Mason's reference to property rights,
added a nod to the unnamed Creator and provided a different spell-
ing for "inalienable," but otherwise simply cleaned up Mason's prose.

> We hold these truths to be self-evident, that all men are
> created equal, that they are endowed by their Creator with
> certain unalienable Rights, that among these are Life, Lib-
> erty and the Pursuit of Happiness.

Style matters. The Declaration of Independence is deservedly remembered, the Virginia Declaration of Rights not, and not just
because of the difference in political importance. Mason needed

an editor, and got a superb one in Jefferson, who himself benefited from Benjamin Franklin's pen. Nevertheless, the importance of Mason's draft as the inspiration for the language of the Declaration of Independence can scarcely be minimized.[22]

Mason and Jefferson took their republicanism to the next level by seeking to subvert aristocratic institutions. Section 4 of Mason's Virginia Declaration took aim at aristocracy's claim of political preference.

> No man, or set of men, is entitled to exclusive or separate emoluments or privileges from the community, but in consideration of public services; which, not being descendible, neither ought the offices of magistrate, legislator, or judge to be hereditary.

Jefferson too sought to eradicate aristocratic privileges. After serving in the Continental Congress, he returned to Virginia, where he served in the House of Delegates. One of his first acts as a Virginia politician was to sponsor a bill to reform the state's private laws, and he took particular aim at the system of primogeniture. This was a presumptive rule under which, if a person died without a will, all his property descended to his first-born son. The point was to preserve the integrity of family fortunes, and made an otherwise unappealing first-born son a very eligible bachelor in Jane Austen's *Persuasion*. Primogeniture was received in Virginia as part of its common law inheritance, even though it was much resented by younger sons such as Jefferson. Whether the rule really made a difference has been doubted, since a father could avoid it through an explicit devise in a will to his younger children.[23] Nevertheless, default rules have an expressive effect, signaling what the state regards as a reasonable rule of succession, and it was this that Jefferson wished to change in 1776. What he sought, he later recalled, was a "republican" code of laws, one in which "every fibre would be eradicated of ancient or future aristocracy."[24]

Mason was a wealthy planter from Virginia's Northern Neck, and a confidante of Washington. Jefferson's father owned a smaller farm, but his mother was a Randolph and he was related to many of the First Families of Virginia. How was it, then, that the two were so hostile to aristocracy? It's not as though we'd think either of them to be democrats today. The right to vote was severely limited, and Virginia adopted universal suffrage only in 1851, when landowning qualifications were abolished. Even then, women could not vote, nor could Mason's and Jefferson's slaves, of course.

Voters could not elect governors either, since they were chosen by the legislators under the 1776 Virginia Constitution that Mason had drafted and for which Jefferson had signaled his approval. "It would be as unnatural to refer the choice of a proper character for chief Magistrate to the people," said Mason, "as it would, to refer a trial of colours to a blind man."[25] Madison proposed the same thing in his Virginia Plan at the 1787 Philadelphia Convention. Senators would be chosen by the House of Representatives, and Presidents would be chosen from Congress, which Madison described as a "policy of refining the popular appointments by successive filtrations."[26] The lower orders would take their places in the state legislatures, while "the purest and noblest characters" in society would occupy the more senior places in the federal government.[27] That indeed was how the Framers thought that presidents would almost always be chosen, in the Constitution they gave us.[28]

All this would seem like an aristocratic form of government to us. But the Framers did not see themselves as aristocrats. They knew they would survive the filtration process, but they did not think their traits were heritable. Our own descendants, said George Mason, will in a short time be distributed "throughout the lowest classes of Society."[29] Those who wished well for their children would therefore want a constitution that worked for everyone, for the character and talents of one's children were hidden behind a veil of ignorance.

In the fullness of time, the Framers' constitution would become democratic. The president would come to be popularly chosen, and after the Seventeenth Amendment senators also would be elected by the people. The 1848 Seneca Falls Declaration echoed the Declaration of Independence in its demand for equality for women,[30] and the promise of equality in the Declaration of Independence was the promissory note that Martin Luther King, Jr. presented for payment at the Lincoln Memorial in 1963. The Framers' constitution was a sealed train, speeding through the night and emerging into the light on arrival.

The Invention of the
American Dream

NOT ALL OF THE DELEGATES TO THE 1787 PHILADELPHIA
Convention were the demigods Jefferson took them to be, and
George Mason looked down on some of them with the aristocratic
disdain of a Virginia planter.

> You may have supposed they were an assemblage of great
> men. There is nothing less true. From [New England] there
> were knaves and fools and from the states southward of Vir-
> ginia they were a parcel of coxcombs and from the middle
> states office hunters not a few.[1]

That's how people from other states have often seemed to Virginians. However, the delegates included sixteen lawyers, four judges,
seven politicians, four planters, and two physicians.[2] Twenty-
nine of them had undergraduate degrees, nine from Princeton,
four each from Yale and William and Mary, and three each from

Harvard and King's College (Columbia). Three had attended college in Great Britain, at Oxford, St. Andrews, and Glasgow. Six had been trained as lawyers at the Inns of Court in London.[3] Half were on Mrs. John Jay's dinner invitation list, the Social Register of the time.[4] By any standard, most were the aristocrats of America.

Did they know that the document they signed would sound the death knell for their class? Very likely not. They could not have imagined the changes in our politics, let alone the changes in our society, that would transform America.

A Natural Aristocracy

None of the Framers would have anticipated the social upheavals and political changes that have taken place since their day. They took aim at one kind of aristocracy, a hereditary one, but expected that a different kind of aristocracy would survive, an aristocracy of talent and republican virtue that would survive Madison's process of filtration and ascend to the highest political offices. What such a "natural aristocracy" would look like was, famously, the subject of a series of letters between John Adams and Thomas Jefferson in 1813. Friends at first during the Revolution, then antagonists in politics, they were at last brought together in retirement through their mutual friend, Benjamin Rush.

The reconciliation delighted Adams, who wrote long, teasing letters to his old friend. For his part, Jefferson wrote serious letters that acknowledged the differences that still separated them, taking up Adams' hint "that we ought not to die before we have explained ourselves to each other." The natural aristocracy, said Jefferson, was one of virtue or talents, and he contrasted this with an artificial aristocracy founded on wealth and birth. The latter, he said, was a "mischievous ingredient in government," which he trusted would

be rejected in popular elections.[5] All very well, replied Adams imp-
ishly, but "what chance have Talents and Virtue in competition
with Wealth and Birth?" Or beauty, he added, no doubt recalling
how he had been mocked as 'His Rotundity.' "Beauty, Grace, Figure, Attitude, Movement, have in innumerable Instances prevailed
over Wealth, Birth, Talents, Virtue and every thing else."[6] Then
there was the natural deference paid to eminent families.

> Our Winthrops, Winslows, Bradfords, Saltonstalls, Quin-
> cys, Chandlers, Leonards, Hutchinsons, Olivers, Sewalls etc
> are precisely in the Situation of your Randolphs, Carters and
> Burwells, and Harrisons. Some of them unpopular for the
> part they took in the late revolution, but all respected for their
> names and connections and whenever they fall in with the
> popular Sentiments, are preferred, ceteris paribus to all others.[7]

Yet suppose, added Adams, that Jefferson's natural aristocrats
overcame all of the prejudices of family names, and the preference
for beauty. Suppose that, as Jefferson imagined, voters would prefer
genius to birth, virtue to beauty, and that a meritocracy of intelligence and character were chosen to lead the country. Even then, said
the skeptical Adams, I would wish to place a check on their ambition.
No class of people can safely be given unlimited power over others.

More than Jefferson, the conservative Adams had a better grasp
on what the future would hold. Where Jefferson foresaw the popular election of natural aristocrats, Adams understood that voters
would be looking for things other than republican virtue in their
politicians. And where Jefferson thought that his natural aristocrats
would promote the public interest, Adams predicted the rise of modern interest group politics in which everyone looks out for number
one. Most of all, Adams expected that a form of hereditary aristocracy would survive, in the country's leading families.

Adams' Boston is more democratic today than in his day, or in the recent past. Cleveland Amory's *Proper Bostonians* told of a letter of recommendation written a hundred years ago for a scion of the city. "You will be more than satisfied with him. His father was a Cabot, his mother a Lowell, and further back there were Saltonstalls and Peabodys." From Chicago the prospective employer wrote back "unfortunately we were not contemplating using Mr. _____ for breeding purposes."[8] Even today, however, dynasties may still be found, for who can doubt that family connections matter in a country whose leaders bear names such as Clinton and Bush, and where the Kennedys and Pauls begin with a leg up. We like to think we live in an egalitarian society, but there's less social mobility than we imagine, and less we can do to change this than we think.

The Transformation of America

Neither Adams nor Jefferson anticipated how democracy would transform America in the nineteenth century. While both men still lived, states began to depart from the system of filtering presidential candidates by letting state legislators pick the electors. In the 1824 election, only a quarter of the states chose electors in this way, and four years later only two states did so. The 1824 election was also the last one in which the House of Representatives chose the president because no candidate obtained a majority of votes in the Electoral College. The prescient George Mason had predicted the rise of democracy. "Notwithstanding the oppressions & injustice experienced amongst us from democracy; the genius of the people is in favor of it, and the genius of the people must be consulted."[9] But even Mason failed to anticipate just how profoundly America would change over the next 50 years.

American society had indeed begun to change with the

Revolution. An early effort to create a hereditary social elite amongst members of the Revolution's officer class proved to be a major embarrassment for George Washington. After surrendering his sword in 1783, Washington enjoyed the company of his old comrades and allowed himself to be elected the president of their group, the Society of the Cincinnati. The problem, however, was that its members were seen to constitute an American aristocracy. Writing from France, Jefferson warned Washington that a single fiber left of the Society "will produce an hereditary aristocracy which will change the form of our governments from the best to the worst in the world."[10] Jefferson's fears proved unfounded, however. Today the Society's Washington headquarters, largely unused, may be seen across Massachusetts Avenue from the considerably more popular and meritocratic Cosmos Club, whose walls are graced with the pictures of members who have won Nobel or Pulitzer prizes or Presidential Medals of Freedom, people such as Henry Kissinger and Colin Powell, people not to be found in the club across the street. The Founders' descendants had returned to the general mass, as George Mason had predicted.

The change was most obvious to foreigners. Before the Revolution, English visitors to colonial America felt very much at home, especially when they came to Virginia. Its people, reported a British officer, were well-bred, polite, and affable.[11] By the 1830s, however, American society had radically changed, as a new set of visitors discovered. Now Americans seemed to embrace the world of business with an eagerness that appalled the European. Captain Marryat, the author of popular novels such as *Mr. Midshipman Easy*, visited America in 1836–37 and observed that "time to an American is everything, and space he attempts to reduce to a mere nothing.... 'Go ahead' is the real motto of the country."[12] It was democracy that had made the difference, said Alexis de Tocqueville. "In democracies there is nothing greater or more brilliant than commerce; it is what attracts the regard of the public and fills the imagination of the crowd; all energetic passions are directed toward it."[13]

Commerce had made ordinary Americans wealthy, but to the European visitor this had seemed a Faustian bargain, where culture and refinement had been traded away for money. The mother of Victorian novelist Anthony Trollope lived for several years in the States, and reported that the "polish which removes the coarser and rougher parts of our nature is unknown and undreamed of" in America.[14] Marryat had no better opinion of Americans. "Honours of every description, which stir up the soul of man to noble deeds—worthy incitements, they have none," he observed.[15] All of that had been bartered away in the pursuit of wealth. Politicians were the worst. "No high-minded consistent man will now offer himself" for public office, said Marryat. "The scum is uppermost.... The prudent, the enlightened, the wise, and the good, have all retired into the shade, preferring to pass a life of quiet retirement, rather than submit to the insolence and dictation of a mob."[16] Themselves the product of an aristocratic age, the Founders had created a society that had little use for men like themselves.

Not every American celebrated what had happened to their country, and the revolt against the new commercial democracy was nowhere stronger than in the South, especially when slavery was in question. Beginning with John C. Calhoun in 1837, southerners argued that poor northern workers, though free, were nonetheless "wage-slaves" of their employers. The slaveholders' scorn for northern life came naturally to them, and its roots maybe found in their long-held contempt for trade. One saw it in Washington's Rule 35 ("Let your Discourse with Men of Business be Short and Comprehensive"), and in Jefferson's paean to farmers in his *Notes on the State of Virginia*. "Those who labour in the earth are the chosen people of God, if ever he had a chosen people, whose breast he has made his peculiar deposit for substantial and genuine virtue."[17] Compared to them, thought Jefferson, the mobs of Northern factory workers were "cankers" that subverted laws and society.

By the 1850s, Southern apologists for slavery went further still to defend an aristocratic vision of society that came to be called the mud-sill theory. "Every social structure must have its substratum," wrote George Fitzhugh.

> In free society this substratum, the weak, poor and ignorant, is borne down upon and oppressed with continually increasing weight by all above. We have solved the problem of relieving this substratum from the pressure from above. The slaves are the substratum, and the master's feelings and interests alike prevent him from bearing down upon and oppressing them.[18]

The mud-sill is the base of a building, on the bare earth. Above it, by stages, the mansion is erected, to be inhabited by those superior people who are the carriers of civilization.

> Domestic slavery in the Southern States has produced the same results in elevating the character of the master that it did in Greece and Rome. He is lofty and independent in his sentiments, generous, affectionate, brave and eloquent; he is superior to the Northerner in every thing but the arts of thrift.[19]

Fitzhugh had taken aim at every institution of liberal democracy, from the English Revolutionary Settlement of 1689 with its Bill of Rights to the sentiments in the Declaration of Independence. His theory of class struggle resembled that of the *Communist Manifesto*, which he had read, with the difference that Fitzhugh sided with the upper classes. His attack on the materialism, individualism, and greed of a northern mercantile society is one which today's Occupy movement might applaud, did they not know where it came from.

Most Southern apologists for slavery were merely racists, sometimes taking their inspiration from biblical texts, sometimes seeking
a more up-to-date foundation in what passed for scientific racism.
Fitzhugh was a racist, of course, but he was also something more
than that. He simply liked slavery, and thought it inevitable. In de-
fending the institution, he foreswore any advantage he might derive
from what he saw as racial inferiority. Whites made good slaves too,
he thought, and he would not discriminate on the basis of race or
color. His was an equal opportunity slavery, and when he spoke of
northern wage-slavery he meant real slavery. Nineteenth century
industrial society had created a new class of slaves, with the difference that the callous Northern wage-slavery was so much worse
than the paternalistic slavery of the South.[20]

However it reads now, Fitzhugh's *Sociology for the South* was not an
especially radical book in its day. Today we would think Fitzhugh the
most extreme of right-wingers, but had not his British contemporary
Thomas Carlyle said much the same thing, and used the N-word to do
so?[21] On what might be taken for the Nineteenth Century British Left,
writers such as Carlyle, Charles Kingsley, and Charles Dickens (with
Mrs. Jellaby, his "telescopic philanthropist" in *Bleak House*) argued that
England's poor merited more concern than African slaves. Fitzhugh
had placed himself in the mainstream of a nineteenth century attack
from the Left and Right on the egalitarian political ideals of George
Mason and Thomas Jefferson. And his attack on social mobility required an answer, which it would receive from a most unusual place.

The Promise Renewed

The farmers who gathered in Milwaukee on September 30, 1859 for
the Wisconsin state fair were treated to displays and speeches about
modern agricultural improvements. There were presentations on

how to make champagne from gooseberries, prizes for the best pig, and a report on that noxious bird, the sapsucker. Some of the visitors might have stopped to listen to a visitor from Illinois, who had recently made a name for himself in a series of debates with Senator Stephen Douglas. Abraham Lincoln had accepted an honorarium of $100 to come to the fair, and one of the organizers, thinking they might as well get their money's worth, asked him to give a speech. Lincoln joked that he had not a platform to stand on, whereupon someone brought him an empty dry-goods box.[22]

Finding himself before an agricultural fair, a rising politician could be expected to dwell on the virtues of agrarian life, the honesty, industriousness, and high-mindedness of farmers. That's certainly what a Jeffersonian Republican would have said. But then Lincoln wasn't a Jeffersonian Republican. He came to politics as a Whig, and his beau ideal of a statesman was always Henry Clay.[23] Lincoln liked "internal improvements" (federal support for infrastructure projects), high tariffs to pay for them, and most of all the idea of social mobility in which everyone is provided with the opportunity to flourish. Besides, he had seen farming life back in Kentucky, and got out of it as quickly as he could. His views on agrarian society could be expressed in three words, says Lincoln historian Allen Guelzo: "I hate farming."

Lincoln was not unprepared when asked to speak. He had frequently hit the lecture circuit, with talks on discoveries and inventions, and spoke for three-quarters of an hour in a speech that revealed his deepest thoughts on politics and society. What he didn't do was pander. Farmers, he told the crowd, are wonderful people, but they're really no better or worse than other people. What was exciting about agriculture was how it had progressed, thanks to scientific experiments and new technology. Steam power, he said, now *that's* the ticket! What new technologies do is lighten the burden of physical labor while increasing production, and who could be opposed to that?

No group more needed new technology or could profit more from book-learning than farmers, said Lincoln. There were the new harvesters, which substituted capital improvements for human labor and made farms much more productive. Then there were the new seeds, which might increase a harvest twentyfold. Farming had become an intellectual endeavor, and what made agricultural fairs so valuable was the way in which they spread the news of new discoveries and inventions. So said the only American president who ever held a patent in his name (for a barge that could navigate the shallow rivers of downstate Illinois).

From his talk about labor and technology, Lincoln turned to labor and democracy, and to mud-sills. His law partner, William Herndon, had given him a copy of *Sociology of the South* and reported that no book had more angered Lincoln.[24] And as Lincoln tended to ramble in his talks, the leap from threshers to George Fitzhugh was an easy one. What Lincoln objected to, in the mud-sill theory, was the idea that mental and physical labor were the work of different classes of people.

From that idea so much was to follow. It meant there were no sharp class distinctions between capitalists and laborers, since laborers use their minds and most capitalists labor for their profits. And since everyone uses their minds, education should be open and available to all. Crucially, one's lot in life should not be fixed, and everyone should be permitted to ascend from the lowest stations in life, as Lincoln had himself had done, rising from the grinding and desperate poverty of a hardscrabble farm. Through his own efforts he had bettered himself, read voraciously, and became a lawyer; and from his personal rise he took an understanding of society that led in time to the Emancipation Proclamation and the Thirteenth Amendment's abolition of slavery. That by itself would have made Lincoln the greatest leader of his time, but even apart from that, and the Civil War too, Lincoln's domestic policies would have made him the dominant nineteenth century American president. From his premises about individuals and society, as expressed in Milwaukee and repeated in his July 4, 1861 Address to Congress, came land grant colleges, an open-border system of immigration, and free land for farmers under a Homestead Act that transformed his country. It was how, he told Congress, the fight to preserve the Union should be seen.

> This is essentially a people's contest. On the side of the Union it is a struggle for maintaining in the world that form and substance of government whose leading object is to elevate the condition of men; to lift artificial weights from all shoulders; to clear the paths of laudable pursuit for all; to afford all an unfettered start and a fair chance in the race of life.

"All honor to Jefferson," Lincoln had written earlier that year.[25] Two years later, on his way to his inauguration in Washington, he told a gathering at Independence Hall in Philadelphia that "I have never had a feeling politically that did not spring from the sentiments embodied in the Declaration of Independence."[26] Jefferson had introduced an abstract truth about equality, applicable to all men and all times. What Lincoln had done, however, was to give new meaning to the Declaration. First, and most obviously, Lincoln understood that Jefferson's egalitarianism was incompatible with the institution of slavery. In addition, Lincoln had a different understanding about why equality mattered. More than an abstract truth, it was also a guarantee of social mobility.

> This progress by which the poor, honest, industrious, and resolute man raises himself, that he may work on his own account…is that progress that human nature is entitled to, is that improvement in condition that is intended to be secured by those institutions under which we live, is the great principle for which this government was really formed.[27]

Jefferson had spoken of a natural aristocracy in which the most gifted and able might rise to the top, but this was simply a happy by-product of equality. For Lincoln, however, it was more than that. Rather, the central idea of America, as expressed in the Declaration, became through Lincoln the promise of income mobility and a faith in the ability of people to rise to a higher station in life. There was nothing base about labor, as Fitzhugh had thought. Instead, what was ignoble was an aristocratic disdain for work and the failure to attempt to better oneself. That was his idea of what America meant, and his ideal of self-improvement and mobility has come down to us as the American Dream.

That was our dream—but has our dream now fled?

PART II

The Way We Are Now

I no longer wished for a better world, because I was thinking of the whole of creation, and in the light of this clearer discernment I had come to see that, though the higher things are better than the lower, the sum of all creation is better than the higher things alone.

— ST. AUGSTINE, *Confessions, Book VII*

Unequal and Immobile

IN 2008, BARACK OBAMA WAS ELECTED PRESIDENT AFTER a largely issue-free campaign. There were serious issues out there, to be sure. The war in Iraq continued, but after the surge U.S. combat fatalities had fallen from 126 in May 2007 to thirteen in July 2008. The military mission would be scaled back, whoever won the election. The financial crisis, which began with the bankruptcy of Lehman Brothers in 2007, would turn out to be a defining challenge for the Obama administration; but it was not an issue that much divided the parties the next year, and the government bailout was authorized by legislation signed by George W. Bush.

The principal issue of the campaign was nothing so boring as that. Instead, the issue was the candidates, and in particular Obama, who ran as a charismatic leader. He had virtually nothing by way of legislative background, but offered hope and change and the promise that his election would signal "the moment when the rise of the oceans began to slow and our planet began to heal." There was also the prospect of absolution for America's historical racial injustices, coupled with the sly suggestion that his opponents were tinged with racism. They would dwell on his faults, he said, and then they would add, "Did I mention he was black?"

To many pundits, the election of a rock star president in 2008 seemed a one-off, not to be repeated. In future elections, Democrats would not be faced by a tired John McCain and life and politics would go on, not much changed. "This was a good Democratic year," observed Bill Kristol, "but it is still a center-right country."[1] Within two years, however, Democratic majorities in the House and Senate had passed far-reaching progressive legislation: the Patient Protection and Affordable Care Act (Obamacare) and the Dodd-Frank Wall Street Reform and Consumer Protection Act.

The Tea Party irruption and the 2010 Congressional election, which returned control of the House to Republicans, might have seemed to evidence Kristol's beliefs about a conservative country, but if so the 2012 presidential election would have been a rude awakening. If the 2008 election was largely content-free, the 2012 election was fought over a single issue, that of income inequality and immobility, in which Obama and the Democrats employed the rhetoric of class warfare to pit the bottom 99 percent against the top one percent. The 2014 mid-term elections were again a turn to the Right, but the impuissance of Congress in a country with an increasingly presidential form of government focuses attention on 2016, and the prospect of another election for the highest office fought over income disparities by candidates both Left and Right.

In a signature 2011 speech in Osawatomie, Kansas, Obama described income inequality as the defining issue of our time. America's grand bargain, he said, was that those who contribute to the country should share in its wealth. That bargain had made the country great, the envy of the world, but now it was betrayed by the "breathtaking greed" of the super-rich.

> Look at the statistics. In the last few decades, the average
> income of the top 1 percent has gone up by more than 250
> percent to $1.2 million per year.... And yet, over the last de-
> cade the incomes of most Americans have actually fallen by
> about 6 percent.[2]

The problem was worsened, he said, by a tax system whose shel-
ters and loopholes gave the super-rich lower rates than the middle
class. "Some billionaires have a tax rate as low as 1 percent. One
percent. That is the height of unfairness. It is wrong." And how did
this happen? Because inequality gave the superrich who contribute
to political parties an outsized voice in the way in which tax and
other laws are written. Worse still, he said, the promise of income
mobility, that a child born in poverty might through his own efforts
rise to the middle class, had been broken.

Mitt Romney sought to deflect Obama's message with a promise
of a more entrepreneurial society, but this failed to arouse much
enthusiasm. The Republican candidate, with his 59-point recovery plan, didn't connect with the voters. What they wanted instead
was a candidate who would speak to the issues of income inequality
and income immobility. The Republicans weren't interested in inequality—but inequality was interested in them. And so Romney
lost, and this at a time when the economy was so weak that pundit
George F. Will opined that, if Obama won, the Republicans should
find another line of work.

The voters' concerns were magnified by the severe job losses of
the Great Recession. In the twenty-six months between December 2007 and January 2010, the economy shed 7.2 million jobs and
those with a high school education or less accounted for four-fifths
of the job losses.[3] The community organizer—Obama—told them
he had their back, while the asset fund manager—Romney—came
across as the boss who was about to give them the pink slip.

The Great Recession of 2007–09, and the job losses that en-
sued, threatened a core belief of ordinary Americans, the idea that
this is a country of economic promise where everyone can get ahead.
If that's no longer the case something seems drastically wrong. Let's
start, then, by asking whether income inequality is really the problem it's cracked up to be. We'll never have perfect income equality,
so long as people sort themselves out by their industry and talents,
and any government that tried to mandate it would, if successful,
deprive its citizens of the incentive to produce wealth. Everyone
would be equal, but they'd also be very, very poor. Income disparities in themselves are not a problem, then, unless they rise to the
levels described so effectively by Obama, where we've become immobile, where the rich shape the contours of the laws and prevent
those at the bottom of the ladder from getting ahead. Is Obama's
America our America, then?

Inequality

To measure income inequality, one must first ask what one is looking for. Income might be pre-tax earnings, or it might be take-home
pay after taxes. Pre-tax income provides a better measure of overall
changes in the economy; post-tax income provides a better measure
of the effect of the government's tax and welfare policies. Taking it
a step further to include the government's entire safety net would
have one include non-cash, in-kind government transfers, such as
food stamps, school lunches, and subsidized housing.

All of these measures are of interest. We'd like to know whether
recent changes in the economy have increased income inequality,
and we'd also like to know what the government has done about it
through its tax and welfare policies. For the moment what I want
to know is whether current economic trends, excluding taxes and

government safety nets, can explain the rise of inequality. I'll sub-sequently look at what the government has done to adjust for this through its tax policies and welfare benefits.

Measuring Pre-tax Earnings

Pre-tax income might be raw income, one's salary before taxes (including business income from partnerships and pass-through S corporations). Then there are capital gains, the benefit derived from the appreciation of one's assets. Capital gains in turn might either be realized (where an asset is sold above cost during a fiscal year) or unrealized (where the asset isn't sold but has simply appreciated in value).

It's not really possible to measure pre-tax income shorn of how it's affected by government policies. When marginal tax rates are higher than 90 percent, as they were in the 1950s, the very rich are going to slack off and earn less, or at least report less income on their tax returns.

Have we seen a run-up in pre-tax income inequality, then? The short answer is yes, at the very top end. If income were equally divided across households and we all earned the same, the top 5 percent of earners would get 5 percent of the country's income. That's never been the case, however, and especially today. Between 1968 and 2011, the top 5 percent's share rose from 16.3 to 22.3 percent.[4] That's quite striking, but when Thomas Piketty and Emmanuel Saez looked more closely at the data they found that the strongest sense of inequality comes from the wealthiest million-plus American households, the much-reviled one percent who earned more than $394,000 in 2012.[5] That's an average Wall Street salary, more than what federal judges and 90 percent of law firm partners make. It's also more than the average salary of a doctor with a medical specialty. As seen in Figure 4.1, the one percent take home about 17 percent of everyone's earnings, and 20 percent when realized capital gains are included.

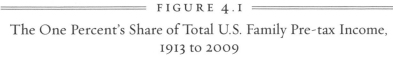

FIGURE 4.1

The One Percent's Share of Total U.S. Family Pre-tax Income, 1913 to 2009

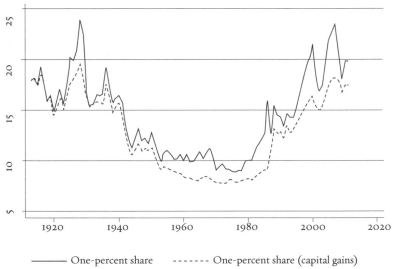

——— One-percent share   - - - - - - One-percent share (capital gains)

SOURCE: Facundo Alvaredo, Anthony B. Atkinson, Thomas Piketty, and Emmanuel Saez, The World Top Incomes Database, at http://topincomes.g-mond.parisschoolofeconomics.eu/.

Even amongst the one percent, there are enormous income disparities between the 1.35 million households earning $394,000 or more and the 135,000 households earning $1.6 million or more a year. The latter are the 0.1 percent. They include professionals at the top of their field, business executives, and your average NHL hockey player. The one percent earned 20 percent of the country's household income, but of that nearly half went to 0.1 percent. Then there's the 0.01 percent, who make more than $5.5 million a year, 100 times more than the median American (at the midpoint of the distribution). There are 13,000 of them, and they include finance executives, asset managers, and your average New York Yankee ballplayer. Together, they walked off with 4.5 percent of the household income of all Americans.

It wasn't always been like this, and Figure 4.1 portrays the rollercoaster the one percent have been on. The Roaring Twenties were a great time for them, one of instant millionaires and of Great Gatsbys who rose from obscurity to riches. Beginning with the Great Depression and the New Deal, however, their share of the income stream fell by more than half, only to rise again after 1980 and return to heights not seen in 60 years. The 1950s and 1960s were a halcyon period of relative income equality, interposed between the bookends that preceded and followed them, with the one percent's share increasing from 10 to 20 percent of the national income over the last 30 years.

By itself this might explain why income inequality became a hot issue in 2012, but that wasn't the half of it. It wasn't simply that the one percent became wealthier—it's that no one else seemed to move up very much, even *after* progressive taxes meant to shift wealth from the rich to the poor. The non-partisan and highly-respected Congressional Budget Office (CBO) reports that the top one percent enjoyed real after-tax income gains (including realized capital gains) of 275 percent over 1979–2007. The 81st to the 99th centile gained only 65 percent, and Americans in the middle of the distribution at the 21st to the 80th centile gained only 37 percent. For the 20 percent of Americans in the lowest quintile, the increase was only 18 percent.[6]

More recently, the wealth gap became greater still. After the Great Recession of 2007, the one percent took a hit. Much of their earnings come in the form of realized capital gains, which shrank because of the decline in share prices. Nevertheless, over 1993–2011 they enjoyed real pre-tax income gains of 57.5 percent, ten times more than the 5.8 percent of the bottom 99 percent.[7] The one percent fared even better over 2009–11, when *all* the income gains went to them. Their income grew by 11.2 percent while that of the remaining 99 percent fell by 0.4 percent.[8]

Apart from inequalities in income streams, there are stark differences in American wealth holdings. Thomas Piketty estimates that the top ten percent of wealth holders own more than 70 percent of the country's assets, and that the top one percent hold more than 30 percent.[9] That's down from Gilded Age heights of 1910 (80 percent for the top ten percent, 45 percent for the top one percent), but it's still a remarkably unequal split in wealth.[10]

The American middle class has been hardest hit in all of this. The very rich are doing well, and the poorest Americans are propped up by a generous welfare system as we'll see in Chapter 11. At the bottom end of the income distribution, people are also finding jobs. It's the jobs in the middle that have cratered, a phenomenon economists call "jobs polarization." Highly paid jobs have expanded, but then so too have poorly paid, low-skilled jobs.[11] We're talking about hands-on jobs such as food service workers, janitors and gardeners, cleaners, home health aides, hairdressers and beauticians. They don't require a high degree of education, they're not unionized, and they won't make you rich, but the jobs are there. It's all very well to be in the one percent, but one still needs people to mow the lawns and mop the floors, and that's not going to be done by computers or machines. What we haven't seen, however, is job growth for the kinds of people whose high school diploma used to get them a decently paying factory job.[12]

Today, America has the smallest middle class in the First World, defined as households with an income between 75 and 150 percent of the country's median (midpoint) income. Only 38.6 percent of

Americans are in that category, fewer than in Sweden (59.7%), Canada (46.2%), Britain (45%), and *all* of the twenty-four other First World nations surveyed.[13] There's also been a shift of wealth to the very rich in all advanced economies, as seen in Figure 4.2, but it's happened more in America. Over the last twenty years, the one percent increased their share of total income (including realized capital gains) in each of Canada, Germany, and Sweden, but not nearly as much as America's one percent.

===== FIGURE 4.2 =====

The One-Percent's Share of Total Pre-tax National Income: Four First World Countries

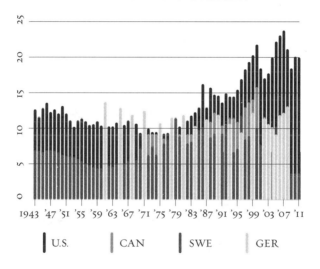

SOURCE: Anthony B. Atkinson, Thomas Piketty, and Emmanuel Saez, The World Top Incomes Database, at http://topincomes.g-mond.parisschoolofeconomics.eu/.

America and Europe have traded places. While there was greater wealth inequality in Europe in 1910, now there's more of it in the United States. That doesn't mean that America's 99 percent, or even the average American, is poor, by world standards. It's only when ordinary Americans are compared to the top American one or five percent that the inequalities stand out. Were the median American family, with its earnings of $50,000 a year, matched against people across the world, it would find itself in the global one percent. In the lottery of life, nearly all Americans are amongst life's great winners, and seem poor only in comparison with the richest Americans. But then it wouldn't occur to compare oneself with the average Kenyan.

The picture that emerges from all of this is of a society that offers tremendous financial rewards for the very rich. It's also a picture of a middle class that has been squeezed from both ends. The rewards of a sound economy have flowed disproportionately to those at the very top end, with generous welfare benefits going to those at the bottom.

Immobility

Income inequality might not seem much of a problem if everyone had an equal shot at the prize. That's how most conservatives respond to liberal concerns about inequality. But what if there really isn't much income mobility in the United States? What if Lincoln's promise of opportunity for everyone proves false? In that case Americans might join in comedian George Carlin's bitter laughter: It's called the American Dream, he said, because you have to be asleep to believe it.

So just how much mobility is there in America? Historically, a lot, in Ragged Dick's America. The nineteenth century was a golden age for income mobility, and in the 1950s and 1960s more people than ever before went to college, aided by the G.I. Bill. On graduation, they found good jobs waiting for them, and better homes than the ones they grew up in. Discriminatory barriers continued to impede women and minorities from moving up, but these began to recede with the rise of feminism and the civil rights movement. Since then, however, income mobility has slowed, and today there is much less chance for a family to move up the ranks.[14]

========== TABLE 4 ==========

Cross-country Immobility Rankings

COUNTRY	IMMOBILITY
United Kingdom	0.50
Italy	0.48
United States	0.47
France	0.41
Spain	0.40
Germany	0.32
Sweden	0.27
Australia	0.26
Canada	0.19
Finland	0.18
Norway	0.17
Denmark	0.15

SOURCE: http://www.economicmobility.org/assets/pdfs/PEW_EMP_US-CANADA.pdf.

Table 4, taken from the Pew Economic Mobility Project 2011, ranks countries on an immobility scale, where a higher score means less mobility (a closer correlation between the incomes of fathers and sons). At zero there is no correlation and the society is perfectly mobile. Denmark has a ranking of 0.15 and is relatively mobile, while an immobile Britain has a ranking of 0.50. Surprisingly, the U.S. comes in at a relatively immobile 0.47. To put this in dollar terms, imagine a father who earns $100,000 more in income than the average family. Danish children will earn only $15,000 more than their peers, but British children will earn $50,000 more and American children $47,000 more.[15] Remarkably, the U.S. is now one of the least mobile societies in the First World.

Over time, the earnings advantage dissipates, but for rich Americans it would still persist for several generations. At a ranking of 0.47, a father earning $400,000 (just over the one percent threshold) would assume that it would take four generations (great-great grandchildren) before his descendants fall into the middle class. Using more sophisticated estimation techniques, Bhashkar Mazumder reports that it would be more like five generations (great-great-great-grandchildren).[16] That might not seem like a lot, but it's a good run even when compared to the British aristocracy. Few British nobles can trace their titles back much before 1800, and before then most of their ancestors lived in obscurity.

This has to be troubling for Americans, who don't want to see permanent classes of peers and peasants. That's our idea of what Europe is or was, and we've always seen the U.S. to be better than that. We see America, not Denmark, as the land of opportunity. If it turns out that we are more class-ridden than the Europeans, then a core understanding of what it means to be American will have been lost.

Inequality Hardens into Immobility

A high measure of income immobility magnifies concerns about income inequality. People who think that there's a lot of income mobility in America—children doing better than their parents—don't worry about income inequality. They're willing to accept it so long as their kids have an equal shot at getting ahead. That's why the United States resisted socialism, thought Marx. As the most advanced capitalist country, America should have been the first place where socialism triumphed, according to Marxist theories of history. If that didn't happen it was a bit of an embarrassment, which Marx tried to explain away by pointing to American social mobility. "True enough, the classes already exist, but [they] have not yet acquired permanent character, [and] are in constant flux and reflux, constantly changing their elements and yielding them up to one another."[17]

But that was then. Today America is both unequal and

immobile. As that becomes more apparent, we might begin to see the kind of class-consciousness that Marx thought was missing in 1850s America, and with this a greater support for wealth redistribution schemes. Perhaps that's already started to happen. It's what the 2011 Occupy movement and the one percent protests were all about, and the 2012 election too.

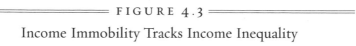

Income Immobility Tracks Income Inequality

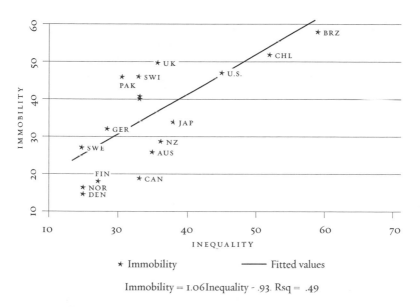

Immobility = 1.06Inequality - .93. Rsq = .49

SOURCES: Miles Corak, "Inequality from Generation to Generation: The United States in Comparison," in Robert Rycroft (ed.), The Economics of Inequality, Poverty, and Discrimination in the 21st Century, ABC-CLIO (2013); CIA Fact Book.

It's not just that people worry more about inequality when there's little income mobility. There's also more real inequality in immobile societies. Immobility entrenches inequality. That's the message from Figure 4.3, where the immobility rankings from the Table 4 data set (times 100) are paired against a cross-country measure of

How to Measure Inequality

The Gini coefficient is a single number between zero and one, with higher numbers representing more inequality. If everyone earned the same income (perfect equality), the Gini value would be 0; and if all the income went to the highest paid person (perfect inequality), the Gini ratio would be 1. No country is at 0 or 1, and in practice the range of Gini ratios is between .25 and .65. Clear data are hard to come by and there are significant measurement issues, but the Gini coefficient nevertheless provides a commonly accepted measure of cross-country income inequality.

inequality (the economist's Gini coefficient times 100).[18] At the Figure's lower left, Denmark is an egalitarian and highly mobile society. Brazil, on the upper right, is an unequal and immobile society. The United States is in the upper right quadrant, closer to Brazil than to Denmark.

Figure 4.3's straight line reveals a nearly one-to-one relationship between immobility and inequality. (I explain how the line is derived in Appendix C.) Alan Krueger, the former chief White House economist, has labeled the line the "Great Gatsby Curve," with a nod to F. Scott Fitzgerald's tycoon. With more accuracy, it might be labeled the anti-Gatsby curve, since Fitzgerald's eponymous protagonist came up from nowhere, and the message from the line is that this is less likely to happen in the United States than in Denmark. What the Figure portrays is inertia: egalitarian countries are likely to stay egalitarian, and unequal countries are likely to stay unequal. For highly unequal countries, that's a recipe for peasants with pitchforks.

Does this describe the United States? To answer that, we'd want to move beyond cross-country comparisons to look at the relation between inequality and immobility at the local level in America. That's what Raj Chetty and his co-authors did, and what they found is that unequal American communities are also more immobile, as the Great Gatsby curve would predict. Explaining what happened is more complicated, however. Were Obama right, the fault would lie with the one percent, who sucked all the oxygen and the money out of the room. But that's not what Chetty et al. reported. Instead, they didn't find any relation between the one percent's share of the economy and income immobility in local communities.[19] They also found that the chances of an individual child moving up from his parents' earnings quintile hadn't much changed in the last twenty years.

Chetty et al. also found that the chances of an individual child moving up from his parents' earnings quintile hasn't changed in the last twenty years, and more recent scholarship tells us there hasn't been much change since 1980.[20] Perhaps that's not surprising. Always ahead of his time, Irving Kristol described the emergence of an aristocratic New Class in 1978, a term that Christopher Lasch also employed before his death in 1994.[21] The causes I attribute to the rise of immobility in the last part of this book—the weakening of the public education system, a flawed immigration law, legal barriers to advancement—are moreover things that go back to at least 1980. The more recent rise of the one percent seems to be an epiphenomenon that serves to draw attention to the emergence of a class society without much explaining how we got where we are.

So why did we become so immobile, if it wasn't the one percent? What happened, suggested Chetty and his co-authors, was the jobs polarization phenomenon, the shrinking of the middle class and the shift of people towards lower income jobs.[22] In the bottom end of the income distribution, each person had the same chance to move up the ranks as he did twenty years ago, but now there were more people in the bottom end. That's why, in absolute numbers, more people remained in the lower class.

Then there were the social pathologies that kept people back. The strongest predictor of upward mobility was family structure, such as the fraction of single parents in the area. Not merely is it better to come from a two-parent family, but children of married parents also have more upward mobility if they live in communities with fewer single parents. That's not a novel insight. It's one that conservatives have voiced at least since Charles Murray's *Losing Ground* in 1984,[23] without identifying a means of returning to the norms of an earlier, more hopeful society, and without persuading voters to follow them there. The other things contributing to immobility include the weakening of public education, a flawed immigration law, legal barriers to advancement, and these we'll look at in the last part of this book.

The Great Gatsby curve has been seen as an invitation to despair. If we are so immobile as that, then we might be passing on our inequalities to future generations. But the curve moves in both directions. Suppose that we could, as suggested in the book's last part, return to a country of high mobility. Then the promised land of equality might follow.

Why Republicans Should Care About Income Immobility

INCOME DISPARITIES ARE OBVIOUSLY AN ISSUE FOR THE LEFT, and not just the Occupy movement. In *Ill Fares the Land*, the dying Tony Judt mourned the loss of cohesion, the sense that we're all in this together, in an unequal economy.[1] It's not a new complaint. The title of the book was taken from Oliver Goldsmith's *Deserted Village*, his romantic lament for the destruction of the Irish peasantry by rich landlords and the enclosure movement.

> Ill fares the land, to hastening ills a prey
> Where wealth accumulates and men decay.

Scholars of the Left offer a variety of diagnoses for the malady. The *New Republic*'s Timothy Noah decries the tax breaks and legal arcana that advantage the rich,[2] and the same charge has been made by a host of similarly minded commentators.[3] Harvard Law professor Larry Lessig points to the baneful influence of money on politics,[4] while in *Billionaires* (which sadly is not a self-help book), Darrell West makes the similar complaint that the super-wealthy have an outsized influence on politics.[5] Then there are structural changes to the economy: the shift from a highly paid industrial to a lowly-paid service economy that has left Americans *Nickel and Dimed*, according to political activist Barbara Ehrenreich.[6] Finally, Senator Elizabeth Warren has risen to political prominence for her description of a middle class pushed to the edge of financial ruin by economic instability and an overly-harsh bankruptcy regime that strips debtors of their assets.[7] Today Democrats campaign for the White House on the theme of income inequality, and Bernie Sanders has shown that voters of that party are not unprepared to support a self-proclaimed socialist.

People on the Left obviously need no persuading about any of this. Instead, it's people on the Right who dismiss concerns about a society increasingly fragmented by wealth. They're wrong to do so.

Not Just the Left

The problem of economic disparities requires an answer from Republicans, and indeed all Americans, whatever their political label. The problem, however, is that the Republican Party tends to sniff its delicate nose at the issue. That's not surprising, for were it to declare class warfare it would be clobbered by the majority of people who haven't shared in the wealth gains of the super-rich. But by ignoring the question, the Republican establishment has handed the Democrats a hammer with which to pound it. Obama's Osawatomie speech about income inequality proved highly attractive to voters, and the 2012 election showed that no viable political party could wish away the issue.

Obama's speech spoke to the greatest worry of the voters,

that of economic insecurity. The unemployment rate had risen to its highest level in 30 years, and appeared to have declined only because millions of Americans stopped looking for work. Were they to be counted as jobless, the unemployment figure would be much higher. Five years after the Great Recession began, the unemployment rate was 7.6 percent in 2012. That's not good, but if one included the "discouraged workers" who wanted a job but had given up looking for one the figure was 8.1 percent. Add to that people "marginally attached to the labor force" who weren't working or looking for work but who did work sometime in the prior 12 months and the figure was 8.9 percent. Finally, toss in people working part time because they could not find full time work and the figure jumps to 13.8 percent.[8] That's 21 million people who were un- or under-employed, as many as the total number of adults in New York and New Jersey. Of those employed, many were given the choice between a pink slip and a "permatemp" job in which they were given their old job back as an independent contractor, but without employment benefits and sometimes with a cut in salary. Even if they kept the same pay as before, what they lost was the sense of a secure job and faith in the future. Today, permatemp jobs account for about 10 percent of the American workforce. Add them to the number of un- or under-employed people and now you're talking about the total adult population of New York, New Jersey and Pennsylvania.[9]

Yale political scientist Jacob Hacker has developed an Economic Security Index that measures the percent of Americans who experienced a major drop in their available family income.[10] This is defined as a 25 percent decline in income, after deducting for medical expenses and excluding people with the financial resources to deal with the decline. Fourteen percent of Americans experienced such an income loss in 1986, but that number gradually and steadily rose over the next quarter century, and by 2010 included 62 million Americans, more than 20 percent of the total population and more people than the total population of twenty-seven states. For African-Americans, the figures were even more alarming: 27 percent of them lost a quarter of their income in 2010, and 22 percent lost a third of their income.

The Economic Security Index is an objective measure of income decline, and understates the number of Americans who *feel* insecure. During the Great Recession, many of us learned that we were at risk of losing our jobs, and that sent a chill up our backs. In addition, most people have seen their wealth decline, leaving them with a sense of life on the edge. A quarter of Americans reportedly have no emergency savings, nothing to fall back on, while only 40 percent have enough to last three months without any income.[11] Americans at the median (or midpoint) of the earnings scale had a family net worth of $77,300 in 2010, a decline of nearly $50,000 from 2007 and less even than they had in 1989 (in inflation-adjusted dollars).[12] In comparative rankings, this had moved the average American down several notches, below the Norwegians, Australians, Danes, Swedes, and Canadians.[13] The loss of wealth magnifies concerns about insecurity, for as Amy Sullivan observes, "a shriveled nest egg can turn a stint of unemployment from an inconvenience into a catastrophe."[14]

All this helps to explain the growing sense that America is in decline, that its glory days are a thing of the past. We have had many economic downturns in the past, but what is different this time is the fear that we will not bounce back, that something is structurally wrong, and that we must adjust to diminished expectations. A CNN poll reports that six in ten Americans believe that the American Dream is out of reach, that children won't be better off than their parents.[15] That's new, and it's an omen of a transformative political change, particularly for the most fragile of Americans.

Income immobility wasn't a hot political issue in the immediate past. In 2005 Alberto Alesina and George-Marios Angeletos reported that Americans believed that where you end up depends on your own skills and efforts. In Europe, people thought otherwise: They believed it was more a matter of luck, family ties and whom you know. The difference in beliefs about mobility, said Alesina and Angeletos, accounted for why Europeans were more likely than Americans to support governmental wealth redistribution schemes.[16] But is this going to continue? The question is what will happen to American politics when reality sinks in. Perhaps it already has, and that was what the 2012 election was all about. In a 2014 survey, 60 percent of Americans and 75 percent of Democrats told the Pew Research Center that the country's economic system unfairly favors the wealthy. Only 38 percent said that the rich acquired their wealth because they worked harder than others. What mattered, said 51 percent, was that the rich had had more advantages.[17] It's not the same country that Alesina and Angeletos had described only a few years earlier.

The Fragiles Come out to Vote

In 2012 people brought their anxieties to the polling stations. Four years after the Great Recession began, with the most anemic of recoveries, voters overwhelmingly thought the economy was the most important issue facing the country. So did the two parties, but they offered different messages to voters about what was to be done. Republicans campaigned on a platform of entrepreneurship and wealth creation, while Democrats countered with a message that spoke to economic insecurities and the safety net provided by the government. Mitt Romney announced a 59-point economic recovery plan, while the Democrats projected a sense of concern for the poor and an outrage at the malefactors of great wealth. And the Democrats won.

In the midst of the campaign, Jimmy Carter's grandson secretly taped Mitt Romney at a Republican fundraiser, recording the candidate's innermost thoughts about the campaign.

> There are 47 percent of the people who will vote for the president no matter what. All right, there are 47 percent who are with him, who are dependent upon government, who believe that they are victims, who believe that government has a responsibility to care for them, who believe that they are entitled to health care, to food, to housing, to you name it. That's an entitlement. And the government should give it to them. And they will vote for this president no matter what.[18]

The video, released by the liberal *Mother Jones* magazine, was a bombshell. In a troubled time, voters believed they had heard how Republicans really felt about the country's poor,[19] and this from the person who had said, "I like to fire people" and, "I'm not concerned about the very poor." The 47 percent included the infirm, the elderly, those who had paid their way in the past and those who could not find work despite their best efforts, but all were seen as shiftless wastrels. The 47 percent figure was even too low—much too low—since it excluded those who had benefited from the disguised government subsidies of what Suzanne Mettler calls the "submerged state"—the home mortgage interest and pension tax deductions, the student loan programs, the government support for the drug industry.[20] Romney came away looking heartless and mean-spirited, and in his rich-versus-them pitch to wealthy right-wing donors he also seemed divisive, contemptuous of the ordinary voter whose support he was soliciting. More than that, if he thought that the Democrats had a lock on nearly half the voters, he had seemingly just conceded the election. In his book about the 2012 presidential election, Dan Balz describes the video as the campaign's turning point.[21]

The Republicans could not recover with a platform of wealth creation which fell flat amongst those who thought that any wealth that was created would go to the super-rich and not to them, that the promise of equal opportunity was tarnished and that a class system had insinuated itself in the folds of what was supposed to be a classless society. And so the Democrats succeeded in shifting the blame for a bad economy from their shoulders. Fifty-nine percent of voters said the economic system favors the rich and of these 70 percent supported Obama. Forty-seven percent (Romney's number again) thought that taxes should be raised on those making over $250,000, and of these 70 percent voted for Obama.[22] The 2012 election was not the best of times for the Republican Party to nominate a wealthy asset fund manager as its candidate.

Unsurprisingly, Obama won big with poorer voters. Those with a family income of less than $30,000 gave 63 percent of their votes to him, and he also won a sizable majority—57 percent—of households with an income between $30,000 and $50,000.[23] These were the voters most at risk in a weak economy. When asked by a pollster, an overwhelming majority of Americans believed that middle class people were more likely to drop into the low-income class than were low-earners to rise.[24] The election was a referendum, at a time of economic distress, between security and growth, and given the choice, voters preferred security.

The issue isn't going away. Voters remain very concerned with the state of the economy, eight years after the Great Recession began, and the Democrats have made it their issue. Nearly 90 percent of Americans think they belong to the middle class, reports the conservative American Enterprise Institute, and of them a clear majority believe that the Democrats will do a better job helping them.[25] Unless the Republicans can connect with the voters on the issue, it's not hard to predict future presidential elections.

Curiously, Obama and Romney resembled each other in important ways. Both had the royal jelly that seeks to command—but then no one would run for president today without that. More importantly, both men enjoyed risk-taking. Obama had left Harvard Law School and the presidency of its law review not to take up a job on Wall Street, but to become a community organizer. At 43 he ran for the Senate and four years later mounted an uphill battle for the highest office in the land. Romney, the child of privilege, left Harvard Business School to lead an asset management firm that invested in troubled companies and sought to turn them around. Both men are examples of a character trait writer Nicholas Taleb calls *antifragility*.[26]

Taleb distinguishes between three kinds or people or institutions, according to how they react to the stress of very high magnitude, extremely low probability events. These are the events at the extreme ends of a probability distribution, either for good or ill. For the fragiles, the golden upsides won't help and the downside risks are like a fearful tornado swooping down on them. They are ill-prepared for the losses and when they occur feel them intensely. The second group is the resilient, those who can ride out the storm and not be affected by it. These are government employees, academics with tenure, most professionals. The third group, that of Obama and Romney, is composed of the antifragiles who thrive on the unforeseen event and profit from it. They are the risk-takers, who emerge wealthier than before. They'll exploit the golden upside, while the downside risk is simply a learning experience from which they bounce back stronger than ever. "I wouldn't be where I am now if I didn't fail a lot," billionaire Mark Cuban tells us. "The good, the bad, it's all part of the success equation."[27]

The Great Recession of 2008 was just the kind of unexpected, high magnitude event that illustrates the difference between Taleb's three archetypes. The 0.01 percent of Americans, the super-rich, were antifragiles who were poised to make enormous gains from economic distress, while those below them in the one or two percent were the resilients who were little affected by it. But the rest, the 99 or 98 percent of Americans, were mostly fragiles. They lost their jobs and houses, or sensed that they were at great risk; and to them what Obama promised was safety from the storm, resilience. The promise was possibly an illusion, but it was nevertheless believed. What Romney offered was antifragility, entrepreneurship, a growing economy, yet more risk. And resilience beat antifragility at the polls. It usually does, and almost invariably in times of great stress.

What answer do establishment Republicans have for any of this? They can pick holes in some of the overstated claims about inequality—and holes there are, as we'll see in Appendix B. They can point to our generous welfare policies, as I do in Chapter 11, and tell us that the progressive's policy responses are mostly self-defeating. But if they think they can wish away the issue, in the face of its compelling appeal to voters, they are deluded and deserve the label John Stuart Mill applied to the Conservatives of his day: the stupid party. They are doubly stupid if they fail to recognize that the real issue is not inequality but immobility, and that that issue belongs to them, for they only have the answers to how we can return to Ragged Dick's America. And that is the subject of the last part of this book.

Why Conservatives Should Care About Income Immobility

NOT ALL REPUBLICANS ARE CONSERVATIVES. AND SOME
Democrats are conservatives. What makes one a conservative is the
belief that, in the realm of public policy, there are institutions interposed between the individual and the state that matter. A libertarian who believed that only individuals count, and that their
rights must be respected whatever harm they impose on society,
would not be a conservative. Neither is the liberal who is suspicious
of Edmund Burke's "little platoons" of families, churches, and social
groups that do things which the liberal thinks the state should do,
and often by imposing what he sees as illiberal values.

Conservatives see things differently. Like Alexis de Tocqueville,
they will celebrate the fact that Americans are the world's greatest
joiners. We'll join churches, the Rotary, professional organizations,
much more than people in other countries.

Why We Need Intermediate Organizations

Unless suppressed by the state, intermediate organizations and clubs will arise spontaneously, for they serve four basic needs. First, they permit people to unite around projects that voluntary groups can perform more *efficiently* than the state. Think here of the Red Cross, civil liberties associations, or simply the neighborhood association that picks up litter on the street, groups that do things the government can't or won't do. Such groups serve as focal points for individuals who wish to perform a task in common, and who otherwise might free ride and let the other fellow do it.

Second, by doing what the state might otherwise have to do, intermediate organizations shrink the size of the state and in this way preserve *political liberty*. Societies with weak civic associations find it difficult to resist the intrusion of state power, and this helps explain the different paths of Russia and Poland, post-communism. In 1721 Peter the Great had subjected the Russian Orthodox Church to government control, and when they came to power the Soviets simply continued the policy of suppressing rival social groups. On the fall of communism, there weren't any subsidiary organizations around, and that made Vladimir Putin possible. By contrast, the Catholic Church remained a vibrant, independent force in Communist Poland, and today that country is much more democratic than Russia.

Third, social groups connect people to each other and satisfy the desire for *solidarity*, which is one of the deepest of human desires. We need other people to flourish. We need their friendship, their understanding, their love. After the 9-11 tragedy we took comfort from sharing our grief, and the sense of union with others helped ease the pain. We are strengthened, too, when bound to others, which was the point of *The Gift Outright*, the poem that Robert Frost recited from memory at the inauguration of President Kennedy.

Something we were withholding made us weak
Until we found out that it was ourselves
We were withholding from our land of living,
And forthwith found salvation in surrender.

The land was ours before we were the land's, explained Frost. We owned it, nothing more. But then we came to belong to it, and this defined us as Americans. We belonged to it, even as it belonged to us, and by giving of ourselves were made stronger.

Lastly, intermediate groups promote *trust*, as people learn to rely on each other through joint participation in a group, and this is crucially important in fostering economic growth. I am wealthier when I live in a society composed of honest, reliable people. Because I can trust them, I find it easier to reach agreements with them. I can also count on them to perform the kinds of promises that courts imperfectly enforce, such as doing a workman-like paint job; or promises that are uncertain and hard to measure, such as taking care of my child; or promises that the promisor opportunistically tries to renegotiate when he has a threat advantage down the road. Given the less than perfect reliability of the judicial system, this includes many of the promises made in America today.

That's not to say that intermediate groups are always admirable. After the Civil War, the Ku Klux Klan was wondrously effective in getting people together for a nighttime ride, and today the New Black Panther Party is noted for bringing out poll-watchers come election time.[1] And don't get me started on bicycle groups: in Italy the fascists goose-step; in my Alexandria VA they pedal. Organizations that pit one group against another don't always serve the kind of community values that Tocqueville had in mind. On balance, however, most Americans would agree that we have too few and not too many civic associations, and in that sense we're nearly all conservative. Every libertarian I know prizes Tocqueville's civic associations, for example, and simply thinks they flourish better when they're organized from below. Libertarians also suspect that a too-large state would crowd out civic associations by assuming burdens best left for them.[2]

The question, then, is whether the rise of income immobility threatens our willingness to support civic associations and our sense of membership in the nation. That in turn is really two questions. First, has there been a decline in civic participation; and second, if that's the case, is income inequality to blame?

Have Intermediate Organizations Declined?

The first question was the subject of a famous debate sparked by Robert Putnam's *Bowling Alone*, first a magazine article in 1995 and then a book in 2000.[3] What the title referred to was the decline in bowling leagues: formerly one bowled as the member of a club, but now one bowls alone. What made people (including non-bowlers) take the book seriously was the wealth of empirical evidence which Putnam presented about declining membership in clubs of all kinds, from high points in the 1950s and early 1960s. Memberships in associations with local chapters fell, as did club meetings and PTA membership.

Since Putnam wrote, things haven't gotten better. In the 2012 election, the rise of the "nones"—people who said they belonged to no organized religion—helped reelect Obama. From 2 percent in 1950 to 15 percent in 2007, they now comprise a fifth of all adult Americans.[4] Families have also declined. Between 1950 and 2010, the number of American households containing only one person increased from 10 to 27 percent, and this has weakened our sense of membership in a community. Families root one to a place, to its schools, parks, and sports teams. They also produce the sense of connection to others that is a cure to loneliness. For years television has celebrated a fantasy world of happy singles. In the last episode of the *Mary Tyler Moore Show*, for example, "Mary Richards" told her co-workers:

> Sometimes I get concerned about being a career women. I
> get to thinking that my job is too important to me, and I tell
> myself that the people I work with are just the people I work
> with, and not my family. And last night I thought "What is
> a family anyway?" They're just people who make you feel
> less alone and really loved. And that's what you've done for
> me. Thank you for being my family.

The reality, however, is that the unmarried are lonelier than married people. In an American Association of Retired Persons survey of the 45+ population, 51 percent of the never-married respondents reported that they were lonely, much more than the 29 percent of married people.[5]

Lonely people are more likely to kill themselves, and more people have done so in recent years. Amongst Americans aged 35 to 64, the suicide rate rose by nearly 30 percent between 1999 and 2010. For men in their 50s, suicide rates increased by nearly 50 percent.[6] Other things, such as economic decline and the loss of jobs, no doubt contributed to this morbid statistic, but divorce, family break-ups, and the loss of community likely played a role as well.

We might spend time on Facebook and other social media outlets, but that doesn't seem to make us feel less lonely,[7] or provide the sense of intimacy and companionship that face-to-face friendships provide. Concentered all in self, the video gamer and Web addict often live solitary lives, dispensing with what Marc Dunkelman calls "middle ring" relationships. These are the people who, not as close as near relatives but not as distant as mere acquaintances, link us to our communities and give us a sense of belonging to something greater than ourselves.[8] Between 1985 to 2004, the number of Americans who told a friend something of personal importance to themselves during the prior six months fell from 73 to 51 percent, while the number of people who had no such confidants rose from 10 to 25 percent.[9] That is a staggering loss in social solidarity.

Putnam's claims about declining civic participation rates have not gone unchallenged. Putnam's problem, said Everett Ladd, was that he was looking at organizations that flourished in the past, and not the new ones that have since arisen for causes such as environmental protection that were much less of an issue 50 years ago.[10] Perhaps so, but overall our sense of community has declined, and that's evidenced by the loss of a sense of trust.

Trust in the federal government has fallen off a cliff since 1960, particularly during the Johnson, Nixon, and George W. Bush administrations. When asked "how much of the time do you trust the government in Washington," 26 percent of respondents said "just about always" or "most of the time" in 2013, down from 73 percent in 1958.[11] We also trust other people less.[12] In *Bowling Alone*, Putnam reported that the percent of people who agreed that "most people can be trusted" fell from 55 in 1960 to 34 in 1998.[13] Similarly, the University of Chicago's General Social Survey found that between 1976 to 2006 there was a 10 percent decline in the number of Americans who believe other people can generally be trusted. The decline is sharpest amongst the 18–33-year-old Millennials, according to a recent Pew Research poll. When asked, "would you say that most people can be trusted," only 19 percent of Millennials agreed, compared to 40 percent of Boomers and 31 percent of Generation X'ers.[14] Unless the Millennials develop a hitherto unnoticed trust gene as they age, one can expect Americans to be less trusting in the future.

Voter turnout rates provide one measure of trust and civic engagement. Fifty years ago, most people who could vote did vote, as seen in Figure 6.1.[15] Using adjusted figures for the eligible voting population, the Figure shows a sharp decline in voting rates since 1952. Moreover,

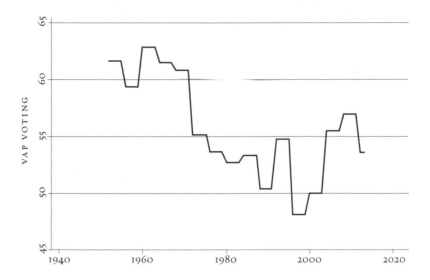

FIGURE 6.1

Voter Participation Rates, 1948–2012 Presidential Elections

SOURCE: Michael P. McDonald, United States Elections Project, at http://elections.gmu.edu/voter_turnout.htm.

the 2008 election, in which an African-American ran for president and more voters turned out at the polls, seems something of an outlier.

So what's changed? It's not that presidential power has declined. Over the last few decades, as the executive branch has amassed more power, the choice of who will be president has become increasingly consequential. And while we'd also expect to see lower turnout rates in states that are overwhelmingly Democratic or Republican, where there isn't much campaign advertising, voter polarization isn't a new phenomenon. In the past, the "Solid South" voted Democratic, the North-East voted Republican, and there weren't all that many swing states. If anything, we'd have expected greater voter participation over the years, as formerly disenfranchised African-Americans came to the polls. That's not what happened, and the lower turnout rates can be plausibly be attributed to the general decline in civic partici- pation described by Putnam, the sense that we're members of a com- munity and owe something to it.

What's Immobility Got to Do with It?

Let's assume, therefore, that there has been a loss of trust and so- cial solidarity. Even so, did perceptions about income inequality and immobility have anything to do with this? One way to test this is to plot the voter participation levels from Figure 6.1 against the one

=== FIGURE 6.2 ===

More Income Inequality, Less Voting... Up to a Point

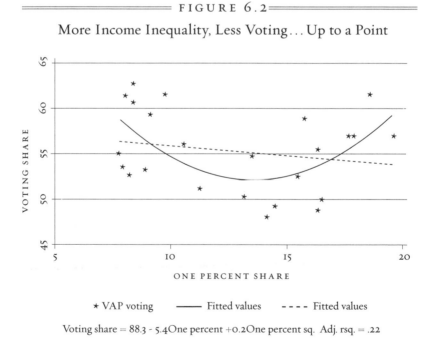

★ VAP voting ——— Fitted values - - - - Fitted values

Voting share = 88.3 - 5.4One percent +0.2One percent sq. Adj. rsq. = .22

SOURCE: Michael P. McDonald, United States Elections Project, at http://elections.gmu.edu/ voter_turnout.htm.

FIGURE 6.3

More Inequality, Less Trust

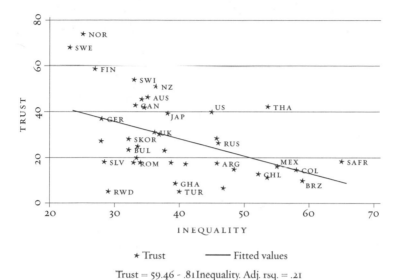

* Trust   —— Fitted values

Trust = 59.46 - .81 Inequality. Adj. rsq. = .21

SOURCE: World Values Survey, at http://www.wvsevsdb.com/wvs/WVSAnalizeQuestion.jsp.

percent's share of the national income, which I take as a proxy for general perceptions about income disparities. While the superrich didn't get wealthy off the backs of the poor, America is unequal and the one percent have been taken as the symbol of its inequality. Perceptions matter, and there's hard evidence of inequality to back up the perceptions. Accordingly, I want to see if Americans are less likely to vote when they think the country unequal. This I do in Figure 6.2's scatterplot, which looks at voting patterns for each election year from 1916 to 2008, and which reveals a decline in voter participation rates when the one percent's wealth increases. Given data limitations these findings are suggestive at best, but they're what one would expect. People are more willing to participate in a club—or a nation—when they believe the gains are equitably shared.

What's interesting in Figure 6.2 is the U-shaped curve that initially bends downward and then upward when the one percent's income level exceeds 14 percent of total household income. The curve (which represents voting rates when these are estimated from both the one percent's share and the squared value of the one percent share) picks up how people are motivated to vote at extreme levels of income inequality. *Fewer* people vote as the one percent receives an increasing share of the nation's wealth, but only up to 14 percent. Above that, *more* people vote. For the voters, first alienation, then outrage. Below 14 percent people withdraw from politics, but above 14 percent inequality rankles and voters experience a Howard Beale moment from the movie *Network* ("I'm as mad as Hell and I'm not going to take this anymore!"). When that happens they're more likely to vote. That's the story of the Occupy movement and the Tea Party, and it's one that political parties ignore at their peril.

Income inequality also appears to reduce levels of trust. Between 2004 and 2007, the World Values Survey asked respondents whether they agreed that most people can be trusted, and received answers ranging from 4.9 in the case of Rwanda and Turkey to 74.2 for Norway, out of 100. What Figure 6.3 shows is that countries with more equality (as measured by the country's Gini coefficient seen in the Chapter 4) also have higher levels of trust (as measured by the World Values Survey).[16] The U.S. is roughly at the midpoint, less trusting and more unequal than most First World countries. Moving along the downward-sloping straight line, a 0.81 percent increase in inequality is associated with a one percent decline in trust. The same relationship holds within the United States: people in states with higher degrees of inequality are also less trusting.[17]

There has thus been a decline in various measures of social solidarity in the United States, from voter participation rates to trust. There are likely several different reasons for this, but one of them appears to have been the increase in income inequality and immobility. That's something that should bother conservatives, and indeed all Americans.

Why Libertarians Should Care About Income Immobility

LIBERTARIANS OFTEN PICK THEIR BATTLES ABOUT THE erosion of personal freedom over concerns that, for most Americans, are a little obscure—motorcycle helmets, overhead cameras, and the like. The purists amongst them are apt to take pride in how they've never voted Republican. And yet the libertarian should not be indifferent to general politics either, and especially to the growing appeal of the kind of populism seen in Obama's Osawatomic speech and the 2012 election.

The question, then, is whether income inequality and immobility can lead to the loss of the freedoms the libertarian prizes. That's an argument attributed to Supreme Court Justice Louis Brandeis. "We can have a democratic society or we can have great concentrated wealth in the hands of a few. We cannot have both."[1] Alan Greenspan made a similar point on the *Charlie Rose* show. "You cannot have a market capitalist system if there is a significant mood in the population that its rewards are unjustly distributed."[2]

It doesn't take a great deal of imagination to see how the danger to political freedom may arise. The Chavismo movement in Venezuela, which has weakened freedom and outlived Hugo Chávez, would not appear possible in countries with Swedish-style income equality. Chávez rose to power with the support of a desperately poor underclass that was willing to trade off political freedom for the promise of economic equality. Once in power, Chávez embarked on a wealth-destroying attack on the rule of law that frightened away investors and curbed the political freedom of opponents.[3]

To what extent did Venezuela lose its freedom? One of the most widely-respected freedom rankings is Freedom House's index of liberal democracies. Freedom House is a Washington-based non-governmental organization that each year evaluates 195 countries according to their political rights, relying on a process of analysis and evaluation by a team of regional experts and scholars.[4] The rankings are based on a series of questions such as: are there free and fair elections, are there competitive political parties, and are minority groups excluded from the political process? The rankings run from 1 (most free) to 7 (least free). The year before Chávez came to power Freedom House gave Venezuela a respectable score of 2, the same ranking as Brazil today. By 2014, however, the country had fallen to 5, putting it in the same unwholesome company as Kyrgyzstan.

While Venezuela isn't much of a democracy today, Chávez came to power in 1998 through a fair and square election where wealth redistribution was a winning ticket. That's not surprising, since the *median voter theorem* explains why there will be a demand for wealth redistribution in any democracy. Where voters express their preferences over a single issue, such as redistribution, opinions will vary from the most liberal to the most conservative, and the voter at the exact middle determines the outcome.[5] He is the median voter, and he plus those below him in the distribution constitute 50 percent plus one of the voters, a majority of the electorate. Unless everyone earns exactly the same income, there will always be some people earning more than the median voter, and he'll have an incentive to take advantage of his majority status to elect politicians who will impose higher taxes on the rich.[6] The temptation will be strongest where (as in Venezuela and America) the distribution of income is skewed towards people at the top end, the one percent.

America is not Venezuela, or even close, but it's also a different country, with a different style of politics, than it was fifty years ago. In *The Once and Future King*,[7] I describe the recent expansion of the executive branch as a form of Crown government: rule by a powerful president who governs as the tribune of the people, with the moral and political authority of the only person elected by the country as a whole. Crown government is worrisome, and when presidents run on a platform of income inequality they can become even more powerful. That's something the libertarian should find troubling.

Leaving aside populist demands for a dictator to equalize wealth, on the model of Venezuela, or the rise of Crown government, there is a further way in which income inequality threatens political freedom, this time from a wealthy and excessively powerful upper class. If the libertarian might fear a bottom-up populist revolt, liberals on the Left have an equal and opposite concern about top-down plutocrats who buy elections, and this especially after the Supreme Court's *Citizens United* decision.[8] More broadly, both Left and Right have complained that large corporations tilt the free market in their direction through special governmental subsidies and tax loopholes, and this, argues Nobel laureate Joseph Stiglitz, explains the rise of the one percent.[9] Similarly, respected academics such as MIT's Daron Acemoğlu have described how income inequality might breed a vicious circle in which the super-rich employ their wealth to buy political power, and then use that power to augment their wealth.[10] We've seen more than enough of this in the Obama administration's love affair with the "green energy" firms in its donor base.

Does income inequality threaten political freedom, then? In Figure

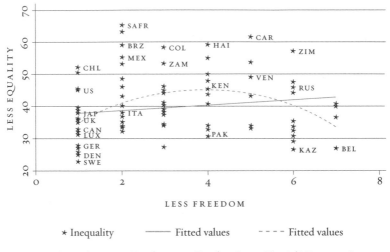

FIGURE 7

Less Equality, Less Political Freedom

* Inequality   —— Fitted values   - - - - Fitted values

Inequality = 9.32 Freedom - 1.19 FreedomSq. +26.89. Adj. Rsq = 0.16

SOURCES: CIA Fact Book, Freedom House, Freedom in the World.

7, income inequality (the Gini ratio from Chapter 4) for 100 countries in 2010 is portrayed on the vertical axis and their Freedom House score for the same year on the horizontal. The upper right quadrant is the danger zone (little freedom, little equality), while the lower left is the happy zone (more freedom, more equality). Sweden, on the lower-left side of the diagram, has the highest level of freedom and greatest equality, while Zimbabwe on the upper-right is both unfree and unequal.

What the Brandies theory predicts is that less equality would lead to less freedom, and that's what the upward-sloping straight line in Figure 7 portrays.[11] Moving from left to right and upward on the line, countries are both less equal and less free. It's more complicated than that, however. The upward sloping line running from Sweden to Zimbabwe is consistent with the Brandeis story, but we'd also want to see what happens to equality in extremely unfree countries. I do that by estimating inequality using both the Freedom House rate and its squared value, and when I do that I get the upside-down U-shaped curve of Figure 8. Moving upward on the curve from Sweden, more inequality means less freedom, as Brandeis predicted,[12] to the midpoint around Kenya. Moving further along on the curve, however, towards Belarus on the lower-right side, less freedom means more equality. That's not what Brandeis had in mind, and it requires an explanation.

One explanation is that unfree countries are really good at destroying wealth and impoverishing everyone. That might be the Belarus story. It's a kind of equality, but it's not one that will appeal to many people, and something else must be going on if voters get to choose. Suppose then that there is a general desire for income equality, of the kind that helped elect Obama in 2012. Voters will back candidates who promise greater equality, but there are two ways of getting there. The first is the Swedish route, with a democratic government that accepts income equality as a desirable goal to be achieved through democratic means. The second is the Venezuela route, where voters trade away their freedom for an attack on the rich and the promise of greater equality.[13] For a country such as Kenya, poised at the midpoint of the diagram, the move to greater equality might take the country towards either greater freedom on the Swedish model or the less free, one-party rule of Belarus president Alexander Lukashenko.

The same choices potentially face every country with high inequality, and the 2012 election has shown that American politics is not without its strong egalitarian impulses. Income inequality was certainly on the ballot and proved a winning ticket for the Democrats. What should one take from this? Obama's supporters will likely be cheered by what seems to them a move to a more socially just and progressive Swedish-style economy, while Republicans are apt to bemoan the concentration of power in the executive branch, the rise of Crown government, and the loss of political freedom. For libertarians, either possibility would be troubling.

That's not to say that the libertarian would be willing to do anything about it. He might recognize that the promise of income equality gave Obama a winning hand, and that this gave the country things he hates: Obamacare, Dodd-Frank, and a regulatory state on steroids. Nevertheless, he might also believe that any attempt to take the inequality issue away from the Democrats in order to preserve liberty would be self-defeating. State intervention to promote income equality must necessarily be liberticide, he might think.

He might think that—but he would be wrong. Many First World countries have both more income equality and more economic freedom than the United States, as freedom is measured by the libertarian Cato Institute. These include New Zealand, Switzerland, Canada, Australia, and Finland. If the libertarian would have us believe that income equality is incompatible with economic liberty, he's simply mistaken.

Such arguments might nevertheless fail to persuade the libertarian. "You don't understand America," he might say. "We don't do Grand Bargains here." We can't trade off measures to increase equality against progress on economic freedom on other fronts, because people can't be trusted here. Raising marginal tax rates (which are already high) on the one percent might simply raise tax rates, without producing a rollback of wasteful laws and regulations. It's all very well to talk of more economic freedom, if we can't get there from here.

That leaves other ways of addressing income inequalities, to which the libertarian might happily sign on, and which we'll see in the book's last part. Inefficient policies which hinder entrepreneurs and which disproportionately benefit the one percent are condemned by the Left as well as the Right, and some movement on that front might thus be feasible. And while marginal tax rates are high, we might look to progress in scaling back the tax loopholes of which Obama rightly complained. Grand Bargains to fix these problems would leave almost everyone better off—but then, Grand Bargains are hard to do in America.

Why Everyone Should Care
About Income Immobility

PEOPLE ON THE RIGHT ARE APT TO THINK THAT ANY attempt to equalize incomes would make us all poor and unhappy. We are given a choice between today's America, with all its inequalities, and an egalitarian but wealth-destroying and miserably unhappy Belarus. If so, we'd take inequality over equality. But those aren't the only choices open to us.

Wealth

We've been told that income inequality and immobility is the price countries pay if they wish to be wealthy. That's what Arthur Okun argued in his 1975 book, *Equality and Equity: The Big Tradeoff.* A country might be rich and unequal or equal and poor, and to the extent that it opts for equality it must trade off wealth. Okun described government wealth transfer programs as "leaky buckets." They never pass on everything

they take from the economy to the poor. Some money disappears in
transit through a poverty industry staffed by bureaucrats, social workers,
and public-private organizations, and some wealth doesn't get earned
because the added tax burden saps the incentive to create it. As a consequence, money is carried from the rich to the poor in leaky buckets.[1]

If Okun were right, efforts to equalize income are always a drag on
the economy, and we'd expect the richest societies to have the thinnest
of social safety nets. That's not the story of America, however. In absolute terms, the United States spends more on welfare per capita than
almost any other country (as we'll see in Chapter 11), and yet it's also
one of the wealthiest countries. Then there are the Nordic countries,

FIGURE 8.1

More Inequality, Less Wealth

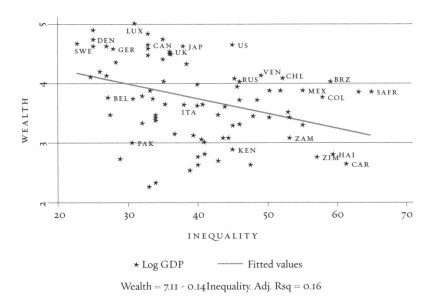

* Log GDP ——— Fitted values

Wealth = 7.11 - 0.14 Inequality. Adj. Rsq = 0.16

SOURCE: World Bank, United Nations, at http://unstats.un.org/unsd/snaama/dnllist.asp, CIA
Fact Book.

as wealthy as or wealthier than the United States, but with welfare policies that are a byword for generosity.

Okun's leaky buckets would also leave one to suppose that rich countries are more unequal, but that's not what the evidence shows. Figure 8.1 maps inequality levels (the Gini ratio) against a country's wealth (the logged value of per capita Gross Domestic Product for 2010), and the downward-sloping line is inconsistent with Okun's leaky buckets. As countries become more unequal, they became poorer, not richer. Most other empirical studies come to the same conclusion.[2]

There is a simple reason why rich countries feature greater income equality: economic growth can make almost everyone wealthier. That's not a matter of government wealth transfer schemes, with their leaky buckets, but of real, across-the-board wealth gains. A rising tide lifts all boats, in short. The global lowering of trade barriers has also helped, since free trade has made countries both wealthier and more equal, especially in the poor countries to which low-tech manufacturing jobs have moved. In addition, the "green revolution" in agriculture, which has made farming much more efficient, has lifted many millions of people in poor countries out of poverty. Finally, if wealth has anything to do with the basic goods of life, such as how long people live, there is greater equality between rich and poor today than in the past. In a model that incorporated the value of increased life expectancy, Gary Becker and his colleagues reported that, between 1960 and 2000, wealth inequalities between rich and poor countries sharply contracted. The 90 countries they studied registered average annual income gains of 2.8 percent, which is impressive. For the poorest countries in the bottom half of the list, however, the income gains were 4.1 percent a year.[3]

Happiness

That's not to say that a country's sole goal should be to maximize national wealth. Other things—freedom, families, culture—matter too, and in any event wealth isn't desirable in itself, but only as the means towards something more fundamental. It's an *instrumental* good, valued insofar as it promotes the sense of well-being that we associate with happiness. "In the end," says Paul Krugman, "economics is not about wealth, it's about the pursuit of happiness."[4]

There are two ways in which income inequality might make people unhappy. The first is the economist's *declining marginal utility* of money.

Explaining Declining Marginal Utility

Economists offer two psychological explanations for diminishing marginal utility. First, our *aspirations* may increase along with our wealth. With more money we simply want more things, and the Promised Land recedes as we approach it, an insight that Émile Durkheim employed to explain why people in advanced, wealthy societies commit suicide. Alternatively, it's been suggested that we might have innate *adaptation set-points* of happiness, determined by character or genes, to which we revert after every gain or loss. Major events, such as a marriage or job loss, will move us from our equilibrium, but we quickly return to our natural state, neither particularly happy or unhappy, joyful or joyless. If happiness levels are coded in our genes, trying to make ourselves happier is as futile as trying to make ourselves taller. David Lykken and Auke Tellegen, Happiness is a Stochastic Phenomenon, 7 Psych. Sc. 186, 189 (1966). In either case, more money is never entirely what it's cracked up to be. See generally Daniel Kahneman, "Objective Happiness," in Daniel Kahneman, Ed Diener and Norbert Schwarz (eds.), Well-Being: The Foundations of Hedonic Psychology 3 (New York: Russell Sage, 2003).

Subjective Well-being Rankings

The U.S. General Social Survey asks people "Taken all together, how would you say things are these days—would you say you are happy, pretty happy, or not too happy?" Such self-reported well-being rankings are necessarily subjective and prone to uncertainty, but most people answer the surveys, and not everybody answers "very happy." As far as empirical evidence of happiness goes, it doesn't get much better than this. See generally Bruno S. Frey, Happiness: A Revolution in Economics ch. 2 (Cambridge: MIT Press, 2008).

Utility for the economist simply means happiness or well-being, and marginal utility refers to the added happiness one gets from one more dollar. To say that that money has a declining marginal utility is thus to say that happiness gains from more money get smaller as people get richer. If you gave Bill Gates $1,000, he'd enjoy it less than I would. This is a commonly accepted idea, and it powers the not very controversial idea that our tax system should transfer wealth from the rich to the poor, rather than the other way around.

Declining marginal utility therefore predicts that, other things being equal, countries with extreme income inequality are less happy than more egalitarian countries. Imagine two states, alike in every way save one. In the first, nearly all the country's wealth is held by a single person. The national wealth is the same in the second country, but it is distributed much more evenly. What declining marginal utility would tell us, and what we would expect, is that the second country is happier than the first. The top dog will be a bit happier in the first country, but everyone else will be vastly less happy.

Given declining marginal utility, more money doesn't translate one-to-one into more happiness, and that's what experimental psychologists report from surveys about people's well-being. Figure 8.2 shows that people are happier (subjective well-being rankings) in richer (the logged value of GDP per capita) countries. That's not surprising, since higher income correlates with better access to basic material goods such as better schooling, food, and health care. The curve is not a straight line, however. Increases in happiness become smaller with more wealth,[5] and that's consistent with diminishing marginal utility.

People with ten times the money we have aren't ten times happier. The lifestyles of the rich and famous are not, after all, so very different from those of the rest of us. People work, they go home, they turn on the television. At $9 a month, they now have vastly more viewing

FIGURE 8.2

Diminishing Marginal Utility

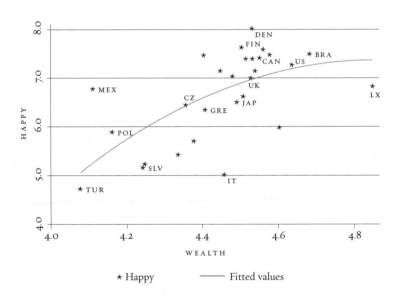

* Happy   —— Fitted values

SOURCE: Source: Gallup World Poll 2001–06.

===== FIGURE 8.3 =====

More Inequality, Less Happiness

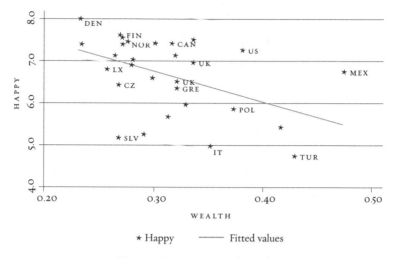

* Happy   —— Fitted values

Happy = 8.91 - 7.20 Inequality. Adj. Rsq = .18

SOURCE: Source: Gallup World Poll 2001–06.

options with a Netflix subscription than anyone in Manhattan had a decade ago. When it comes to simple pastimes, technology has been a great leveler. Not merely have the choices expanded but the gap between rich and poor has shrunk. Think of the web, on which people of every class entertain themselves for the price of an Internet connection. It's the same YouTube for everyone, the same cat videos.

As for their dinners, the difference between a Red Lobster and most downtown Washington D.C. restaurants, with their power tables, is mostly about status, and not the quality of the food. At home, a middle class couple might crack open a $10 bottle of wine from Trader Joe's, but it wouldn't taste all that different from a $100 bottle purchased at a boutique wine store. Then there's our homes. The average American house is 2,100 square feet. Were it 6,000 square feet, there'd be a lot more empty rooms, but it's hard to see how that would make anyone a great deal happier. For the middle class, a holiday might be an ocean cruise, and is that really any worse than upper class jaunts to the Galápagos? "What's great about this country," observed Andy Warhol, "is that America started the tradition where the richest consumers buy essentially the same things as the poorest....A Coke is a Coke and no amount of money can get you a better Coke than the one the bum on the corner is drinking. All the Cokes are the same and all the Cokes are good."

Apart from declining marginal utility, income inequality might affect happiness levels in a second way, through the *relative preferences* people have. I have absolute preferences when I simply want more for myself. I have relative preferences when, in addition to wanting more for myself, I want to have more than other people to whom I compare myself. With absolute preferences I'll be made happier if my employer gives me a $100 raise. With relative preferences the raise might leave me feeling worse off if everyone else at work got a $10,000 raise. Relative preferences explain why America's poor, who are as well off as the poor in Nordic countries, are nevertheless upset at the contrast between their poverty and the wealth of the people to whom they compare themselves: America's one percent.

Economists and moralists both dislike relative preferences. For economists, relative preferences get in the way of efficiency gains that leave at least one person better off and no one worse off. That's a definition of efficiency proposed by Vilfredo Pareto, and so defined it would be inefficient of me to block a $10,000 raise for each of my co-workers even if I don't get a raise. The moralist is also a Paretian, to the extent that he identifies relative preferences with the sin of envy. The envious feel resentment towards those who possess something they want, such as a $10,000 raise.

The problem, however, is that we all have relative preferences. Paretian principles don't begin to describe what motivates us, and we can't label relative preferences sinful when they seem an ineradicable part of our nature. As a spur to self-improvement, relative preferences are even wholesome when they prevent us from lapsing into a Merovingian, slothful supineness. Relative preferences also inform our sense of fairness, when we see injustice in an unequal split of gains. A well-known example of this comes from the *ultimatum games* of the experimental psychologist, which show how people are willing to "pay to punish" another party for unfairness. In an ultimatum game, one party (the "sender") divides up a fixed amount of money and the other (the "receiver") must either accept or reject his share. If he accepts it, he gets what the sender accorded him; if he rejects it, neither party receives anything. Given $1,000 to divide between them, the sender might thus decide to keep $900 and leave the receiver with $100. Were he a Paretian, the receiver would accept this, as the split makes everyone better off and no one worse off. However, most receivers are troubled by unfairness and reject sharply unequal splits even when this means giving up large offers.[6]

Cornell economist Robert H. Frank, who more than anyone else has popularized the idea of relative preferences, imagines a thought experiment to illustrate that we care about how others fare. Suppose that we were offered a choice of living in one of two worlds.

> *World A*: You have a house with 6,000 square feet, in a neighborhood where everyone else has a house of 8,000 square feet.
> *World B*: You have a house with 4,000 square feet, in a neighborhood where everyone else has a house of 3,000 square feet.[7]

We all have basic needs for shelter, but after a certain point it's importantly about status, and given the choice between the two worlds, says Frank, most people would opt for the second.

Given relative preferences, then, we would expect to find that people are happier when income disparities are smaller. That's what experimental psychologists report, from surveys about inequality and people's well-being.[8] And that's what I find in Figure 8.3, where I map a measure of inequality (the Gini ratio) against reported happiness levels. The Danes aren't really melancholy. Instead, they're positively giddy—and equal. It's the Turks who are sad and unequal.

At this point, conservatives are apt to roll out the banner of American Exceptionalism. People in other countries might have relative preferences, says the conservative, but not Americans. We don't do envy. Mean life satisfaction in the United States has remained fairly constant over 1940–2000, notwithstanding the sharp increase in income inequality seen in Figures 4.1 and 4.2. From this, concludes the conservative, Americans aren't bothered by people who are richer than they are.

On examination, however, that looks very much like special pleading. Over the same period, Americans became much wealthier, and from that one would have expected greater happiness levels. Correcting for increased wealth, then, income inequality may plausibly have dampened happiness levels. So economist Richard Layard has argued: unhappiness from rising income inequality simply cancelled out happiness from rising average income.[9] That's also what researchers found when they investigated the relation between income inequality and happiness over a 37-year period in the United States. Within the borders of their country, Americans were happier when there was less inequality.[10] In particular, low-income Americans felt their society to be fairer and more worthy of trust when income inequality was reduced, and the perception of unfairness made people unhappy. Finally, there's the 2012 election, where income inequality was an issue that propelled Obama to victory. It gets harder and harder to argue that Americans aren't bothered by income inequality.

That's no longer the question. The question, rather, is what we can do about it.

PART III

Things We (Mostly) Can't Change: Technology, Taxes, Welfare, Culture, Genes

I conceive that there are two kinds of inequality among the human species; one, which I call natural or physical, because it is established by nature, and consists in a difference of age, health, bodily strength, and the qualities of the mind or of the soul: and another, which may be called moral or political inequality, because it depends on a kind of convention, and is established, or at least authorized by the consent of men.

—JEAN-JACQUES ROUSSEAU, *The Origin of Inequality Among Men*

The Move to an Information Economy

FOR ALL OF THESE REASONS, THE LEFT HAS CORRECTLY identified income inequality as a troubling social and economic problem. The tragedy of America, however, is that while the Left often asks the right questions, it almost as often provides the wrong answers. Income inequality is no exception. If we might prefer a society where income disparities were lessened, there are some things we would not want to do to get there. "For every complex problem," observed H.L. Mencken, "there is an answer that is clear, simple, and wrong."

Let's start by recognizing that some inequalities don't raise our hackles or call for correction. Even Jean-Jacques Rousseau, the first of the moderns to put inequality on the map, conceded this. In his *Discourse on Inequality* (1754), Rousseau distinguished between two kinds of inequality: natural and political. Natural inequality refers to differences in people's strength of body or mind. By contrast, political inequality describes the further differences that arise when people live in civil society, where some people are more honored than others, some more powerful, and some richer, not because of natural differences but because of how society ranks them. Rousseau's point was that what accounts for inequality matters. If the super-wealthy got there because of natural inequalities, because they were more gifted or worked harder, we wouldn't want to take that away from them. That's why it's important to understand just why America's super-rich got that way.

The leading explanation that's been offered for the rise in inequality is *skill-based technological change* (SBTC). We've moved to an information economy in which new technology favors high-tech people in a high-tech world.[1] Poorly skilled workers used to expect that decent middle class jobs would be waiting for them, but now they've been left behind. That looks like Rousseau's natural inequality, and if so he'd tell us to leave things alone.

Since technological change seems so apparent, SBTC explanations won ready acceptance. Technology-based theories rest on three assumptions, however. First, if there's been technological change, is it really "skill-based"? That is, does technology on net transfer jobs to the highly skilled as opposed to the low-skilled? The answer, very likely, is yes, but the other two assumptions are more questionable. Is our sense of technological change an illusion? Is there really more of it today than 100 years ago? If not, SBTC theories can't begin to explain the recent run-up in inequality. Lastly, SBTC explanations assume that the demand for high-skilled jobs has increased and outpaced the supply of high-skilled workers, driving up their wages. Perhaps it's the other way around, however. Perhaps we've seen a relatively smaller supply of high-skilled workers chasing the high-tech jobs. That would also drive up their wages, and if so the rise in inequality might have little to do with technological change.

Is Technological Change Skill-based?

Has technological change advantaged the highly skilled more than the low-skilled? Perhaps not. First, the highly skilled might have been paid more even in a low-tech world. Before there were computers and business software programs, there were office managers, accountants, bookkeepers, and secretaries who served as their firm's memory and information processors. They had to be smart to do their jobs and were better paid to do so. If the highly skilled commanded a wage premium 100 years ago, technological innovations since then might not have changed the relative wage premium they receive today. They were paid more before and they're paid more now.

The second reason why technological change might not be skill-based is because new technologies can benefit low-tech as well as high-tech workers. In the nineteenth century, the steel plow—the Plow that Broke the Plains—allowed farmers to transform an ocean of prairie grasslands to arable farmland in a generation. And not very long ago, George H. Bush was intrigued to learn that a poorly educated sales clerk could price a can of beans simply by scanning a bar code.

To see how new technology can assist even the humblest of low-tech workers, take the deliveryman going about his rounds. Let's say that he has to visit six different houses, and that it doesn't matter in which order he does so. What he faces is called the Fuller Brush Salesman problem, from back when brushes were peddled door to door. With six houses, the deliveryman has to choose amongst six-factorial (6*5*4*3*2) or 720 possible routes. Some are longer than others, and how is he going to know the shortest one? True, there aren't many door-to-door travelling salesmen today, but there are UPS drivers and they have the same problem. Each UPS truck makes around 130 stops per day, and for each mile the trucks cut from their routes the company saves $30 million a year.[2] Solving the travelling salesman problem turns out to be crucially important in keeping costs down.

Before the advent of modern computers, the travelling salesman couldn't be sure which route was the shortest. Today, it is relatively simple for him to run all 720 permutations on his laptop to find the quickest route, and that's an example of how new technology can assist a low-tech worker. But that's only six stops. Suppose that 14 more houses get added to the salesman's route, and that he has to visit 20 houses. Now there are twenty-factorial possible routes, and that comes to 2,432,902,008,176,640,000 possibilities. That's more than 2 billion, billion different choices, and that's not something I can solve on my computer. In fact, a brute force computation and comparison of all possible routes is impractical for even the most powerful of today's computers.

The travelling salesman problem turns out to be one of the most difficult problems on the frontiers of computational mathematics, one with applications in computer chip design, 3-D printing, and computer searches, as well as travel routes. That's beyond the ken of your UPS driver. There's more than one way to skin a cat, however. If brute force calculation of all routes is impossible, there are indirect computational techniques, and in 2006 a team led by Georgia Tech's William J. Cook found the shortest route for an 85,900-city tour.[3] For the UPS driver, Cook also produced an iPhone app that will do the trick for 100 cities. Here's a case where technology has given low-skilled workers the tools to save costs over a problem that would have made the most highly skilled people throw up their hands a decade ago.

Low-skilled workers can benefit from technological change, then. Nevertheless, most economists believe that technology has favored the highly skilled far more than the less skilled, for at least the last

100 years. In part, that's because new technology has eliminated a lot of low-skilled jobs through automation. Taylorism—the assignment of repetitive tasks in early twentieth century factories—took a major hit, as robots moved onto the assembly line and replaced humans. More recently, computerization has permitted firms to dispense with the institutional memory and index cards of long-term employees, as happened to Jack Nicholson's character in *About Schmidt*. Similarly, the scanning devices that puzzled George H. Bush in 1992 are now replacing sales clerks in stores like The Home Depot, where shoppers scan purchases themselves. Next on the list are the servers at fast food restaurants, who are losing their jobs to touchscreen kiosks.

Eastman Kodak's downfall is a good example of how new technologies can account for the loss of middle class jobs and the jobs polarization phenomenon we saw in Chapter 4. Not very long ago, Kodak dominated the photography business and employed 140,000 people, but now it's gone through a bankruptcy and has only 8,000 workers left. What happened was technological change, and the digital cameras on our cellphones. The new technologies are great, but they don't employ the same number of people. In 2012 Facebook paid $1 billion for Instagram, a photo-sharing app, which had only 13 employees at the time.

There's also been a remarkable decline in U.S. private sector union jobs, which are mostly low-skilled. Private sector union membership fell from 24.5 percent of the work force in 1973 to 6.7 percent in 2013. The union movement remains strong, but today most union members work in the public sector, where 35 percent of government workers are unionized, more than five times the rate of private sector workers.[4] As we saw in the disastrous 2013 Obamacare roll out, the politically well-connected public sector isn't exactly the poster child for new technology. Even Obama admitted that "one of the things [the federal government] does not do well is information technology procurement."[5]

It's therefore generally assumed that technological change is "skill-based" and biased in favor of the highly skilled. New technologies tend to increase the demand for highly paid, high-skilled workers, while reducing the number of low-tech jobs. That's what the Organization for Economic Cooperation and Development (OECD) reported, after a cross-country survey of its members:

> The median hourly wage of workers who can make complex inferences and evaluate subtle truth claims or arguments in written texts is more than 60% higher than for workers who can, at best, read relatively short texts to locate a single piece of information. Those with low literacy skills are also more than twice as likely to be unemployed.[6]

As for what's ahead, the Bureau of Labor Statistics tells us to expect more of the same over 2010–20.[7] All the signs point to the continued displacement of many thousands of low-tech jobs, including even UPS truck drivers. Until recently one couldn't imagine truck deliveries without a person at the wheel. In 2004, the Defense Advanced Research Projects Agency (DARPA) offered a prize for a self-driving car that could navigate a 150-mile stretch through the Mojave Desert, but the best car broke down after only 8 miles. Three years later, however, six teams finished a 60-mile course, and today three states permit self-driving cars on their highways. One of them can be seen on a YouTube video of a blind man taking a self-driving Prius through the drive-through at Taco Bell and then to the dry cleaners.[8] The vehicles rely on Google Maps and Street View as well as radar and video messages that are fed into a computer, and have been said to provide a safer drive than any a human driver could provide. The possibility of self-driving trucks—to say nothing of books delivered by Amazon's drones—is something that has to worry the Teamsters Union.

On net, therefore, recent technological changes have likely shifted jobs from low to highly skilled employees, as SBTC theories would have it.

Has Technological Change Recently Increased?

That doesn't prove that technological change caused the rise in inequality, however. The rise of the one percent and the cratering of middle class jobs are recent phenomena, and SBTC theories can't account for them unless there's been a striking increase in the rate of technological change over the last 20 or 30 years. Is that what's happened?

We've certainly seen a good many recent technological innovations, as anyone knows who's shopped for personal computers over the last 25 years. IBM broke the 1-gigabyte barrier in 1980, with a hard drive that weighed 550 pounds and was the size of a refrigerator. Today I am writing on a MacBook Air with 256 gigs of hard drive space, more than enough for me, since I use the Cloud (something not even dreamt of in 1980) for additional storage. If I really wanted to show off I could buy an external hard drive with a terabyte (1,000 gigs) of memory for $60. And I know it'll be cheaper next year.

Along with the increase in storage space, there's been an increase in computational ability. Yale economist William Nordhaus estimates that over the last 60 years the real cost of performing a computational task fell by a third to a half *annually*.[9] Things that were extraordinarily difficult as recently as 30 years ago, such as the multiple regressions of Appendix C, can now be done with the touch of an Enter key on a statistical software package such as STATA. The amount of data that's on the web has also transformed empirical research. Twenty years ago, I had to enter data manually from a printed copy of the Statistical Abstract. Now one simply copies or downloads it.

It's not just storage space or computational ability. Anyone who does research, who has to look up a problem, can now do so in a fraction of the time that it used to take. No trips to the library are needed, soon perhaps no bricks-and-mortar libraries; instead, just a few clicks on a powerful search engine like Google with its Chrome browser. For historical research, there's Google Books. For academics, there's JSTOR, with its enormous collection of scholarly articles. Or maybe one might just ask Siri, Apple's iPhone navigator. Someone with tennis elbow, for example, might be directed to a list of exercises he might try. Siri has sense enough to deflect profound questions, and can even display a sense of humor:

> Do you believe in God? *Siri*: "It's all a mystery to me."
> Do you believe in Santa Claus? *Siri*: "He's as real as I am."

It's never a good idea to bet against emerging technologies. Back in the 1970s, French film director Jean-Luc Godard thought that things would never get better than the new IBM Selectric typewriter (seen in the Costa-Garvas film, Z). Twice the size of an old manual typewriter, with a soothing electric hum and a thrilling click when its keys were pressed, it produced a typescript that looked almost as good as a printed page. And so Godard bought 40 of them, just enough he thought to last him the rest of his life. We've seen how that turned out.

That doesn't make the case for SBTC theories, however. The rise in inequality occurred after 1980, and SBTC theories can't account for this unless there wasn't a lot of technological progress prior to 1980 and it all happened afterwards. Is that what happened? The assumption of a post-1980 step-up in technology has been challenged in the most important recent book on U.S. labor markets,

Claudia Goldin and Lawrence Katz's *The Race between Education and Technology*.[10] Goldin-Katz report that skill-based technological change was far more rapid and continuous during most of the twentieth century than we had previously thought. Jonathan Huebner takes this one step further in arguing that technological changes peaked in the nineteenth century and sharply declined after 1965.[11] If they're right, that demolishes SBTC theories. It's hard to measure any of this, but taking the shifts in inequality as evidence for technological change merely begs the question.

Even if Goldin-Katz and Huebner were wrong, even had there been a pattern of rapid technological change in the last 30 years, this might explain the rise of a technically sophisticated class, but not of the one percent. Of the million-odd members of the top one percent, nearly 70 percent are salaried executives in nonfinancial businesses, people working in finance, or doctors and lawyers. Only 4.6 percent of the one percent were in the tech-savvy fields of computers, math, engineering, or non-finance technical work.[12] SBTC theories are also unable to account for the very sharp income increases for people in the 0.001 percent bracket, such as hedge and asset fund managers.[13] These are risk-takers who got lucky, Taleb's antifragiles, and that doesn't sound like an SBTC-driven change.

As for what's ahead, one can only speculate. Technology skeptics such as Robert Gordon argue that we're on a plateau and that the pace of innovation has stalled.[14] Similarly, Tyler Cowen suggests that the gains from innovation were like low-lying fruit that have all been eaten, and that we have to accept a future of economic stagnation.[15] As evidence of a slowing in innovation, techno-pessimists point to slower gains in productivity (output per hour) and per capita GDP. A decline in innovation has even been thought to explain the difficulty the United States experienced in emerging from the Great Recession.[16] That's not good for the economy, but it might be good news if all you're worried about is inequality. If SBTC theories explain inequality, and if Gordon and Cowen have correctly predicted a slow-down in technological change, we can expect to see a more egalitarian future.

Other economists, including Gordon's colleague at Northwestern, Joel Mokyr,[17] take a much more sanguine view of the future. Perhaps the wealth gains of an information economy haven't even begun to kick in yet, as Erik Brynjolfsson and Andrew McAfee argue.[18] In a Brynjolfsson-McAfee world, the spillover gains from digitalized information will give rise to powerful new networks of minds and machines. With a small number of users, a network isn't much good. When telephones were first introduced, for example, Clarence Day's father didn't want one in the house. "Since almost nobody had them but brokers, there was no one to talk to."[19] But as more people are added to the system, the telephone's value increased exponentially, and under "Metcalfe's Law" the value of a network is proportional to the square of the number of the connected users. We saw an example of what network effects can mean in Egypt's 2011 "Facebook Revolution," where the unpopular Mubarak government was ousted by protests coordinated through social media.

As more people become connected through the Internet, then, the network gains can be expected to increase dramatically. So Brynjolfsson-McAfee think, for they tell us that "the second machine age will be characterized by countless instances of machine intelligence and billions of interconnected brains working together to better understand and improve our world. It will make a mockery of all that came before."[20] Maybe so.

A Supply-side Explanation?

SBTC theories also assume that the run-up in top salaries can be attributed to demand exceeding supply. New technologies increased the demand for highly skilled workers, and there weren't enough of them around. What happened next is what always happens when demand outstrips supply: the suppliers (or workers) are paid more.

Is that what happened? The wage gap between college and high school graduates increased from 1980 to 2000, as SBTC theories would have predicted. There's another possible explanation, however, one to which Claudia Goldin and Lawrence Katz incline, which looks to the supply and not the demand side. The wage premium for highly skilled workers may have increased not because there was a greater demand but because there was a smaller supply of them.

The supply of U.S. college graduates has increased over the last 50 years, along with the population. The greatest rate of change occurred in the 1960s, as Baby Boomers went to college. Thereafter, the rate of change slowed, as the Baby Boom mongoose worked its way through the belly of the snake. There was a greater supply of college grads, but the value of a university degree had declined and graduates found that degrees in postmodern literary theories didn't lead to the kinds of jobs they wanted.[21] American higher education is too often a form of generational betrayal, in which tenured, Boomer professors teach their millennial students how to be unemployable. A pathetic picture on the *We Are the 99 Percent* website features a member of the lost generation holding a sign reading "I have a Master of Arts in Women's Studies. However, the only job I can find is as a bartender at a local restaurant. I owe 60k in student loans. I am forced to rely on food stamps and W.I.C. to support my son. Is this the American Dream?"

With the decline in American higher education, relatively fewer skilled workers are chasing high-tech jobs. In what Goldin-Katz called, "the race between education and technology," the demand for high-tech workers has outstripped supply, and that's why high-tech wages went up. It wasn't because there were dramatic technological changes, as SBTC theories would have it.

To the extent that the decline in U.S. higher education explains the rise in American inequality, as Golden and Katz argue, this might account for the greater income equality in countries whose universities are more likely to stress technical education. One doesn't find courses such as Columbia's "Zombies in Popular Media" in France, or the University of Virginia's "GaGa for Gaga: Sex, Gender, and Identity" in Germany. In those countries, there are relatively more high-tech graduates, who command less of an income premium.

In sum, SBTC explanations of the rise of American inequality are unpersuasive. They assume that there's been a sharp increase in technological change over the last 30 years, and that's anything but clear. Less clear still is what the future might hold, when it comes to technological improvements. Then there's the matter of who the super-rich are. They're mostly corporate executives and risk-loving financial investors, not high-tech geeks. Finally, even if new technology made the difference, it's not something we'd want to change, or even could. No one is going to pry our iPhones away from us.

Globalization

THREE THINGS ACCOUNT FOR AMERICA'S ECONOMIC
success in the twentieth century. First, unlike most of Europe, the
United States invested in public education, and during what Goldin and Katz call the "human capital century" this paid enormous
dividends. For most individuals, and for everyone who is young, the
greatest source of wealth is anticipated future earnings. What these
will be depends upon what economists call human capital: the intelligence, education, work habits, and personal virtues that correlate
with a person's economic success. National wealth in turn is a function of the human capital of its citizens, as well as social capital: the
spillover benefits of living in a country where other people have high
human capital. I am better off if I live in a country whose citizens
are intelligent, well-educated, and trustworthy.[1]

The second factor was the very size of the country. During the
twentieth century, America was the beneficiary of an enormous free
trade zone—the United States of America. Other countries, such
as Australia, New Zealand, and Canada, made equal investments

in public education, but lacked access to America's broad markets. Together with its investments in education, the country's national free trade zone made it the *stupor mundi*. By 1910 it produced 48 percent of the world's wealth, up from 16 percent in 1870. By 1920, when Europe lay prostrate from the effects of the First World War, America's share of the world's wealth would rise to 62 percent.[2]

Third, the United States derived a further spillover benefit from the English language. Americans, along with Britons and citizens of its former colonies, spoke the same language, and because much of the world's foreign trade was amongst them English became the language of global business. That helps explain why top incomes are higher in the English-speaking world.

America's relative advantages have been dissipated in recent years, however, through increased investments in public education elsewhere, expanded free trade arrangements across the globe, and the way in which English has become the *lingua franca* of business across the globe. All this goes a long way towards explaining not only America's rise but also its relative decline after the Second World War, as other countries played catch-up. From 62 percent of the world's wealth in 1920, the U.S. has fallen to 17 percent today. Could these changes also account for the country's growing income inequality?

The Loss of Low-tech Jobs

Free trade ships jobs to countries that can produce goods at a relatively low cost. Economists call this "comparative advantage," and it was first identified by Adam Smith. "If a foreign country can supply us with a commodity cheaper than we ourselves can make it, better buy it of them with some part of the produce of our own industry, employed in a way in which we have some advantage."[3]

This has served to shift low-tech jobs from America to poorer countries with lower wage rates, and through globalization—the spread of markets across the world—the process has intensified over the last twenty years. In the first decade of this century, U.S. multinationals shed 2.9 million U.S. jobs while increasing employment overseas by 2.4 million.[4] General Electric provides a striking example of this. Jeffrey Immelt became the company's CEO in 2001, with a mission to advance stock price. This he did, in part by reducing GE's U.S. workforce by 34,000 jobs. During the same period, however, the company added 25,000 jobs overseas. Ironically, Obama chose Immelt to head the president's Jobs Council.[5]

That's not to belittle the good globalization has done around the world. It has proven an astonishing blessing for most of world's people. This is especially true for China, whose workers saw average income gains of 178 percent in constant dollars over 1988–2008, compared to 29 percent in the more mature economies of the First World.[6] Over the last 30 years, the number of Chinese people living in extreme poverty (less than \$1.25 a day) fell from 84 to 12 percent of the population, from 835 to 156 million, an expansion of wealth unmatched in history.[7] And it's not just China. The World Bank reports that over the same period extreme poverty in the developing world dropped from 52 percent to 14.5 percent, this despite a 59 percent increase in population.[8] But if globalization has brought people in other countries into the middle class, it has also meant the loss of low-tech, middle class jobs in America. Not only have U.S. firms such as GE shipped jobs offshore, but American consumers are increasingly buying foreign manufactured products. By 2010, low-wage imports accounted for more than half of all manufactured imports,[9] and import competition has been found to explain a quarter of the decline in U.S. manufacturing jobs.[10]

The New Global Super-rich

If free trade and globalization lowered wages at the bottom end in America, what about the top end? As we saw, the move to an SBTC information economy doesn't seem to account for why the one percent cleaned up. In conjunction with globalization, however, SBTC theories help explain what happened. That's because many of the new technological advances are *scalable*, and can be expanded in scale at low cost. That goes for management services, and corporate executives who formerly found it difficult to manage anything bigger than a small firm can now bring their skills to oversee global corporations.

As recently as 1966, no more than 138 long-distance calls could be placed at the same time between the United States and Europe.[11] Back then, one picked up a rotary phone, dialed zero, asked the operator for a number, and was told to hang on and be ready to answer when she phoned back in an hour or three to say a line was open. Or else to call back after midnight. Since then, however, communication satellites, digitized information, worldwide access to the Internet, and the ease of travel have made it easier for Wall Street managers to do their deals around the world, and for business managers to oversee plants in other countries.

When globalization interacts with technological change, firms spread across the world and become larger. At the same time, the number of managers needed to oversee a global business becomes relatively smaller, and this explains why executive pay has increased along with firm size.[12] This in turn helps account for the rise of the one percent.[13] It wasn't the information economy by itself, but its interaction with globalization, that made the difference.

What this tends to produce is what Robert Frank and Philip Cook call a "winner-take-all" society. One hundred years ago, entertainment and sports stars depended for their earnings on the number of people who paid to see them in person. The best actor in New York might appear before 10,000 people in a season, the best ballplayer (along with his teammates) might thrill a few hundred thousand fans. New technologies, television, digital recordings, the Internet, now bring the same people before audiences that can number in the billions, and give rise to "superstar" compensation where the rewards for those at the top of their fields vastly exceed those a single step below.[14]

In book publishing, for example, a very small number of authors will make the best-seller lists, with royalties falling off the cliff for everyone below them. The same thing happens with bookstores. A hundred years ago a successful bookseller might stock 10,000 books on its shelves. Twenty years ago, Tom Hanks' *You've Got Mail* portrayed how big-box outlets, with as many as 200,000 titles and revenues of more than $2 million per store, were running Meg Ryan's small niche store out of town. Now, however, it's the big-box Borders bookstores that have folded, and a single bookseller, Amazon, dominates the market. Its founder and CEO, Jeff Bezos, reportedly has a net worth of $25 billion, many thousands of times more than Tom Hanks' character could have dreamed of making. As for small used-book stores, they're thriving as third-party sellers on Amazon.

Ironically, free trade and globalization might in time threaten the American one percent, by shifting high-end as well as low-end jobs to other countries. Indeed, high-end jobs are doubly threatened, since the cross-country pay differential is greater than with low-tech jobs, and since high-tech workers rely on digitalized information that is easily transferred across borders. "In theory," observes the British Institute of Directors, "anything that does not demand physical contact with a customer can be outsourced to anywhere on the globe."[15]

In the future, then, the high-end jobs might increasingly be found in Bangalore rather than Boston. Jobs in computer, accounting, legal, and medical services that were formerly thought to be rooted in the U.S. are already moving offshore. After all, it's a simple matter to send digital X-Ray scans to India, where radiologists make far less than American specialists, and given the heightened U.S. regulatory environment financial services might be the next on the list. I experienced the phenomenon myself, when Oxford University Press in New York sent a book of mine to Coimbatore, India, where Viswanath Prasanna edited it quickly and very skillfully.

In the past, location was all-important: a researcher needed to work closely with colleagues on the cutting edge of his discipline. Papers were shared slowly, and generally only with close colleagues. Scholars worked in "clusters," geographically related networks of universities, research institutions, think tanks, and companies.[16] High-tech development was centered in Silicon Valley, and great universities such as Stanford and MIT spun off research firms in Palo Alto and Cambridge, where intellectual breakthroughs came not from solitary geniuses but from creative teams bouncing ideas off each other.[17] In the future, however, location will matter less. Travel is cheaper, of course, but more importantly papers are accessible worldwide and immediately though Internet publishing sites such as Social Science Research Network (SSRN). Scholars can also collaborate in real time on papers, and 3D virtual reality conferences can be expected to replace the faculty workshop. We'll still want to talk to colleagues down the hall, but we'll also become accustomed to virtual visits with our peers in India or Japan.

The next move may be to nowhere at all. The University of Florida's Tom Lin has described the rise of "cyborg finance," in which investment decisions are increasingly made through computerized programs that employ mathematical algorithms.[18]

That's bad news for both New York and London. What's bad news to lawyers, wherever they are, are computers that can replicate their work. Lawyers who run up many thousands of billable hours reviewing documents are increasingly being replaced by computers that do the same job in a faction of the time at a fraction of the cost. In 2011, for example, one software company helped analyze 1.5 million documents for $100,000, vastly less than what a law firm would have billed.[19] The computers don't get bored or get headaches, and they're probably a lot more accurate. Then there are software programs such as TurboTax that are taking jobs away from tax preparers and accountants. The iron law of the new economy is that any task that can be turned into an algorithm will be done by computers and not by people.

For the moment, however, the interaction between technological change and globalization provides a persuasive explanation for part at least of the rise of the American one percent. We'd expect to see the one percent to pull away from the 99 percent in a technologically advanced, global economy, and especially in rich countries such as the United States. But that can't be the only thing going on. In a truly global economy, location matters less than ever before, and the same economies of managerial scale can be found in Copenhagen and Toronto. The cross-border patterns of income distribution and immobility which I'll discuss in the following chapters require a very different explanation, one which I'll provide in the last part of the book.

Finally, even if new technologies and globalization help explain the rise of the one percent, we wouldn't want to change things. We're even less likely to want to return to 1930s, with their disastrous high tariff barriers. If there is one proposition to which virtually every economist would subscribe, it is that free trade on average makes people better off, including the poor.[20] It provides consumers with cheaper goods and permits manufacturers to

specialize in what they do best and take advantage of scale economies in production. Free trade also discourages the wasteful competition for political advantage in which domestic manufacturers
court politicians for subsidies and special tariffs against foreign
firms. To the extent that technological change and globalization
account for the rise of the superrich, that's something we're going
to live with.

The Limits of Public Policy

IF WE'RE UNHAPPY WITH THE HAND THE HIGH-TECH, global economy has handed us, our first instinct might be to reach for three simple policy responses: increase welfare benefits for the poor, raise marginal taxes on the rich, and pass campaign finance laws. All three policies are espoused by populist politicians, but none of them carries us very far. Our welfare system is already very generous and our tax rates high. As for campaign finance laws to take money out of politics, there's good reason to think that won't make things any better.

Stingy Welfare Benefits?

The clamor over the one percent obscures the fact that the United States has a very generous welfare system, administered through more than 80 federal programs, and this doesn't include private charities and state and local government programs. The non-partisan Congressional Research Service reports that the federal government spent $745 billion on welfare (excluding Medicare) in 2011, more than on defense spending.[1] Quantifying this, the Heritage Foundation reported that the average household headed by someone who lacks a high school degree received more than $46,000 in benefits and services and paid about $11,500 in taxes.[2] And that was before Obamacare kicked in.

Federal Welfare Benefits

The extensive list of federal programs for the poor includes Medicaid (plus the requirement that hospitals permit anyone to use their emergency room as a drop-in clinic); food stamps (the Supplemental Nutrition Assistance Program); the Children's Health Insurance Program (CHIP); the Special Supplemental Nutrition Program for Women, Infants, and Children, for pregnant women and mothers with small children; the School Breakfast and Lunch programs; the Emergency Food Assistance Program; and federal housing assistance (including Section 8 and the Making Home Affordable programs). The old New Deal era Aid to Families with Dependent Children (AFDC) is now the Temporary Assistance for Needy Families (TANF) program, which pays cash mostly to single mothers with children. Then there is the Earned Income Tax Credit (EITC), which sends low-income workers checks even if they owed no taxes to be credited against. There are also the kinds of hidden wealth transfer programs that most people don't associate with government welfare, such as Social Security and Obamacare.

European countries are generally thought to have more generous welfare policies than those of the United States. But even in absolute dollar numbers America spends about the same as the ostensibly more generous Nordic countries.[3] And as a percent of GDP, the United States spends more on welfare than Britain, Canada, Australia, Denmark, Norway, the Netherlands, Japan, and all but four European countries. The U.S. comes in at 27.5 percent, just a little behind Sweden's 27.8.[4] So much for the myth of stingy welfare benefits.

Few Americans realize just how generous their welfare system is. We don't pride ourselves on living in a welfare state, like Sweden. Instead of direct grants to the poor, in the European manner, American welfare is given interstitially, through the cracks of countless, lengthy and confused statutes and regulations, invisible even to its recipients, as described in Suzanne Mettler's *Submerged State*.[5] In short, America is a pretty good country to live in, if you happen to be poor.

Had the American welfare system been designed by a single person, we might think him embarrassed by his liberality. Rather than provide the benefits directly, he does so in a circuitous manner, through a plethora of programs, that his left hand might not know what his right has given. That's not what happened, of course. The different programs simply grew like Topsy. Or perhaps they proliferated in an underground manner, so that they might be obscured from the view of penny-pinching conservatives. But covert tools are never reliable tools, as Karl Llewellyn observed.[6] With so many different programs, there is going to be some overlap amongst them, and some recipients who double-dip. The effort to hide to rabbit also gives us legislative monstrosities such as the 1,000-page Obamacare bill, full of hidden goodies for favored senators and interest groups.

Low Tax Rates?

Changes in *marginal income tax* rates explain a fair bit of the changes in the one percent's share of household wealth over the last 80 years.

The fisc took 92 cents of every dollar at the top end during the 1950s, and until the 1982 Reagan tax cuts the top marginal rate on income was 70 percent. In 1988 it fell again to 28 percent. During the Clinton years it rose to 39.6 percent, where (after the interregnum of the George W. Bush tax cuts) it is today.[7] Not surprisingly, the one percent's share of household after-tax income fell from 1930 to 1980 and rose thereafter. The same changes in the marginal tax rate explain the fluctuation in *pre-tax* income. When taxed at 92 percent, an executive won't seek a higher salary as avidly as he would when taxed at 28 percent. At the higher tax rate, he'll also shift more of his remuneration from income to non-taxable pension benefits.

That's not to say we'd want higher income tax rates. The Reagan era tax cuts powered a dramatic increase in the U.S. economy,[8] and spread worldwide as other countries lowered their marginal tax rates to copy the U.S. Indeed, most other countries lowered tax rates even more than the U.S. Today, the top U.S. federal rate of 39.6 percent on personal income remains lower than that of several other First World countries, but this understates the tax burden when state taxes are added to federal ones. The effective combined state and federal rate is 51.9 percent in California and 50.3 percent in New York,[9] which is higher than Germany and most of Canada (federal and provincial). In 2012 the Democrats got a lot of traction out of claims that personal tax rates were too low, but they don't seem so when Germany and Canada are relative tax havens.

Progressive tax rates have greatly reduced American income inequalities. Even with the prior federal rate of 36 percent, the wealthy paid most of the income taxes. The top one percent earned 18.9 percent of total household income in 2010 and paid 37.4 percent of total federal income taxes. The top ten percent earned 51.9 percent of household income and paid 68.8 percent of the taxes. Households in the bottom quintile received 5.1 percent of income and paid 0.4 percent of taxes. Remarkably, the bottom three quintiles actually

A Tax Law Wrinkle

Harvard economist Martin Feldstein points to a little-noticed tax law change that helps explain the run-up in the salaries of small businessmen. Prior to Reagan era tax reform, corporate earnings were subjected to a lower tax rate than personal income, and businessmen sheltered their earnings by leaving them in the corporation. Such earnings wouldn't have appeared in the Saez and Piketty personal income figures we saw in chapter 4. By 1986, however, personal income tax rates had fallen and the incentive to shelter earnings behind a corporate veil had disappeared. Taking the earnings out of the corporation artificially inflated the taxpayer's reported income. See Martin Feldstein, Piketty's Numbers Don't Add Up, Wall Street Journal, May 14, 2014.

received more in federal government transfers (such as Social Security and Medicare) than they paid in taxes. The entire income tax burden was born by the top 40 percent, and especially by the top quintile.[10] That's a story of an economy whose benefits are strongly tilted towards the top end, but it's also a story about a government that aggressively equalizes end-states.

Marginal income tax rates are only part of the story. In recent years the Tax Code has prompted the super-rich to shift their earnings from income to *capital gains*. Until the George W. Bush tax cuts expired, capital gains were taxed at 15 percent, and on average they're still only 27.9 percent at the top end (federal and state, including Obamacare's 3.8 percent investment tax). That's 10 percent less than the top federal income tax rate, and the top 0.1 percent—executives, hedge fund mangers and asset managers such as Romney—was quick to take advantage of this. Together, they account for half of the country's capital gains, and that has reduced their tax burden.

That's not to say that the super-rich have gamed the system to give themselves lower capital gain rates, however.[11] Were that the case, the U.S. capital gains rate would be lower than that of other countries. It's just the opposite, however. The top U.S. rate of 27.9 percent is far higher than the 16.4 percent average for OECD countries of the First World. If the United States were to compete with

═══════════════════ FIGURE II ═══════════════════

Corporate Tax Rates

SOURCES: Doing Business 2012: Doing Business in a more Transparent World, International Bank for Reconstruction and Development. Paying Taxes 2012: The Global Picture, Appendix 4, Table 1, at http://www.doingbusiness.org/~/media/FPDKM/Doing%20Business/Documents/Special-Reports/Paying-Taxes-2012.pdf. The figures include social contributions and labor taxes paid by the employer, property and property transfer taxes, dividend, capital gains and financial transactions taxes, waste collection, vehicle, road and other taxes, and excludes employee withholding taxes. See Paying Taxes 2012: The Global Picture, Appendix 4, Table 1, at http://www.doingbusiness.org/~/media/FPDKM/Doing%20Business/Documents/Special-Reports/Paying-Taxes-2012.pdf.

the rest of the world on capital gains taxes, then, it would have nowhere to go but down.[12]

Then there are *corporate taxes*, a favorite target for American progressives. For example, the Institute for Policy Studies reports that in 2013 29 of America's 100 highest-paid CEOs received more in pay than their company paid in federal income taxes. Boeing and Ford Motors both paid their CEOs more than $23 million while receiving large tax refunds.[13] That's very troubling, to be sure, but it's a consequence of generous loopholes and not of low marginal corporate tax rates. The loopholes are indeed a scandal, as we'll see in Chapter 18, but the tax rates aren't the problem. The U.S. federal corporate tax rate is 35 percent, but to this should be added state taxes (4.1 percent on average) as well as property taxes. Add them all up and America's marginal tax rate on corporate income is 46.7 percent, one of the highest in the first world. According to the World Bank, 130 countries have lower marginal corporate tax rates, which doesn't much sound as if the American one percent had manipulated the rules to their advantage. What our corporate tax rates have done instead is given firms an incentive to park funds offshore in other countries,[14] or to escape U.S. tax law entirely by changing their residence through a merger with a foreign corporation in a lower-tax country such as Canada.

Taking America's entire tax system into account, the Tax Foundation ranks it second from the bottom amongst the 34 members of the OECD, and "a good example of an uncompetitive tax code."[15] Other countries have worked hard to make their tax systems competitive, but there hasn't been a major tax reform in the U.S. since the Reagan years.

Campaign Finance Reform?

For many on the Left, campaign finance reform is a silver bullet that would cure political corruption and promote income equality. Because candidates must solicit campaign contributions if they're to win an election, donors will have an outsized voice in determining the kinds of policies their candidate supports. Corporate donors will push for laws that benefit them, including inefficient laws designed to hinder up-and-coming business competitors. More political corruption, more income immobility, in short, and it doesn't take a cynic to think that there's a lot of this in Washington.

Most of the countries that rank higher than the U.S. on measures of economic freedom have strict campaign finance laws, and they're also reported to be less corrupt. On Transparency International's Corruption Perceptions Index, the U.S. comes in at number 19, behind most of the rest of the First World.[16] But then politically unfree countries also restrict campaign contributions. Try to fund an opposition party in Russia, for example. Restrictions on campaign spending in America might therefore go either way. They might open up the political process, as those on the Left assert; but they might also limit freedom by protecting incumbent politicians from political challengers, as those on the Right counter. In fact, incumbents of both parties favor campaign finance restrictions. The common enemy is the outside insurgents, such as the Tea Party groups that defeated House Majority Leader Eric Cantor in a 2014 Republican primary. Cantor had spent $5.7 million on the primary, his opponent only $231,000, less than Cantor's restaurant tab.[17]

For now campaign finance reform is on the back burner, less a political debate than a legal one, for the Supreme Court has ruled in *Citizens United* that corporations have First Amendment rights to make political contributions.[18] The case also blessed unlimited donations to independent Super PACs. But then Supreme Court decisions on contentious issues are never fully settled, for they're always open to reversal when new members are appointed to the bench. That's what the Right hopes will happen to *Roe v. Wade*, and what the Left hopes will happen to *Citizens United*; and so campaign finance reform remains a real if somewhat remote possibility.

Whether that would make for a more equal and mobile society is another matter, however. And it's not just that campaign finance restrictions can look like incumbent protection laws. Election laws are highly technical, and the political party that enacts them can be expected to impose a disproportionate burden on the other party. There are different kinds of donors, and different kinds of finance

RAGGED DICK.

"Dick is...smart enough to profit from the book's simple messages: that all labor is respectable, that poverty is no bar to advancement, that getting ahead requires education and saving one's money." Page 4.

"The Carter's Grove [pictured above], Sabine Hall, and Shirley plantations of the Carters, the Westover of the Byrds, the Stratford of the Lees and the Mount Vernons left no doubt that their owners were masters of large fortunes." Page 23.

"Lincoln joked that he had not a platform to stand on, whereupon someone brought him an empty dry-goods box." Page 39.

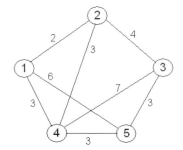

"Solving the travelling salesman problem [pictured left] turns out to be crucially important in keeping costs down." Page 102.

"[Self-driving] vehicles rely on Google Maps and Street View as well as radar and video messages that are fed into a computer, and have been said to provide a safer drive than any a human driver could provide." Page 104.

"In one well-known family, then, the daughter represented not merely an *r* of 0.5, but a sum of 2.5 over only three generations." Page 152.

"A costumed Knight of the Swan challenged the Knight of the Golden Lion to battle." Page 183. Photo: "The Challenge, Eglinton Tournament," by James Henry Nixon.

ABOVE LEFT: "[Booker T. Washington] never attended school, though he sometimes went as far as the schoolhouse door with his white mistresses, carrying their books." Page 187.

ABOVE RIGHT: "'I can see ye don't know what it means to be up to yer neck in nuns.'" Page 206. Photo: Graduation at St. Joseph's School, Petersburg VA.

"He begins as a 'greenhorn,' unable to speak English, but soon finds himself selling hardware from a pushcart on the lower East Side." Page 232. Photo: Mulberry Street, New York City.

regulations, and it's not beyond the skill of the draftsman to produced one-sided rules. In particular, the politician who demands restrictions on campaign contributions, and tells us he does so to defund his political opponents, is the very last person to be trusted to come up with a set of fair and evenhanded standards.[19] Even ostensibly neutral rules that give the regulator a degree of discretion can be employed in a partisan manner. That was the story of Lois Lerner's IRS and its targeting of conservative Tea Party groups, after all.

In America, corruption is a two-way street. We're apt to see it as a matter of donors soliciting wasteful favors from politicians, and forget that corrupt politicians can solicit money from donors with threats of harmful laws. Better still for politicians are laws that give the rule-maker the discretion to extract donations on a continuing basis, for they're the gift that keeps on giving. Peter Schweizer calls this "extortion," and that's an apt label for the shakedowns he describes.[20]

We might also expect partisan criminal prosecutors to pursue political enemies, as they do in Russia. That's what happened to the Wisconsin Club for Growth, a conservative 501(c)4 "social welfare" organization under the Tax Code. It's by no means unusual for politicians to speak at meetings of sympathetic 501(c)4's or suggest that donors support them, and senior aides to Wisconsin governor Scott Walker did just that for the Club for Growth. But this time Democratic prosecutors charged the Club and its members (the "Unnamed Movants" in the subsequent litigation) had unlawfully "coordinated" with Walker. Police wearing flak vests conducted paramilitary predawn raids on club members, turning floodlights onto their homes and seizing their computers and phones as well as those of their families. They were not allowed to call their attorneys, and prosecutors subsequently demanded the names of the club's donors (which such groups are permitted to keep confidential). The breadth of the search was "amazing," said the Wisconsin Supreme Court.

Millions of documents, both in digital and paper copy, were subpoenaed and/or seized. Deputies seized business papers, computer equipment, phones, and other devices, while their targets were restrained under police supervision and denied the ability to contact their attorneys. The special prosecutor obtained virtually every document possessed by the Unnamed Movants relating to every aspect of their lives, both personal and professional, over a five-year span …. Such documents were subpoenaed and/or seized without regard to content or relevance to the alleged violations.…As part of this dragnet, the special prosecutor also had seized wholly irrelevant information, such as retirement income statements, personal financial account information, personal letters, and family photos.[21]

We wouldn't know much about all this, but for the fact that the club director, Eric O'Keefe, revealed it, thus breaching a state gag law and opening himself up to criminal prosecution. O'Keefe has now been vindicated by the Wisconsin Supreme Court, which held that the Club's activities were constitutionally protected speech. It was a bittersweet victory, however, for it came only after extensive and expensive legal proceedings in five Wisconsin counties and numerous interlocutory motions, in three levels of Wisconsin courts and two levels of federal courts. During all this time, the Club's donor support dried up and the prosecution very effectively shut down the club's issue advocacy during Wisconsin's 2014 gubernatorial election. When you're charged with a breach of campaign finance laws, says O'Keefe, "the process is the punishment."

Gov. Rick Perry of Texas can tell a similar story. When a Democratic District Attorney was caught driving drunk, her blood alcohol three times above the legal limit, Perry asked for her resignation, and when she refused he vetoed funding for her public integrity unit. That earned him an indictment for coercion and abuse of office, two felony counts carrying up to 109 years in prison from another Democratic District Attorney. All this came as Perry was considering a bid for the 2016 Republican nomination for president, and it's one of the reasons why he dropped out of the race.

Cases such as these illustrate how four features of American campaign finance laws might invite more corruption than they cure. First, prosecutors are often highly political animals, elected by the voters, and not a few of them have a taste for the kind of publicity that a high profile case might generate. Second, many are elected at the local level, and that increases the likelihood of finding a partisan prosecutor. For example, John Chisholm, who initiated the investigation of the Wisconsin Club for Growth, was elected District Attorney for the very liberal Milwaukee County, while the prosecution of Rick Perry was brought by the District Attorney for the very liberal Travis County (Austin), Texas. Third, the sanctions for prosecutorial misbehavior are extremely weak, and the partisan prosecutor can expect to be celebrated by his political allies. Bad faith prosecutions can be a good career move. Finally, the legal standards are often extremely vague, giving the prosecutor the discretion to discriminate between political friends and foes.

In less corrupt countries, campaign finance laws appear to be enforced in a more politically neutral manner. Prosecutors are career civil servants, who almost never run for office. They are appointed by the government, and in civil law countries they enjoy a quasi-judicial status. In short, they're far less likely to target political opponents. But that's because they're less corrupt to begin with. With campaign finance laws there's a tipping point. At low levels of corruption, stricter rules mean less corruption; but at high levels of corruption stricter rules may result in more corruption.

In America, therefore, it's a nice question whether stiffer campaign finance laws would give us less rather than more political corruption. Those who argue that we'd see less corruption seem to assume that campaign finance laws would never be abused, that corruptible politicians will do the bidding of their donors but will be models of integrity when it comes to enforcing election laws against their political opponents. Nothing could be more naïve, and while campaign finance reformers might burn with honest zeal, they may have picked the wrong country. They seem to be thinking they're living in Nirvana—or New Zealand. Campaign finance laws might work well in less corrupt countries, but in America First Amendment guarantees of free speech are very possibly the best we can do.

There's a deeper problem with campaign finance reform. It seeks to diminish corruption, but attacks the symptom and not the disease. The symptom is campaign spending. The disease is the wasteful legislation and regulations that are drafted to benefit donors. A simplified tax system, shorn of all of the incentive features dictated by special interests, would go a long way towards eliminating corrupt incentives to contribute to political campaigns. So too would simplified legislation, without the earmarks that so disfigured Obamacare, the special payoffs demanded by Senators from Florida, Louisiana, and elsewhere. Too often, the people who support targeted government investments that attract political donors are the same people who propose restrictions on campaign spending. That's not supposed to happen. You can't suck and blow.

CHAPTER

12

Living with Immobility

IN CHAPTER 4 WE SAW HOW AMERICA WAS ALMOST AS aristocratic as Britain. In a measure of income immobility between fathers and sons, America came in at 0.47 and Britain at .50. Denmark was a very low 0.15, the most mobile of all the societies canvassed. But that's not to say that the goal should be an elasticity of zero, with perfect mobility between the generations.

There are three reasons why perfect income mobility is a false ideal, why it would require massive social engineering of a kind that only a despotic tyranny would seek to impose. First, so long as there are income inequalities, rich kids will have a leg up because of their *inherited wealth*. No society imposes 100 percent death duties, and even if it did that wouldn't eliminate the advantages the children of the wealthy enjoy during their parents' lifetime.

Second, *environment and culture matter*. Rich kids are more likely to have been nurtured in homes that prize education and instill the bourgeois virtues that make people wealthy. A child who observes his parents reading books, using sophisticated language, working hard and saving for retirement learns to emulate them. She is also less likely to fall into the traps that are a gateway to lower class status: unwed motherhood, drug use, crime. In all these ways, it helps to have a wealthy parent. That was Ann Richard's line about George H. Bush. "He was born on third base and thought he had hit a triple."

Third, the developing field of *genoeconomics* suggests that rich parents have wealth-promoting genes and that earning ability is in part inherited. That's something that Charles Murray and Richard Herrnstein claimed in their controversial *Bell Curve* nearly 20 years ago,[1] where they attributed the rise of income immobility to the heritability of intelligence. If an information economy offers greater rewards to the highly intelligent, and if intelligence is a heritable trait, then the children of the wealthy will be wealthy themselves, relative to everyone else. The book also reported on what it saw as racial differences in I.Q. levels, and this ignited a firestorm of protest that wholly obscured its message about income immobility. More recently, however, genoeconomics has become more respectable, in part because factors other than I.Q. scores are now seen to explain wealth differences.

Inherited Wealth

Does money help? Not especially for the very wealthiest Americans, as we saw in Chapter 4. When Steven Kaplan and Joshua Rauh looked at the Forbes 400 list of the richest Americans, they found that most had pulled themselves up by their bootstraps. Nearly 70 percent had built their businesses by themselves, up from 40 percent in 1982.[2] At the very top end, amongst the 0.0001 percent, America has never seemed more open to advancement.

That's not to say that inherited wealth doesn't matter. Let me count the ways. Kids with rich parents have better health care and straighter teeth. They'll go to better schools, be taken to after-school activities, and will graduate from better universities. Compared to middle class kids, they have better clothes and a more appealing life story. They can tell you about trips to Brazil to save the rain forest, jokes they shared with the Dalai Lama, and guitar riffs Bono taught them. When interviewed by admission officers and prospective employers, they're not apt to flunk lunch. Sophie Tucker, that red-hot mamma, figured it out. "I've been rich and I've been poor, and rich is definitely better."

If rich kids do better than poor kids, then, we shouldn't be surprised. Who says unequal also says immobile.

Environment and Culture

For the one percent, wealth advantages are heightened when other environmental factors are taken into account. Marriage rates have fallen off a cliff, which is worrisome since the institution is society's principal civilizing institution. The U.S. marriage rate has dropped to a hundred-year low of 31.1, meaning there are about 31 marriages a year for every 1,000 unmarried adult women. In 1950, that number was 90.2.[3] In turn, that's going to affect income mobility. Single parents disproportionately live in poverty,[4] and have little means to give their children a head start. In addition, children born to unwed mothers are more likely to drop out of school and commit crimes.[5] Raj Chetty and his co-authors report that the strongest predictor of upward mobility is family structure.[6] Not merely does a child get a head start in a two-parent family, but as we noted he also does better if the neighbor kids also live in two-parent families.

Wealthy parents are also more likely to spend time with their children, and just listening to parents talk makes a huge difference. Researchers report that, over a four-year period, a child from a professional family will have heard an average of 45 million words, compared to 26 million words for children from a middle-class family and 13 million words for a welfare family. The quality of the words matters too.[7] Children in professional families are more likely to hear words describing abstract thoughts that stimulate mental processes, and thus are better prepared to deal with tasks performed by people in the highest income brackets.

Environmental differences are magnified when like marries like, and that happens much more today than in the recent past.[8] In the innocent Doris Day movies of the 1950s, executives wedded their secretaries and doctors married the schoolteachers whose salary paid their med school tuition. Now, however, lawyers and doctors are more likely to inbreed amongst themselves, a phenomenon labeled "assortative mating." Like the eighteenth century aristocrats, when *prince* married *princesse*, today's aristocrats preserve their rank in society by avoiding a *mésalliance* with someone from a lower station. The Doris Day 1950s were merely an egalitarian interlude, and we have reverted to a natural society of class distinctions.

At the other end of the income scale, between members of the lower class, there's another kind of assortative mating and this also increases economic inequalities. In general, marriage encourages the work habits and saving decisions which leave people better off, but that's less likely to happen when poor women marry down to slacker husbands. What with prison, drugs, and unemployment, there is a smaller pool of employed, marriageable men than of marriageable women. Not surprisingly, struggling women are more likely to give up on marriage entirely, as June Carbone and Naomi Cahn have noted.[9]

Class differences come down importantly to culture. The one percent go to college, don't do drugs, and never have children when they're unwed. They are prudent in their life decisions, temperate in their vices, and resist impulse gratification; and they'll pass on these traits to their children. At the other end, lower class parents will pass on their less desirable traits to their children. In *Coming Apart*, Charles Murray reported that the behavioral gap between rich and poor has widened over the last 30 years, and that today fewer low-income people, white or black, adopt the middle class virtues that favor wealth creation.[10] If he's right, the decline in intergenerational mobility is hardly surprising.

In his 1985 *Losing Ground*, Murray had argued that Lyndon Johnson's Great Society programs of twenty years before had changed

===== FIGURE 12 =====

Earnings Deciles of Sons Born to Bottom-Decile Fathers: U.S. and Canada

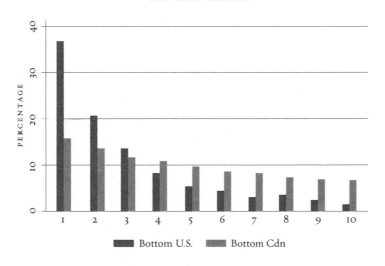

SOURCES: Corak, Curtis and Phipps (2011); Hertz (2005).

the culture and given rise to a permanent underclass.[11] A generation later, when Murray wrote *Coming Apart* in 2012, things were worse still. The unwed birth rate for blacks had increased from 40 to 70 percent, but the bigger news was what had happened to the white unwed birth rate. This had increased from 3.1 to 40 percent, a tenfold increase since 1965.[12] A white underclass had emerged, said Murray, one that had copied the immiserating cultural norms of a black underclass. Poor themselves, the poorest of Americans were increasingly passing on their poverty to their children.

Not all American have followed this downward spiral, however. In *Coming Apart*, Murray presents "Fishtown" as a symbol for the white underclass. That's a real community, a poor neighborhood near historic downtown Philadelphia, and for Murray a proxy for the bottom fifth of white Americans. But then there's the wealthiest 30 percent of Americans, represented by a mythical, politically liberal town called "Belmont"; and between the two towns a chasm has opened, hence the title of Murray's book. In 1960, about 84 percent of Fishtown got married, but that's down to 48 percent now. In Belmont 94 percent got married in 1960, down only to 84 percent today. There's a similar gap when it comes to divorce: 35 percent for Fishtown residents (up from 4 percent in 1960), and 6 percent in Belmont (up from 1 percent). Fishtown and Belmont used to share similar family norms, but today they're like two different countries.

Cultural changes can thus account for much of the rise in American income mobility. They also help explain, what is the greatest puzzle of all, why America is so much less mobile than the similar First World countries, Canada in particular. When income mobility rates are broken down by deciles, there isn't much difference between the two countries for parents in the middle of the distribution. A sharp difference does emerge, however, with the bottom 10 percent of fathers.[13] As seen in Figure 12, American sons born to bottom decile parents are much more likely to end up in the bottom deciles themselves, and less likely to find room at the top, when compared with the sons of bottom decile Canadian parents.

The contrast between the two countries is stunning. We saw in Chapter 4 that Canada is a highly mobile country and America highly immobile, and what Figure 12 tells us is that much of the difference comes from the bottom rung in each country. But just what accounts for this? Part of the answer is the difference in public education, immigration policies, and the rule of law, as we'll see in the next part. But apart from that both countries are democratic, relatively free market, and former British colonies. They have similar legal systems and together form the world's greatest trading block. More than Europeans, both Americans (65 percent) and Canadians (63 percent) think that people determine their own success in life.[14] The cultures are so similar that Hollywood producers bring their films to the Toronto International Film Festival to see how American audiences will react to them.

And yet the cultural norms are different too. American society is more violent and rambunctious, Canadian society more peaceful and ordered. My former colleague, Seymour Martin Lipset, who understood the cultural divide better than anyone I know, described the United States as still Whig and Canada still Tory, the fault lines going back 200 years and more.[15] America was a country formed in a Revolution, individualistic, and populist; Canada was the counter-revolutionary state, taking its character from Loyalists who fled the Revolution, and its people are more deferential to authority. Perhaps so, but that can't explain why Canada is more mobile than the U.S. If anything, the image of Americans as go-getting, self-reliant, and ambitious, as compared to the staid, stick-in-the-muds to the North, would lead one to expect that Americans would be more entrepreneurial and mobile.

When it comes to the bourgeois virtues of moderation and prudence, however, Canada resembles Belmont more than Fishtown. American children are four times more likely to be born to teenage mothers and 50 percent more likely to be born to single, never married mothers, when compared to Canadian children. American children are also more likely to live with step-parents and less likely to live with both biological parents.[16] If Americans seemed more entrepreneurial than Canadians, then, there may be a dark side to American individualism, which Lipset saw as a double-edged sword.[17]

That might lead one to think that there's a simple solution to income immobility: just change the culture. It doesn't take much to get out of poverty, after all. Stay off drugs. Get married. And get a job. Nothing very complicated, in short. But the impediments to the first two are cultural, and that's hard to change. David Hume was not far off the mark when he observed that, "all plans of government, which suppose great reformation in the manners of mankind, are plainly imaginary."[18]

In particular, the federal government has shown itself ill-equipped to engage in the kind of cultural heavy lifting which might encourage bottom decile American parents to adopt the more successful conservative mores of the bottom decile Canadian parents. Welfare reform is a good example. Under the old AFDC program, payments to unwed mothers varied from state to state, and the size of the payment was positively correlated with the unwed birth rate.[19] The greater the payment, the higher the unwed birth rate. That was one of the motives behind the 1996 welfare reform legislation, which placed a time limit on welfare eligibility. As we've seen, however, the unwed birth rate has risen to disheartening levels since then. The cultural norms that made unwed motherhood an acceptable choice were too strong to be much affected by the new law.

Then there's crime. During the 1980s and 1990s, the crack

cocaine epidemic took vast numbers of young men out of the workforce. We might think that the drug culture traps people into poverty and contributes to income inequality, but the last thing we'd want to do is increase criminal penalties for drug use. The United States has five percent of the world's population but 25 percent of the people under criminal supervision, more than any other country, including China. That has to be embarrassing, and if anything we'd want to reduce penalties for drug use, not increase them.

Mobility is downstream from culture. The problem is that we don't know what's upstream from culture, or what can change it. About the only policy levers left are ones which promote economic growth and job creation. If the middle class jobs lost in the Great Recession don't come back, then millions of men will be removed from the marriage market, and that's not something to look forward to. But then job creation was the idea behind Mitt Romney's 59-point plan, and that didn't get very far with the voters.

Genoeconomics

The new field of genoeconomics investigates whether individual and national income is related to genetic factors.[20] Observable traits (phenotypes) such as height and hair color are inherited, and recent studies have shown that psychological as well as physical traits might also be inherited. For example, between 40 and 50 percent of a person's happiness level is said to be inherited,[21] and there appears to be a genetic explanation for violent crime and substance abuse.[22]

What is true of happiness and criminality also appears to be true for the very different traits associated with economic success, and this is evidenced by studies that track family incomes. Brothers are much more likely to make similar incomes than randomly chosen males of the same race and age, even more so if they are identical twins. That doesn't separate out genetic from environmental factors, and it's a mistake to think that they exist in watertight compartments, that a trait can be ascribed to either "nature" or "nurture" and never to both together. Rather, our environment—how we are raised—can affect the genetic advantages with which we are born. "Genetic" does not mean "immutable," as Christopher Jencks noted, and the right family environment can enhance genetic predispositions to economic success.[23]

All the same, genetic factors seem to trump environmental ones. That's the conclusion of economist Bruce Sacerdote, when he looked at Korean-American war adoptees.[24] An Oregon family, the Holts, were moved by the plight of Korean orphans who had lost their parents during the Korean war. They adopted eight of them, and afterwards founded an agency that placed war orphans in American families. In time, over 100,000 children were adopted in this way. It's a heartening story, but what makes it of special interest to the genoeconomist is that children were assigned on a random basis. They were placed in a first-come, first-served manner and the adoptive parents didn't get to pick the children they adopted. By comparing adoptees and non-adoptees in the same family, Sacerdote was then able to compare the contribution of genetic and environmental factors. There was a significant relationship between the incomes of natural, non-adopted children and their parents, but not between the parents and the adopted children. In their case, genetic factors were seemingly more important than environmental ones, in determining income levels. And how important were they? Samuel Bowles and Herbert Gintis estimate that by themselves genes explain a third of the intergenerational wealth correlation between parents and sons.[25]

Just how good genes might contribute to one's income remains highly speculative, however, and the science that maps a person's genetic structure at the molecular level to his observable traits is in its infancy.[26] We're not likely to find a single "income gene" like the single gene for Huntington's disease. There's not even a single character trait that correlates with economic success. In *The Bell Curve*, Richard J. Herrnstein and Charles Murray thought that I.Q. had a major impact on income levels, but Bowles and Gintis report otherwise. What's more important are things like optimism, the sense one isn't stuck in a rut, that one is responsible for one's life. Then there are the virtues of good character—dedication, industry, reliability, impulse control, and an ability to delay gratification. They're what permitted Ragged Dick to rise, and are important elements in what Amy Chua and Jed Rubenfeld describe as *The Triple Package*, the traits that explain economic success.[27] Chua and Rubenfeld offer a cultural explanation for these characteristics, which are disproportionately to be found amongst Mormons, Cuban-Americans, and Chinese-Americans, the book's success stories, but such traits also appear to be heritable.[28] Other heritable traits such as physical beauty and grace doubtlessly help, as the portly and stiff John Adams ruefully concluded.

If that's the case, we're not about to eliminate genetic advantages, in the manner imagined in Kurt Vonnegut's dystopian *Harrison Bergeron*, where a "Handicapper General" erases everyone's natural gifts.[29] In Vonnegut's America of 2081, the beautiful wear masks to cover their faces, the intelligent are fitted with earphones to confuse them, the strong bear heavy "handicap bags." All of that after the 211th, 212th, and 213th Amendments to the Constitution, meant to promote equality. But if that kind of egalitarianism is repellant, this doesn't mean that we'd want to leave things just as they are. As Arthur Goldbeger noted, providing eyeglasses to the myopic would make sense even if the heritability of eyesight were 100%.[30] Other measures to equalize outcome, such as a good public education system, would win nearly everyone's support. Beyond that, however, a country would have to adopt punitive measures to handicap the gifted and talented in order to erase all genetic earnings advantages.

There's one last thing. While genetic explanations help account for income inequality and immobility, what they don't explain are cross-country differences. Why is there is more income mobility in other First World nations, such as Denmark or America's close neighbor, Canada? It's not as if there is a uniquely American DNA. Something else must be going on.

PART IV

Things We (Mostly) Can't Change: The Aristocrat Abides

The great Coprophanaeus beetle will bury me. They will enter, will bury, will live on my flesh; and in the shape of their children and mine, I will escape death. No worm for me nor sordid fly, I will buzz in the dusk like a huge bumble bee. I will be many, buzz even as a swarm of motorbikes, be borne, body by flying body out into the Brazilian wilderness beneath the stars, lofted under those beautiful and un-fused elytra which we will all hold over our backs. So finally I too will shine like a violet ground beetle under a stone.

—W.D. HAMILTON, epitaph

Darwinian Immobility

THE HIPPOCRATIC INJUNCTION 'DO NO HARM' SHOULD be the first precept of public policy as well as of medicine. That's especially the case when it comes to income inequality and immobility, since most of the nostrums that are peddled would make things worse. This includes most of the things we saw in the prior four chapters. In any well-ordered society, we're going to see inequality and immobility, and we're simply going to have to live with them.

But what if we're not such a well-ordered society? We haven't really explained why America is less mobile than most other First World nations, and we haven't answered Obama's charge that the game has been rigged to erect barriers to mobility. There's something else going on, something peculiar to this country, and that's the artificial barriers an American upper class erects to preserve its privileges and to keep the middle class in its place. That's what aristocracies have always sought to do, and today an American aristocracy does this more effectively than people in other First World nations.

We'd like to think that there's something natural about social mobility, that the Ragged Dicks are always bound to ascend the ladder, that nothing need to done to make it happen. That's not what Lincoln thought and it's not what a casual knowledge of history would tell us. Instead, what's natural is aristocracy, a society of stable classes, never wholly fixed but never entirely open either. In the next three chapters I explain why our aristocrats would seek to erect barriers to mobility, and then in the next part I'll discuss how to take them down.

The Bequest Motive

In the last chapter we saw that rich kids have a head start on poor kids. The question, then, is whether we should do anything about this. We could jigger up marginal income tax rates, but they're already high. What that leaves are death duties, the estate taxes to be paid before wealth is passed on at death. That wouldn't eliminate the wealth advantage, since it wouldn't apply until the parent's death, by which time most children from well-off families are well launched. But even apart from that, we wouldn't want to impose confiscatory death duties. That's because we have a *bequest motive* and want to save money for our children, and given this we'd all be a lot poorer if we couldn't pass on our wealth.

With its generous tax credits and tax planning devices, the Tax Code permits most of our wealth to be passed on, tax-free, to our children. Surprisingly, some economists have doubted whether any of this matters. In the Life Cycle savings model proposed by Albert Ando and Franco Modigliani, people don't have a bequest motive and have no desire to save money for their children.[1] Instead, people save only for themselves, putting money aside during their earning years to tide them over during retirement. This would reverse the popular bumper sticker of the 1990s. The person who dies owning the most toys would be a loser, not a winner, for he'd have over-saved. He died earlier than he had thought, and had too many toys left over. Had he timed it perfectly, he would have consumed the last toy just before dying. But even were something left over, the Life Cycle model tells us people wouldn't care if the Taxman took it.

What this comes down to in an empirical question. To what extent, when we save money, do we do so for our old age and to what extent for our children? Surprisingly, when Laurence Kotlikoff and Larry Summers calculated life cycle wealth—how much people spend on themselves during their lifetime—they came up with a figure of only 22 percent.[2] The balance—nearly four-fifths of total savings—was for transfers to others, mostly children, whether as gifts during the donor's lifetime or as bequests to take effect on his death. If all intergeneration transfers were taxed at one hundred percent, this would destroy the incentive to create much of the country's wealth, and Kotlikoff estimated that the country would be 50 percent poorer.

There's an obvious evolutionary explanation for bequest motives, resting on Charles Darwin's theory of sexual selection. The kinds of people who are selected for survival are those who are most successful in having offspring; and these, thought Darwin, were the dominant males and the passive females who paired with them. The male might win the competition in one of two ways: either by driving away other males, or by making himself more agreeable to the female. Amongst humans, the first strategy no longer works. Males don't fight each other for dominance, as stags do. We do, however, compete to make ourselves attractive to females and find that money helps, to the regret of Thomas Love Peacock's nostalgic Mr. Chainmail.

> *Captain Fitzchrome*: We do not now break lances for ladies.
> *Mr. Chainmail*: No, not even bulrushes. We jingle purses for them.[3]

To pass on our genes, we'd want to be rich, and as we'd be concerned about the ability of our children to pass on their genes we'd want them to be rich too. Hence the bequest motive.

The competition to pass on one's genes doesn't seem particularly altruistic. It's all about family, not about other people. This has troubled evolutionary biologists and one of them, W.D. Hamilton,

---

The 'Selfish' Gene

Calling the gene selfish is not to ascribe emotions to it. All it means, instead, is that natural selection favors genes that produce the greatest number of copies of themselves in subsequent generations. We would then expect that the personal qualities (the geneticist's phenotypes) that dispose people to want children will be heritable, along with the desire to see that they and their descendants have the highest degree of evolutionary fitness.

---

is credited with an explanation for how Darwinian natural selection might favor a form of altruism. The competition, said Hamilton, shouldn't be seen at the level of individuals. Instead, he said, evolution should be seen from a gene's-eye view, the perspective of what Richard Dawkins subsequently labeled the *selfish gene*.[4] On this arresting hypothesis, the gene is the decision-making principal, and the individual is merely the agent that from time to time the gene (and its copies) inhabit. The gene gives the command, the individual follows it. And the command is: Be fruitful and multiply.

The selfish gene isn't very altruistic, but what Hamilton recognized was that genes can be transmitted in more than one way. Most obviously, the individual might pass on his genes to his children. In addition, however, we also share genes with our relatives, as geneticist Sewall Wright had noted in 1922.[5] Wright gave a mathematical formula for the probability that two individuals shared a common gene, which he called the "coefficient of relatedness" or r. For one person and any of his direct descendants, r is equal to 0.5^n, where n is the number of generations separating the two. Between father and daughter, for example, r is 0.5; and between father and grandchild it is 0.25. Between siblings, r is 0.5.

From this, Hamilton arrived at a theory of "inclusive fitness,"[6] which he defined to include the contribution to fitness provided by relatives other than immediate children. A person might thus be expected to act altruistically to nephews and cousins, when this would enhance the survival of his genes (and their copies). To operationalize this, Hamilton next applied the coefficient of relatedness r to the economist's cost-benefit ratio: the cost to the donor and the benefit to the recipient, in terms of evolutionary fitness. If altruism is an act that confers a fitness benefit B on the recipient (increasing his probability of reproductive success) and imposes a fitness cost C on the donor (reducing his probability of reproductive success), the decision-making gene can be seen to give the following order to its body:

$$\text{Be altruistic if } rB > C.$$

The selfish gene would therefore sacrifice the individual's reproductive capacity if this increases overall reproductive success through the individual's relatives, both children and other kin. This is "Hamilton's Rule," though it is better known today by the label Maynard Smith gave it: *kin selection*.

By way of example, J.B.S. Haldane had earlier intuited the idea behind kin selection in an aphorism that he would lay down his life for two brothers or eight first cousins. For one brother, $r = 0.5$ and for two of them $r = 1.0$. For one cousin, $r = 0.125$ and for eight of them r = 1.0. When the donor sacrifices himself for either two brothers or eight cousins, it's an even trade.

When it's all tied up like this, the selfish gene is indifferent as between the body it inhabits and those of his kin. But could it ever be more than an even trade? Yes, and this explains the intensity

---

Aristocracy and the Measure of Relatedness

One might ordinarily expect the coefficient of relatedness r to be bounded by 1 and 0. How could the measure of relatedness ever exceed that between identical twins, where $r = 1$? Or be less than 0, where people are entirely unrelated? It can easily happen, however, that $r > 1$ between parents and a large number of their descendants (e.g., three children). Further, r may be less than 0 when people act out of spite to harm strangers with the goal of benefiting relatives, as we'll see in Appendix D.

That's crucially important in explaining the persistence of aristocracy. One can't appreciate the strength of the desire for one's children to do well unless one realizes that r might exceed 1. Similarly, one can't understand why this might take the form of wasteful, beggar-thy-neighbor policies unless one knows that r might be less than 0. The aristocrat might prefer a world where everyone is worse off provided that his children end up on top.

---

of a parent's altruistic feelings for his child, and the desire for an aristocracy. One of the most strongly felt bonds is between fathers and daughters, which could movingly be seen when George VI bade farewell to his newly married daughter, Princess Elizabeth, before she left on a five-month tour with her husband, Prince Philip. The King was gravely ill and knew he would never see his favorite daughter again. He died a week later, and Elizabeth, now the Queen, was

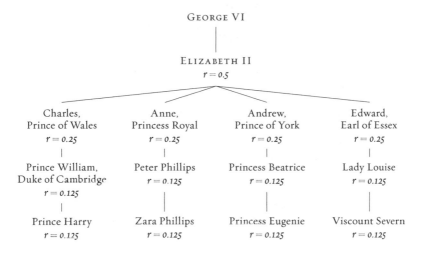

FIGURE 13.1

A Coefficient of Relatedness of 2.5 in Three Generations

recalled from Kenya for her father's funeral and her coronation.

The almost unbearable sadness of the departure scene, captured by cameramen, can be seen on YouTube and does not require a genetic explanation. As it happens, however, there is one. Table 13.1 lists the descendants of George VI, down to three generations, along with their coefficient of relatedness to the king. For Queen Elizabeth it was 0.5; for Prince Charles it was 0.25; and for Prince William it was 0.125. But then they weren't the only descendants. Queen Elizabeth had four children and each of them had two children, and adding all of the coefficients together produces a cumulative coefficient of relatedness that exceeds 1.0. For George VI, his daughter represented not only herself ($r = 0.5$) but also her expected future children: Prince Charles ($r = 0.25$), Anne, the Princess Royal ($r = 0.25$), Andrew, Duke of York ($r = 0.25$) and Edward, Earl of Wessex ($r = 0.25$). Then there are George VI's grandchildren, eight of them in all ($r = .125$ for each), even before getting into the great-grandchildren. In one well-known family, then, the daughter represented not merely an r of 0.5, but a sum of 2.5 over only three generations, and at that point the father is impelled to sacrifice for his child. All this was implicit in Haldane's aphorism. With 8 cousins it was all tied up, but the selfish gene would order the body to sacrifice itself for nine cousins with an r of 1.125.

The insight that r might exceed 1 explains why children don't sacrifice for their parents as much as parents sacrifice for their children. Considered in themselves alone, parent and child both share 50 percent of their genes ($r = 0.5$), and this suggests that they should be equally ready to sacrifice for each other. But if the child's r, relative to one parent, can never exceed 0.5; the parent's r, relative to his descendants, can be larger than 1, as it was for George VI in relation to his daughter and her descendants. That is why the social contract takes this form: we take from our parents and, without repaying them, give to our children. There is always an asymmetry in the relationship, one biased towards future generations. That is why the bequest motive exists, and why aristocracies arise.

A parent will ordinarily recognize the asymmetry, and the father who invests too little in his daughter, or the daughter who invests too heavily in her father, are both unnatural. That should have been the tip-off for King Lear, when he gave away his kingdom to his daughters. He had, first of all, three of them, and might therefore have assumed that, as their combined r was ($3*0.5 =$) 1.5, he could safely retire to their care. His mistake was to rely not on the degree of kinship, but on their professions of love.

GONERIL

Sir, I love you more than words can wield the matter;
Dearer than eye-sight, space, and liberty;
Beyond what can be valued, rich or rare;
No less than life, with grace, health, beauty, honour;

As much as child e'er loved, or father found;
A love that makes breath poor, and speech unable;
Beyond all manner of so much I love you.

REGAN

Sir, I am made
Of the self-same metal that my sister is,
And prize me at her worth. In my true heart
I find she names my very deed of love;
Only she comes too short: that I profess
Myself an enemy to all other joys,
Which the most precious square of sense possesses;
And find I am alone felicitate
In your dear highness' love.

They proclaim, in short, that their devotion will exceed that dictated by a daughter's kinship ratio of 0.5 to her father. With a better sense of human nature and evolutionary psychology, Lear would have recognized that they had lied and that, being untrustworthy, they would betray him in time. Without the third daughter, Cordelia, the play might have been a comedy and called "The Foolish Father." But there is a third daughter, and her fate made the play the supreme tragedy in English literature.

CORDELIA

I love your majesty
According to my bond; nor more nor less.

Cordelia's bond is the kinship bond of daughter to father, no more, no less. It is less than the false, pretended bond of Goneril and Regan, but more than they privately feel, and had Lear relied on the normal evolutionary instincts of fathers to daughters it would have sufficed. It does not, and it will kill him and all of his daughters.

Sadder still are the stories of parents, whether human or animal, abandoning children. In a video that went viral, a newborn elephant cried uncontrollably for five hours after being attacked and rejected by his mother.[7] The video showed tears streaming down his red eyes, as he lay covered with a blanket, a profoundly moving picture of grief, one that any human will recognize.

We should not, then, be surprised or even upset if parents wish well for their children and their children's children. This is what nearly every parent will want. The alternative, parental neglect, is so much worse. The conservative might even take heart. After a national apostasy that leaves an Obama-shaped hole in one's heart, after republican virtue is bartered away for the politics of entitlement, what remains is the dream in Mes Aieux's *Dégéneration* of *une grande table entourée d'enfants*—a big table surrounded by children. When all else fails, that alone may give one to courage to say with confidence *non omnis moriar*.

Relative Preferences

The bequest motive helps account for the persistence of aristocracy. If the point is to pass on our genes, we'd want to do so over more than one generation and we'd wish for the genetic success of our children. That's why we'd want them to be wealthy. For a full explanation of aristocracy, however, one more thing is needed: why might the aristocrat be willing to impoverish future societies, so long as his children end up on top? Why might he prefer to live in seventeenth century France, rather than in Ragged Dick's much wealthier America?

The answer is the relative preferences we saw in Chapter 8. We don't just care about how wealthy we are in absolute terms. We also care about how wealthy we are relative to other people. The result is a rat race, which Robert Frank tells us accounts for income inequality, and why we're happier in a more equal society.[8]

Zoologist Amotz Zahavi explains why this is so from an example in the animal world. The competition for evolutionary fitness, for the ability to pass on our genes, comes at a cost, which Zahavi identified as a "handicap principle."[9] Amongst animals, competing males bear a cost in the competition to make themselves attractive to females, and the classic example is the peacock's tail. Peahens choose their mates by the size and color of their tails, preferring large to small tails, with lots of "eyespots" in the tail.[10] In this way, the genes of individual large-tailed birds are selected to survive. For the species, however, that's a handicap. The large, colorful tail makes birds more visible to predators, and as the tail is cumbersome it is harder for the bird to escape once it is noticed. But what's bad for the species is good for the individual, successful bird. The large-tailed male will seem a good genetic bet if it has escaped its predators notwithstanding its tail, since long-tailed birds with lower survivability will have already have been eaten.[11] As a group, the males would be better off if they could sign and enforce a strategic tail limitation agreement, but that's not about to happen.

For Frank, people's relative preferences are like the peacock's tail. We'd all like to be rich, but the competition for reproductive success leads us to want more money than we otherwise would, since financial success is a signal of evolutionary fitness. This, says Frank, imposes costs on both rich and poor. For the poor, it means the unhappiness that comes from knowing that others are both wealthier and have a greater probability of passing on their genes. For the rich, it means more work accumulating money and less leisure than they'd want in a world where money is not tied to reproductive success. For both rich and poor, Frank argues, the Zahavi handicap principle explains the correlation between income inequality and unhappiness that we saw in Chapter 8.

That's an intriguing suggestion, but Frank overstates things. There are other reasons why unequal societies are unhappy ones, notably an absence of economic opportunities. Unequal societies are unhappy because they're immobile and the poor feel locked in to their economic class. Nor would fiddling with the Tax Code, as Frank suggests, eliminate the competition for wealth if we're hard-wired to pass on our genes by becoming wealthy. What matters is the signal of fitness, after all, and that's a constant whatever the marginal tax rate. When the top tax rate exceeded 90 percent in the 1950s, one could still identify the rich. They weren't buying yachts or private jets, but they did get a new Lincoln every year and were found at the country club on weekends. Compared to today, the income differences between rich and poor were smaller, but for the rich the signal of reproductive superiority was the same.

Spite

Given kin selection, parents will be concerned about the genetic success of their descendants. Add relative preferences to the mix, and parents will also want their descendants to have greater genetic success than their contemporaries. What that means is an aristocracy in which their children will never have to compete with their maid's little urchins or live next door to their gardener's imps.

The parent who wishes well for his children is altruistic, relative to them. He might even be altruistic if he would impoverish everyone else in order to see his children do well. To the people he would impoverish he is spiteful, but then spite can be altruistic. The opposite of altruism is not spite; rather it's the selfish person's indifference to others. The person who wishes well for others is an altruist, but then so too is the person who wishes ill for others. He does care about others, only not in a good way.

Spite is *malicious* where donor *x* incurs a fitness cost simply to impose a fitness cost on *y*. The leading literary example is *Great Expectations'* Miss Haversham,[12] who as a young woman was rejected at the altar and who now seeks to extract revenge on young Pip as the representative of the male sex. She is the local aristocrat, and Pip an orphan raised by his sister and her husband, Joe Gargery, a blacksmith. Pip expects to become a blacksmith himself, and is surprised to be summoned to Miss Haversham's mansion, where he is told to play with the beautiful Estella, a heartless girl of his age. A pack of cards is produced and he is required to play a "Beggar thy Neighbor" card game with her. She mocks his clothes, his lack of education, his working class origins. Until then he had been satisfied with his life and would happily have worked as a blacksmith with Joe, almost his only friend. After a glimpse of life at the Haversham mansion, however, he aspires to be a gentleman. "I had believed in the forge as the glowing road to manhood and independence. Within a single year all this was changed. Now, it was all course and common" (p.107). Through Haversham, Pip has discovered relative preferences. He has also fallen in love with Estella, and is uninterested in Biddy, a working class girl of his age who loves him and whom he would have loved had he not visited Miss Haversham and seen Estella. For Pip and for Dickens, Lincoln's promise of social mobility is a curse.

Miss Haversham's interest in Pip comes at a cost to her, but imposes a far greater cost on Pip. She had wanted Pip to fall in love with Estella, and for Estella to reject him. "Beggar him," she tells Estella (p. 60). She has raised Estella, to whom she is not related, to be a heart-breaker. "Break their hearts my pride and hope," she tells Estella. "Break their hearts and have no mercy" (p. 95). Only Biddy, the voice of common sense, recognizes the trap into which Pip has fallen. Do you want to become a gentleman, she asks Pip, in order to spite Estella or to win her over? I don't know, answers Pip.

> "Because if it's to spite her," Biddy pursued, "I should
> think—but you know best—that it might be better and more
> independently done by caring nothing for her words. And if
> it is to gain her over I should think—but you know best—she
> was not worth gaining over" (p.129).

But Pip is beyond help. Tainted by Haversham's malice, he has perhaps a touch of malice himself, and in his treatment of Biddy reveals how his morals have been corrupted. In the game of Beggar
thy Neighbor, malice is paid back with malice.

Spite might nevertheless be *benign* if people punish with a view to
conferring a benefit on a third party. One example of this is reported
by experimental economists in their study of the ultimatum games we
saw in Chapter 8. Recall that, in such games, senders are given a sum
of money to divide, and receivers are told they can take it or leave it. If
receivers leave the money on the table, they get nothing and are worse
off than if they had accepted a one-sided split that favored the sender
but at least offered receivers something. Given a one-sided split, however, receivers often reject the offer and "pay to punish" the sender
even if they know they'll never see him again. That looks like malice, but the receiver might also be thought to be acting from a sense
of fairness for the benefit of future players who might encounter the
selfish sender, and that would be an example of benign spite. We'll
pay to punish in order to teach the sender to treat others better.[13]

Benign spite can be explained on kin selection theories, if we impose a cost on non-kin to benefit our kin,[14] and that was the theme
of the AMC series *Breaking Bad*. At the beginning of the series, high
school chemistry teacher Walter White, thinking he is dying of can-
cer, becomes a meth dealer to provide for his family after his death.
Bad for society, good for his family. In an early episode he is faced
with the need to murder a rival drug dealer. White lists the arguments, for and against sparing the rival's life, on a sheet of paper.

In the pro column are "It's the moral thing to do," "Won't be able to live with yourself," "Judeo/Christian principles," "Post-traumatic stress," and "Murder is wrong." These count for little, however, next to the single entry in the con column: "He'll kill your entire family if you let him go."

TABLE 13.2

Choosing Future Worlds

	PRESENT	WORLD I	WORLD II
Top Quintile	$150,000	$160,000	$140,000
Second Quintile	$75,000	$150,000	$50,000
Median	$50,000	$140,000	$40,000

Table 13.2 illustrates how kin selection spite might lead to a world of hereditary aristocracy. Imagine that today's top-quintile people are given a choice between moving to either World I or World II. Were they altruists who wished well for everyone, they'd prefer World I, where everyone is made better off and income inequalities are reduced. World II is a poorer society all around, but a kin selection altruist might nevertheless prefer it if he could ensure that he and his children will be in the top quintile. In World II his children will be less wealthy in absolute dollars but they'll be better off in relative terms than they would be in World I.

World I is a society of Lincolnian income mobility where everyone is permitted to advance, while World II is a Beggar Thy Neighbor, aristocratic society where national wealth is sacrificed to preserve the relative wealth of an aristocratic class. It is seventeenth century France, where the pretentious aspirations of the *bourgeois gentilhomme* were ridiculed and where a centralized and *dirigiste* administration stifled the economy. That made the country poorer than it might have been, but served to protect aristocrats from competition from below.

We moderns are apt to discount the strength of family ties. And yet we act upon them, without entirely realizing that we do so. For example, many of the world's largest firms remain family businesses. They include Walmart, Mars, and BMW, and in recent years they have increased their presence amongst global businesses. Family-controlled firms account for a fifth of the world's top 500 firms,[15] and they constitute an even greater percent of America's top firms. We shouldn't be surprised. What families provide, as Christopher Lasch reminded us, is a haven in a heartless world, the assurance that one won't be betrayed by a co-worker, the trust needed before major projects can be exploited.[16] That's why we've always had family firms, and always will have them.

The New Class

IN THE LAST CHAPTER WE SAW HOW AN ARISTOCRAT would want his descendants to retain the privileges of his class, and how, given relative preferences, he'd be willing to sacrifice the wealth of the entire society to make this happen. By itself, that doesn't account for the rise of an aristocracy, however. Its members must first be able to agree on the badges that constitute their class. If it's not their pedigree and Burke's Peerage today, then it must be something else, and what that might be is the subject of this chapter. Second, since they won't be a majority in a democracy, they must make an alliance with other classes, and how they do so we'll see in the next chapter.

America's aristocrats are able to identify each other through settled patterns of cooperation called reciprocal altruism. They are also more likely to be able to recognize each other through their facial signals, networks and reputations. All this permits them to exploit the bargaining gains available to people who can trust each other. Other social groups may seek to form similar networks of cooperative behavior, but cannot do so as easily as the highest classes. In this way, a dominant

New Class has emerged atop American society, jealous of its privileges and both willing and able to resist competition from below.

Reciprocal Altruism

The kin selection effects we saw in the last chapter don't take us very far beyond one's immediate family. In kin selection, the command to be altruistic is discounted by r, the ratio of the probability of genetic identity, and after first cousins the ratio drops away quickly: 0.03125 for a second cousin, 0.00781 for a third cousin. As such, the kin selection model for altruism is severely limited to close relatives.

What we're missing, then, is an account of how people develop loyalty to a broader group of people beyond their kin. Such explanations do exist, however. With experience we can learn whom to trust, without relying on a benign altruism to everyone. Instead, we're more discriminating. *J'aime qui m'aime, autrement non*, wrote Charles d'Orléans. I'll be nice to those who are nice to me, otherwise not.

General altruists who cooperate with everyone flourish when they deal with each other. At the same time, they'll be double-crossed when they encounter a defector who takes them for patsies and welshes on his promises. There are other ways in which trust might be encouraged, however, not by relying on general altruistic genes but rather by invoking institutions or dispositions that sanction defectors. One of these is contract law, where the promise of cooperation is backed by a sanction for non-performance. That won't work in low trust countries that do not adhere to the rule of law, however, and even in high trust countries many promises cannot be enforced by a court. They might be too vague, too indefinite, or too open to opportunistic breaches that courts cannot perfectly deter.

Curiously, a solution to the problem of getting people to cooperate when bargaining is impossible came from the animal world. Large fish have food particles stuck in their teeth, which are bitten away by small "cleaner" fish. This gives the smaller fish a supply of food and the larger fish free dental services, and makes both better off. The puzzle, however, is why the bigger fish don't chomp down and swallow the smaller fish. They'd be sacrificing future teeth-cleaning services, but then they'd be getting the immediate reward of a meal. The mystery is how the two kinds of fish came to cooperate, and an explanation was provided a brilliant evolutionary biologist named Robert Trivers. What Trivers recognized was that, without bargaining, a pattern of trust and cooperation could emerge. Over time, the large fish kept its mouth open, the cleaner fish got its free meal, and everything was copacetic.

A cooperative trait, which Trivers called reciprocal altruism, had seemingly become encoded in the genes of both kinds of fish.[1] The general altruist will be taken for a patsy by defectors and is less likely to pass on his genes. But the reciprocal altruist, who does not tolerate defectors and cooperates only with fellow cooperators, doesn't have the same problem and his traits are more likely to survive. Amongst humans, all that is needed is an instinct of gratitude, the very powerful sense we all have that a gift should be repaid with a return gift.[2]

Trivers' reciprocal altruism shows how a cooperative subgroup of society might emerge. As one begins to deal with people outside the family, relationships of trust begin to develop, even as they do for cleaner and feeder fish. We're most likely to see this happen in a group of well-connected people with similar backgrounds who know each other or see people like themselves on a regular basis. And just such a society is formed by America's aristocrats.

Green Beards, Networks, and Reputations

W.D. Hamilton wasn't satisfied with kinship selection, either morally or intellectually. Moreover, kinship selection ignored the reality of what Hamilton called "foolishly helpful" friends.[3] These were people who went out of their way to cooperate, even where this was costly and there was no kinship bond. Such people existed, and the puzzle was how they were to be explained. They might begin to cooperate, and a pattern of reciprocal altruism might eventually emerge, but even apart from that there might be some way in which cooperators might recognize each other, a mechanism which Richard Dawkins labeled the *green beard* effect. Suppose that cooperators share a distinctive physical trait by which they can recognize each other, he proposed, something like a green beard. They could then begin to rely on each other and share in the gains of joint cooperation.

While Hamilton and Dawkins didn't think there was a genetic explanation for green beard effects, at a weak level one might nevertheless exist, for friends have been found to share genetic traits at the level of fourth cousins.[4] In this way, we might sniff each other out and recognize non-relatives as "functional kin." This would extend the benefits of kin selection beyond members of the same family and permit unrelated people to share in the gains of mutual cooperation.

Then there are facial signals. With very little information, we size up people by looking at their faces. Shown facial photos of candidates for election for only a second, and knowing nothing else about them, people picked the winning candidate nearly 70 percent of the time.[5] Even before clearly perceiving faces, we make snap judgments about whom to trust. One study found that the amygdala portions of the brain which process our emotional responses automatically distinguish between trustworthy and untrustworthy faces that flash before us for only a fraction of a second.[6]

Through joke-telling and observing how listeners respond we can also see whom to trust. In 1862 the French anatomist Duchenne de Boulogne took a series of photographs to illustrate the difference between true and false smiles.[7] In one picture the man was in his normal state; in the second he was naturally smiling; but in the third the smile was false. The lips curled up but the signs of hilarity were absent, suggesting a masked threat. Darwin was struck by this, and when he tested the photos on a small group of subjects, everyone could tell the genuine from the false smile.[8] Sincere friends laugh together in a special way that false friends cannot duplicate. The laughter is open, unreserved, and joyful. The weaker the tie, the more strained the laughter. Between enemies, the listener's cheeks are pulled back and his teeth are barred. His general expression is ironic, and his gaze rests on the joke-teller. The emotional cost of hiding the enmity is simply too great for most false listeners, and the appropriate inference will be made. If you cannot laugh with me, how can I trust you?

While the green beards hypothesis helps explain how a pattern of cooperation might emerge, it doesn't take us terribly far. It didn't work particularly well when George W. Bush looked into Vladimir Putin's eyes and thought he had seen the Russian leader's soul. But to the extent that it exists we're more likely to see it amongst people with similar ethnic backgrounds and similar facial features, and these are typically members of the one percent. Go to the executive offices of a large firm and you'll see the same faces. Go to a law faculty and, for all their professed love of diversity, you'll not find people who resemble the janitor. They'll also share a similar sense of irony and will laugh at jokes that leave those a rung down on the ladder looking puzzled. If there are green beards, you'll find them amongst the members of the New Class.

Genetic similarities and facial signals are not foolproof methods of identifying defectors, which is why we'll also rely on the informational benefits of membership in a *network* or social group. We'll join in a group because we value human company for its own sake, but we'll also do so for the information membership provides about a person. That is why, in a typical Washington conversation, one quickly moves on from "what do you do?" to the shared confidences that reveal common friends. The real Washington question is "whom do you know?"

We always tend to hang out with people like us, and for three reasons we'll trust them more. First, their membership in the group will tell us something about them. The narrower the club, the better the information. While I may not learn much about someone if I find he's a fellow member of the Automobile Association of America, learning that's he is a fellow Mormon might be very useful. Second, I'm more likely to have dealt with a fellow member before, so as to enjoy the benefits or reciprocal altruism. Third, even if I haven't seen him before, I may know of someone else who has dealt with him and who can vouch for his reputation. For this kind of cooperation to be selected to survive, all we need are the common and genial traits of sociability and friendliness.[9]

Network membership strengthens *reputational signals* about whom to trust. If I meet a stranger, a one-time joke might tell me a little about him, but the more I see him the more I'll learn about him. It's difficult to maintain a mask over a period of time, with a network of people. Over time, the car salesman's coprophagous grin is seen to be false, the trustworthy person identified. For good or ill, we acquire a reputation, and the narrower the group the stronger the reputational signal.

Class Markers

Since the benefits of group membership are lost when members cannot be identified, every group needs a members list. This might be drawn with some precision, as it is with English peers, who until recently had the right to sit in the House of Lords and whose titles continue to have a legal status. Beyond the peerage, however, the borders of the English upper classes have become blurred, and this became the subject of an amusing exchange of letters between Nancy Mitford and Evelyn Waugh.[10] At a time when the House of Lords had lost political power, and death duties had deprived the landed aristocracy of its lands, the only remaining marker of class rank, it seemed, was one's vocabulary and pronunciation. The lower classes said "pardon," the upper classes said "what?" The lower classes wiped their mouths with serviettes, the upper classes with napkins.

Even these distinctions are disappearing in England. The received upper class pronunciation of former days has been replaced with the flatter accents of a Tony Blair or David Cameron. In America too, vocabulary and pronunciation no longer signal one's class. When Dexter (Katharine Hepburn) exclaimed "My, she was yar!" in *The Philadelphia Story*, we knew she was upper class, even if we didn't know what yar meant. In 1940, when the movie was made, America's aristocrats talked differently. They swallowed their r's ("we have nothing to fea-ah except fea-ah itself") and spoke with the nasal accent Tom Wolfe called *honk*. There is little left of this now, and one almost misses the exaggerated WASP accent of a Franklin Roosevelt, as transcribed by Wolfe ("*I hate wooouugggggggg-hawwwwwwwwwwwggggggg hhhhhhhh*—meaning *war*").[11]

In times past, a nodding acquaintance with high culture served to signal membership in America's elite, and it still serves that function in France. In Pierre Bourdieu's study of his country's class structure, where one ranked came down importantly to what one liked or read. For the upper class, the *Well-Tempered Clavier*, poetry, avant-garde theatre; for the lower class, *The Blue Danube*, football, boulevard theatre.[12] Bourdieu's Frenchman judges the culture he is offered at the same time that the culture judges him, and without conscious reflection fits himself within a cultural category and social class.

Pronunciation and cultural referents no longer serve as class markers in America, except in a very limited and negative way. Regional accents have largely been dissolved by a standard pronunciation learned from television, and even television accents have been flattened over the last fifty years. Walter Cronkite's orotund delivery is heard no more, nor is Dan Rather's Texas accent. What remains of regional accents, particularly those from the South and Appalachia, are confined to ever-decreasing social milieus, and these are mostly taken to signify lower class membership. Nor does high culture serve as a class marker for the clever barbarians who comprise America's aristocracy. Bach and Strauss are liked equally, or more likely not at all, by people of every class. There is virtually no one who prefers poetry to football, and the *boulvardier* comedy in Paris that signifies lower or middle class status is the Broadway musical in America, enjoyed by people of every class on this side of the Atlantic.

If culture is defined more broadly, however, the upper classes do share a common culture. They might be ignorant as swans about the *Well-Tempered Clavier* and *Adlestrop*, but they can talk intelligently about continuing resolutions and 501(c)3's. They'll know who the Speaker of the House is, and the last Speaker too. They can give a satisfactory definition of originalism, executive privilege, and recess appointments. In their learning, they share enough in common to form a common culture that distinguishes them from other classes, and for class markers that's all that matters.

You can also tell American classes apart just by looking at them. For the upper class, it's not Hapsburg chins or aquiline noses, but the well tended look of people who take care of themselves. The signs of cigarette smoking—the raspy voice, the bad skin, the discolored fingers—will not be heard or seen. The blotchy, red face of the problem drinker, the stumbling disheveled gait of the substance abuser, all these stamp one as a member of the lower classes.

The American upper class can also be identified through the places where it lives, its professions and its politics—the three P's. The acceptable places to live are well recognized, and straying outside them to geographically undesirable neighborhoods simply isn't done. There are more than enough choices within bounds. In the Washington D.C. area, those who want to live in historic areas with Federal period architecture can choose between Georgetown and Old Town Alexandria.

For something rural, where their horses may graze, they have Potomac MD or Great Falls VA For large 1920s houses, there's Chevy Chase MD, Cleveland Park D.C., or Alexandria's Rosemont.

The same concentration of American aristocrats can be seen across the country, from La Jolla (where Mitt Romney lives) to Belmont MA (where Mitt Romney also lives). The wealthy tend to live in a relatively few of America's 4,075 counties, as seen in Figure 14.1. The map portrays the number of households with annual income of more than $200,000, roughly the cut-off for the top 5 percent of earners. The concentration is so marked that, when James K. Galbraith took out earners from just 15 of the counties, income inequality between counties disappeared.[13]

None of that is very surprising. We want to live next to people like us. The schools will be better, the parks cared for, the homes nicer. We won't see beat-up rustbuckets in the driveways. For shopping, we'll go to a local Whole Foods, not a Safeway; or to a Restoration Hardware, not an IKEA There'll be no local 7-Elevens or TGI Friday's. What there will be are charming little bistros and boutiques, places where one can get a real cup of cappuccino. In the bakeries, the pâtissières will have been trained in Paris, as will the coiffeurs at the hair salons. There won't be any street crime to speak of—our local city police will have seen to that. All life will seemingly have been arranged to please our senses.

Best of all, our neighbors will be people like us. They'll have interesting jobs in law, the media, banking, and the senior ranks of government. All will share our cultural and political leanings, and we'll meet them at our children's field hockey matches or going to the candidates' debate. Should we have to stray into underclass neighborhoods, we'll do so in limousines on our way to the airport, or in the sealed Google buses that bring high-tech workers to their jobs past the riff-raff of San Francisco.

America's one percent includes car dealers and real estate salesmen, but those aren't the jobs that serve as green beards. Instead, Charles Murray describes the emergence of a New Class composed of the most successful 5 percent of adults in managerial positions, the professions and in the media, the people with an outside influence on our culture and politics.[14] They constitute what Joel Kotkin, following Samuel Coleridge, call a "clerisy," the priesthood of a secular society that sets the values which everyone is expected to follow. Before Murray and Kotkin, Irving Kristol identified them as a New Class,[15] and in Britain they were called the Establishment, a term popularized by Henry Fairlie. They include the academics who impart their beliefs to college students, the creative elite of artists, playwrights, fashion designers and artists, the leaders at the bar, the trust fund babies who sit on the boards of major philanthropies, the members of the media who move back and forth from journalism to government, and the political appointees and senior government officials in Washington.[16]

Murray's impressionistic definition doesn't lend itself to empirical analysis, and a rougher but more serviceable definition of the New Class would simply include everyone with a professional degree, as

FIGURE 14.1

Household Income of $200,000 or More, by County

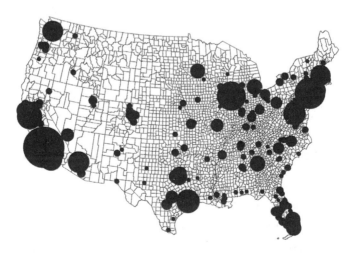

SOURCE: Social Explorer, ACS 2006–10 (5 year estimates)

===== FIGURE 14.2 =====

Holders of Professional School Degrees, by County

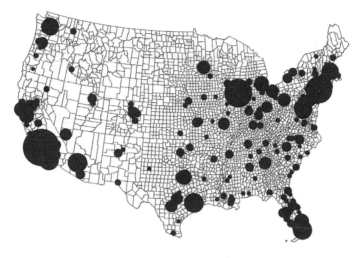

SOURCE: Social Explorer, ACS 2006–10 (5 year estimates).

measured by the Census Bureau's American Community Survey and seen in Figure 14.2. Not surprisingly, it's remarkably similar to Figure 14.1. Professionals are more likely to be in the top income category than less educated Americans. In addition, professionals are more likely to live near wealthy non-professionals, who will require their services, whether in law, medicine, or the other professions.

Amongst one's interests, politics represents the most important class marker. Leaving out the majority-minority counties that understandably voted for an African-American candidate, the districts that voted Democratic in Figure 14.3 are largely the ones where wealthy Americans live in Figure 14.1 and where professionals live in Figure 14.2. When Trulia's chief economist looked at the 100 largest U.S. metropolitan areas, he found that the most expensive communities had almost invariably voted for Obama in 2012. In the most politically liberal cities, houses cost almost twice as much per square foot as those in conservative cities.[17]

=========== FIGURE 14.3 ===========

2012 Presidential Election, Voting by County

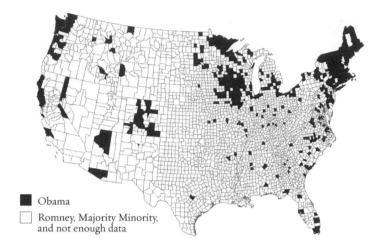

■ Obama
☐ Romney, Majority Minority,
and not enough data

SOURCE: Mark Newman, Department of Physics and Center for the Study of Complex Systems,
University of Michigan, at http://www-personal.umich.edu/~mejn/election/2012/; author.

Over time, the tendency towards political concentration has become more pronounced, in what journalist Bill Bishop has called
the "big sort."[18] We don't care to live on streets where our neighbors think us heartless bigots or preening idiots, and so we settle
amongst people like us. There are plenty of Republicans around,
even in the Washington D.C. area, but when you meet one chances
are he lives in McLean VA if he's inside the beltway. As for the
Democrats, liberals seem to have property rights to the District,
Montgomery County MD, and Alexandria VA. Further out, there
are mega-churches, country-and-western radio stations, and conservatives on one side of the line; Ph.D.'s, bicyclists, and liberals on
the other. On one side chain restaurants, on the other yoga studios.

The geographic concentration intensifies the polarization of
American politics. Over time, liberals become more liberal, con-
servatives more conservative. This was something political scientist
Robert Dahl noticed 40 years ago, before Bishop's big sort. When

people lived in communities where people weren't divided along political lines, they moderated their views. The same was true when church attendance was less likely to signal political beliefs. Once everyone one knew belonged to the same party, however, the instinct to moderation disappeared, and when that happens, observed Dahl, "the man of the other side is not just an opponent: he soon becomes an enemy."[19] What we're left with is a country in which each side questions the good faith of the other side, where liberals attribute opposition to Obamacare to racism, and conservatives see a hidden socialist agenda in every liberal measure.

Bill Clinton, who saw as much of the political divide as any politician, bemoans what he sees as a new form of bigotry—the bigotry of partisan hatreds.

> You know, Americans have come so far since, let's say, the era of Joe McCarthy. I mean, think about it. We're less racist. We're less sexist. We're less homophobic than we used to be. We only have one remaining bigotry. We don't want to be around anybody who disagrees with us.[20]

To what extent are the super-wealthy on one side of the divide? We don't know how they vote. Lower down on the income scale, those earning between $200,000 and $250,000 broke for Romney in 2012, according to an Edison Research exit poll.[21] We're left to surmise how the one percent—those earning more than $400,000— voted, to say nothing of the 0.1 percent. A very tentative survey of Chicago residents, biased towards business executives, reported that members of the one percent were generally more economically conservative than the average American. On the other hand, they were more willing to see federal spending directed towards infrastructure improvements (such as highways and bridges) and scientific research, and less willing to see money spent on national defense. They accepted the progressive nature of income taxes and Social Security, as a means to transfer wealth from the rich to the poor, and were more likely than the general public to support deficit spending when the economy is in a recession.[22] The relatively wealthy are also more socially liberal than the average American over issues such as abortion.[23]

We do know that people with postgraduate study broke 55 to 42 for Obama, as did those who attend religious services only occasionally (55 to 43) or not at all (62 to 34).[24] In addition, wealthy and educated counties disproportionately supported the 2012 Democratic candidate: Cambridge MA (86.1 %); Manhattan (84.2 %); San Francisco (83.4 %); Charlottesville VA (75.8 %); Alexandria VA (71.4 %); Montgomery MD (70.9 %); Los Angeles (68.9 %); and Seattle's King County (68.8 %). In such cities, Charles Murray's New Class has arisen, one that might not include the car dealer who earns $200,000 a year, but that does include the wealthy professionals who live in geographically concentrated areas and who favor politically liberal policies.

We'd like to think that, in a representative democracy, the views of our elected officials will mimic those of the average voter. The evidence, however, suggests that American elections aren't democratic in that sense. Instead, the government's policy decisions are more likely to reflect the preferences of powerful interest groups and the wealthiest of Americans. When Martin Gilens and Benjamin Page looked at the survey evidence about voting preferences, they found that the wishes of the average voter don't correlate with the preferences of interest groups such as the U.S. Chamber of Commerce. That's perhaps not very surprising. It's what "interest group" theorists have long suggested.[25] Indeed, there's a negative correlation: what business groups want—subsidies for their industries, for example—is what the average voter *doesn't* want. And when the economic elites are added to the mix, along with interest groups, their preferences also diverge from those of the average voter. They and the interest groups have a significant influence on government decisions, but not the average voter.[26] The elites get things they want, and the average voters must suck it up. That's a searing indictment of American democracy, which is tilted towards the rich and powerful and which no longer seems to reflect what the average voter wants.

Politics as a Green Beard

A naïve explanation for the voting habits of Murray's New Class, favored by liberals, would have it that educated people are more likely to recognize the greater intellectual appeal of their party. Liberals also pride themselves on their greater concern for social justice. A more cynical explanation, favored by conservatives, is that New Class liberals will be attracted by the prospect of political favors from the Democratic Party. As an example, the conservative might point to the failure of Democrats, in drafting Obamacare, to place a cap on medical malpractice claims brought by their trial lawyer allies.

There may be an element of truth in both these arguments, for when is an element of truth ever absent, but I incline to a third, Darwinian explanation for political allegiance. Politics has become a green beard, by which members of the New Class can recognize fellow members of the club. The conservative might be right in suggesting that their political views permit some liberals to bargain for favors from the state, but in truth how many of them are so well-connected to do so? What liberalism does give them, however, is membership in a club and the ability to trust and bargain with each other, and that is likely of far greater value. At a time when the rule of law in America seems in decline,[27] personal trust substitutes for the dubious legal enforcement of promises, and what trust needs are green beards.

A green beard explanation of political allegiance helps explain two curious features of American political life. The first is the way in which politics intrudes into ordinary life, and the omnipresent display of political views, from bumper stickers to Facebook postings. We don't signal our views about favorite novels or movies but do hasten to tell people how we feel about the Tea Party, and choose one set of friends and exclude another on that basis. A Pew study reports that two-thirds of conservatives and half of liberals say that most of their close friends share their political views. If not we'll drop them, and 44 percent of liberals and 31 percent of conservatives have unfriended Facebook friends because of their politics.[28]

At times, this is beyond parody. For Jews, Passover is one the holiest times of the year, and the most prominent part of the Haggadah ritual is the Four Questions, when people gathered around the Seder Table are asked why this night is different from all the rest. For the 2012 Passover, however, the National Democratic Jewish Council thought to improve on this with four additional questions, to respond to the "many false and malicious emails" attacking Obama. Just why, for example, "has President Obama provided record amounts of military aid to Israel"?[29] Enquiring minds will also want to know how to deal with "your Republican uncle" over Thanksgiving dinner, and the Democratic National Committee has helpfully provided the progressive nephew with a set of talking points in case the conversation over the turkey strays too far from a list of Obama's accomplishments.[30] And lest holiday mirth intrude over Christmas, Organizing for Action's "pajama boy" will turn the conversation from Timmy's new toys to Obamacare. We are to be offered no respite, it seems, from the grimly serious business of politics.

The second distinctive feature of American politics is its rancor. Politics everywhere is the systematic organization of hatreds, as Henry Adams observed, but much more so in America than in comparable First World nations. Political brawls in Britain, France, and Canada can be nasty, but seldom descend to the mud-wrestling contests of U.S. cable talk shows or to the casual personal animosities bred by differences over politics. Somehow, in other countries one meets people from the other side at the water cooler, in the faculty lounge. And it doesn't seem to matter.

If Mitt Romney saw Democrats as spongers at the schnorrer's table, the Left has paid him back with interest. Opposition to Obama is racism, the Catholic's problems with abortion are part of a war on women, and only a Randian greed-head could see a problem with America's income tax rates. Racist, misogynist, and evil is no way to go through life, but then conservatives are also stupid. Universal Medicare might or might not have been a good idea, in the byzantine form it took under Obamacare, but it took an idiot to believe it could happen without a wealth transfer from the rich and middle class to the poor. Happily, there are a lot of idiots around, said MIT's Jonathan Gruber, a lead adviser on Obamacare.[31]

Every class in society might in theory exploit the benefits of green beard membership, but the gains accrue primarily to liberal members of the New Class. Being rich, and with their fingers on the levers of power, they have more to trade and more to gain from cooperation with fellow members of the club. Their networks are also tighter and less dispersed. They're more likely to have gone to the same kinds of schools, to belong to the same profession, to share the same political allegiances, and to live in the same neighborhoods. In John Guare's play, *Six Degrees of Separation*, we're never more than six friends-of-friends links away from everyone else, but for the New Class it's more like one or two degrees.

Somewhere along the line, Lincoln's idea of a meritocratic society of income mobility was turned around. Meritocracy was supposed to be synonymous with income mobility, but instead an ostensibly meritocratic society became self-reproducing. Its members share the same beliefs, flourish in the same networks, feel the same sense of class solidarity, and pass all this on to their children. Between them and those below them a crevasse has opened.[32]

There's nothing novel in the idea that a ruling New Class might emerge in a society that had cast off a titled aristocracy. The very term New Class came from an ex-communist, Milovan Djilas, who argued that the party's ideals had been betrayed by an elite *nomenklatura* that had installed itself in the leadership positions of the Soviet Union and Tito's Yugoslavia.[33] In China, too, the children of the Communist party's revolutionary leaders have been seen as a "red nobility." Earlier still, German sociologist Robert Michels identified an "iron law of oligarchy" in which power passes from people generally to an elite in any organization. Such theories might easily lead one to question democracy, and Michels himself joined Mussolini's Fascist Party. Michels' contemporary, the Italian Gaetano Mosca, remained a democrat but nevertheless described what he saw as the inevitable rise of an elite in his canonical *The Ruling Class*. Mosca's elite would rise to the top, and over time would breed an aristocracy that persists over generations. "All ruling classes tend to become hereditary in fact if not in law."[34]

Mosca offered a psychological explanation for how his ruling class would spawn a hereditary aristocracy. Over time the upper classes will settle into a habit of dominance, he argued, and the lower orders into one of obedience. Whatever might have been the case in Mosca's Italy, however, that doesn't much sound like America. Something else is going on, and it's the way in which the American New Class shapes the contours of our public policies in order to ensure that their children will remain on top, and has done so more successfully than in other countries. To make this work, what are needed are the legal barriers to mobility we'll see in the next part that immunize upper class children from competition from below. In a democracy, however, the upper class can't make that happen without broader political support, and those allies won't be found in the middle class. But what of those one level below the middle class?

Red Tories

IN A MODERN DEMOCRACY, WHERE ALL MAY VOTE, THE aristocrat who seeks to preserve his class standing will find it necessary to ally himself with voters beneath him in society. This he can do if he makes common cause with an underclass that has no aspirations to rise, against an intermediate middle class from which the aristocrat senses competition. And this is how politics should be understood in America today, as a battle waged by the peers above and peasants below against a middle class, fought over Lincoln's vision of a meritocratic and mobile country.

We've seen it all before.

Maypoles on the Village Green

Throughout the British eighteenth century, there were no real political parties, as we understand the term. There was no central office that picked candidates for Parliament, but only a swirling set of friends and mentors, and modern distinctions between Right and Left began to make sense only in the next century. We recall Pitt the Younger (Prime Minister 1783–1801, 1804–1806) as a Tory, but he thought himself a Whig who celebrated the principles of the Revolutionary Settlement of 1689. Edmund Burke we remember as the greatest of Tory philosophers, but he saw himself as a Whig and mentored that arch-Whig, Charles James Fox, in Whiggism. Tory ministries, in both name and conservative philosophy, appeared only after the French Revolution, with Prime Ministers such as the Duke of Wellington (1828–30, 1834) and the Marquis of Salisbury (1885–86, 1886–92, 1895–1902).

Wellington was not without liberal sympathies, and his government gave Catholics the vote in 1829. This in turn brought a very different kind of member from Ireland, and the 1831 election returned the Whigs under Earl Grey to power. With a large majority, Grey was now able to bring in a proposal for parliamentary reform, and the Great Reform Act of 1832 created 67 new constituencies in industrial cities that had been underrepresented and eliminated 143 seats where voters were overrepresented. It also expanded the voting rolls to include middle class homeowners with property valued at more than £10 and renters who paid more than £50 a year. This increased the electorate from 350,000 to 652,000, and over time, as people become wealthier and the £10 property restriction became less of a barrier, the voting rolls increased to 1,056,000 by 1866.[1]

With the Industrial Revolution, Britain was no longer a largely agricultural country. It was increasingly an urban one, and this along with the Great Reform Act transformed British politics. Whigs and Tories would no longer come to power through the influence of great, landowning families, but had to campaign for votes from the newly enfranchised middle class. The factory towns also created a new class of industrial workers and ripped apart the illusion of a country composed of people who, rich and poor, had essentially the same interests. Instead, said Benjamin Disraeli, England was divided along class lines, into Two Nations:

> Between whom there is no intercourse and no sympathy; who are as ignorant of each other's habits, thoughts, and feelings, as if they were dwellers in different zones, or inhabitants of different planets.... THE RICH AND THE POOR.[2]

Thereafter parties had to campaign for votes, as never before. They had had some experience with this, and Georgiana, the beautiful Duchess of Devonshire had offered to kiss people who would vote for her lover, Fox; but now the politicians had to seek support from a new kind of electorate, one with different concerns. These were the middle class voters who elected governments that abolished slavery in the Empire, gave Britain limited liability company laws, adopted free trade, and repealed the protectionist Corn Laws.

The obvious place to look for new votes was amongst the £10 freeholders who were enfranchised by the Reform Act. These were city people, who lived in rising cities such as Birmingham and Manchester. With the farmers who benefited from Corn Law tariffs they had little in common, for what agricultural protectionism meant for city folk was higher prices at the dinner table. The Corn Laws had also led to mass starvation in Ireland, and that was a most powerful argument for repeal. That apart, Tory Prime Minister Sir Robert Peel had always opposed protectionism and sought to re-brand the Tories as a free trade party.

Peel was a free market conservative who was willing to abandon his party's agricultural allies when their legislative gains could not be justified on an economic basis. He was thus the forerunner of future free market Blue Tories, of Margaret Thatcher in Britain and Stephen Harper in Canada. There was another species of Tories, however, the Red Tories one saw in Britain's Edward Heath and

Canada's John Diefenbaker. These were traditional conservatives who identified free markets with Whiggism, and who drew their strength from landowners and farmers. (Blue is everywhere the color of conservatism and red of socialism, everywhere except in the United States, where of late red is taken to refer to Republicans and blue to Democrats.)

Peel's support for free trade cost him his premiership, brought down by Disraeli, who in the process invented the Red Tories. Peel had sought an alliance of aristocratic Tories and country squires with the newly enfranchised middle class. What Disraeli would propose instead was a party composed of both the upper classes and the impoverished lower class, a union of both ends against the middle class. This was an imaginative coalition, one that anticipated future extensions of the franchise, for at this point the lower classes did not have the vote. They had their protest movement—Chartism—but for them the ballot box lay in the future. Nevertheless, Disraeli gathered round him a group of young aristocrats, and voting with the Whigs they defeated Peel's Tory government in 1846. Thereafter the Peelites drifted slowly into the Liberal Party, while Disraeli's allies became today's British Tory Party, led by David Cameron.

Peel was a product of the middle classes himself, the son of a Lancashire cotton manufacturer. With Disraeli, a wit, dandy, and a novelist, he had almost nothing in common, and it is hardly surprising that Disraeli failed to find a place in Peel's cabinet. That more than anything explains why Disraeli turned on him, but there was something more going on. Disraeli had an uncanny ability to absorb whatever was most fashionable at the moment, and in the 1840s this was the novels of Sir Walter Scott and the revival of chivalry that the Young England movement thought provided the solution to their country's problems.

Even in a country that prized its eccentrics, Young England was more than a little bizarre. Like Thomas Love Peacock's Mr.

Chainmail, they wished to relive the twelfth century, and in 1839 organized the Woodstock of the day, the Eglington Tournament.[3] This was a mock-medieval pageant of chivalric splendor, where a Queen of Beauty presided over a tilting-ground and upper class twits (and the future Napoleon III) gathered round the canopies of the Knight of the Burning Tower, the Knight of the Dolphin, and the Knight of the Ram. As the tournament opened, a costumed Knight of the Swan challenged the Knight of the Golden Lion to battle, but then the rains came and all the knights errant and ladies fair repaired home. Absurd as this was, their foolishness had an air of glamor, which is more than could be said for the prosaic good sense of the rising middle class. There was never a grocer errant, which was the point of Francis Beaumont's satire, *The Knight of the Burning Pestle*.

Young England's chief figure was Lord John Manners, a dreamy young man who sought a middle way between the political economists and Whigs on the Right and the radical Chartists on the Left. The Whigs' free markets bade to destroy pre-modern social bonds, he thought, and would reduce personal relations down to what Thomas Carlyle (and later *The Communist Manifesto*) called "cash-payment."[4] The Whigs had also ignored the blight of poverty in the new urban slums. The Chartists, with their demands for universal suffrage and annual elections, would not do either. Instead, Manners proposed an Arcadian Tory radicalism, which saw aristocrats and peasants as natural allies.[5]

Manners and Young England had poured over that monument to mediaeval chivalry, Kenelm Digby's *Broad Stone of Honour*, and found in its celebration of a natural bond between peer and serf a defense against the false doctrines of the Whigs' free trade economics and the Chartists' parliamentary reforms and democracy.[6] Class barriers must exist, but their edges could be softened by a common participation in Maypole dancing, cricket, and religious holy days.

As such, the lower orders had no need for voting rights or annual elections. Rather, they should be offered the substantive results Chartist reforms would give them, without the procedural reforms themselves, through a restored feudalism and a sympathetic aristocracy. Marx and Engels dismissed Young England as "half lamentation, half lampoon,"[7] but things equally foolish were commonly accepted in the 1970s, and doubtless are today as well.

Disraeli swept the younger men under his wing, as a mother goose with her ducklings, and popularized their views in his novels. In *Sybil* (1845), he even defended the high Anglicanism of the Oxford movement, although some Young Englanders suspected that "Dizzy's attachment to moderate Oxfordism is something like Bonaparte's to moderate Mahomedanism."[8] Historian Crane Brinton thought that Disraeli had "the intellectual detachment of the true mime who in a moment captures the essence of a passer-by,"[9] but there was more than mimicry in his dream of an alliance between the aristocrats and the poor. If Peel thought that the Tory Party should make its peace with the middle class after the 1832 Reform Act, Disraeli proposed a different national party based on an alliance between the upper class and then-disenfranchised poor. Later, when Disraeli led his Party in giving the vote to all male heads of households under the 1867 Reform Act, cynics complained that he did so merely to "dish the Whigs." Yet this was simply an application of the ideas he had put forward years before, in *Coningsby* (1844) and *Sybil*.

Nor was Disraeli's concern for the urban poor insincere. Friedrich Engels shocked readers with his description of the wretchedness of East End London in *The Condition of the Working Class in England* (1845), but the year before Disraeli had written no less passionately of economic inequality:

> I had long been aware that there was something rotten in
> the core of our social system. I had seen that while immense

fortunes were accumulating, while wealth was increasing to a superabundance…the working classes, the creators of wealth, were steeped in the most abject poverty and gradually sinking into the deepest degradation.[10]

And in the same year that Engels took his reader through London's wretched East End, Disraeli's brought his eponymous heroine down a nightmare descent into the same slums in *Sybil*.

Disraeli sought to remind the aristocracy that with power came responsibility, that unto whom much is given, of him much shall be required; and this could be seen in the social welfare legislation of his government when he at last climbed the greasy pole of office. His political legacy was a red-tinged Tory Party that supported generous welfare benefits and state intervention in the economy, policies that British Tories continued to embrace until the arrival of Margaret Thatcher.

Heroism and Hubris

Tory Parties are not to be found outside of Britain and Canada, and there was never a Red Tory party as such in the United States. There were, however, echoes of Disraeli's vision of a union of the highest and lowest classes against a rising middle class, at just the same time in the American South, as we saw in Chapter 3. Like Lord John Manners, the southerners had read *Ivanhoe*, and took from it a love of aristocracy. Indeed, Mark Twain thought that without Sir Walter Scott's historical novels there never would have been a Civil War. In their defense of slavery, moreover, the southerners argued that a paternalistic society of rigid class distinctions in which the highest class felt bound to protect the lowest class was superior to the market society of the North. There were classes in the North as well, argued the southerners, and the "wage slaves" of the North fared worse than the true slaves of the South. That was why, argued George Fitzhugh, the true philanthropist would buy slaves.

After the Civil War, the southerner's self-image as a knight errant, the descendant of Virginia's laughing Cavaliers, survived only in the dim twilight of the Lost Cause, with its memories of doomed Confederate heroes. So the southerner became reconciled to defeat, but his romantic illusions ignored the reality of slavery and were debased further by lynch mobs and the Ku Klux Klan. The southerner's ideals were also at odds with the spirit of the age. The country of their dreams was one of social immobility, but it was Lincoln's vision of income mobility that would come to define the country. The America that emerged from the Civil War was commercial more than agricultural, mercantile more than romantic, open and not closed to advancement.

That didn't prevent the emergence of a social elite, the WASP aristocracy of Mrs. Astor's 400, the Boston Brahmins, and the Daughters of the American Revolution. They were rich, for the most part, but money alone didn't suffice, as Max Weber observed. "The absence of barriers in America's political 'democracy'... has not prevented the gradual growth of an estate of 'aristocrats' alongside the crude plutocracy of property."[11] This was a distinctly American kind of aristocracy, for the members of the elite disclaimed the privileges of birth and were sincere republicans. They felt entitled, however, to take a leading role in the republic because they thought they understood republican principles better than the second generation Irish- or Italian-American. They also had a sense of obligation to their country, and were not slow to enlist during the First and Second World Wars. Later, in the Cold War, they supplied the senior ranks of the CIA, just as Cambridge had sent its students and fellows to MI6.

More broadly, their ideals were communicated to the other

ranks, through Boy Scout oaths and Hollywood Westerns. The marshal and outlaw who waited for the other to draw in a John Ford movie were merely repeating Voltaire's account of the Battle of Fontenoy (1745), where out of politeness the English asked the French to fire first.[12] It was right there in Gene Autry's Cowboy Code: The cowboy must never shoot first, hit a smaller man, or take unfair advantage. We saw the same code of gentlemanly conduct in Dink Stover at Yale and the Hardy Boys in their roadsters. One lived in a commercial republic, but still felt shame when one failed to live according to codes of honor learned in Henry Longfellow's *Song of Hiawatha* and James Russell Lowell's *The Vision of Sir Launfal*. Even today, Kenelm Digby's knights-errant can be found in popular films, from *Star Wars* to *Batman*.

There is also a form of heroic capitalism, in which the risk-taker rises through his own efforts and daring, scorning the privileges of birth. The entrepreneur, who gambles on the chance that cannot be measured, whose worth is a hazard, is the knight-errant of our time. In the commonplace world that lies about he sees the romance of ordinary life, the adventure at the end of the street. The steeper the path, the more improbable the quest, the greater our applause. We naturally root for the underdog, the person who beats the system, the team that come from behind in the ninth, the caddy who beats the pro, the man who bets the farm on the longest of long-shots. We reserve our contempt for those to whom success is handed, who tread the safe and narrow, who are too big to fail.

The autobiography of the most heroic American entrepreneur begins "I was born a slave on a plantation in Franklin County Virginia. I am not quite sure the exact place or exact date of my birth, but at any rate I suspect I must have been born somewhere and at some time."[13] Booker T. Washington's boyhood home was a windowless log cabin, his bed a bundle of rags, his floor George Fitzhugh's mud-sill. As a child he never attended school, though he sometimes went as far as the schoolhouse door with his white mistresses, carrying their books. Years later, after the struggle for an education, after founding Tuskegee Institute, Harvard awarded him an honorary degree, the first such honor for an African-American, and before an audience at the university's Memorial Hall Washington summed up his credo.

> In the economy of God, there is but one standard by which an individual can succeed—there is but one for a race. The country demands that every race shall measure itself by the American standard. By it a race must rise or fall.[14]

Booker T. Washington, Batman and the entrepreneurs in the top 0.01 percent of earners were and are the Nicholas Taleb's antifragiles:, people who thrive on chaos and stress. But chaos and stress are carefully avoided by Charles Murray's New Class.[15] These were the A students in high school who went to the best of universities, where they networked with their peers and espoused politically correct causes. They married late, with spouses from similar backgrounds, and waited till their thirties to have children. They abstained from every kind of abuse, and aimed always at the main chance. So far from being risk-takers, they have ordered their lives to minimize risk, both for themselves and for everyone around them. They are deserving (for otherwise they would not be meritocrats), but not so deserving as they think they are. They are Taleb's class of resilients, people who float above the storm and are never harmed by it.

How different these are from Kenelm Digby's chivalrous knights, who disdained artifice and despised crafty calculation, who preferred to serve rather than to command, and who performed the most laborious and humble offices with cheerfulness and grace. Knights were attentive to the call of duty and their spirit was one of sacrifice and obedience.[16] These are arresting fictions, but only fictions of course. The Black Prince massacred 3,000 residents of Limoges in 1370; and Sir John Hawkwood, whose portrait by Uccello adorns the Duomo in Florence, was a mercenary who served the highest bidder. Yet as an ideal of chivalrous service, Digby's knights, the heroes of every old Western movie, had the power to inspire people to perform the most arduous and dangerous tasks.

The same can't be said for the New Class. There aren't any dragons to slay, but one measure of a sense of obligation is provided by charitable giving. In 2008, the eight states whose residents gave the biggest share of discretionary income to charity voted for John McCain while the seven lowest-ranking states supported Barack Obama.[17] One might expect liberals who favor welfare policies to be personally more generous, but Arthur Brooks found that they give only ten percent as much as those who say they strongly oppose government redistribution of wealth.[18] Liberals may sniff at such findings if they think that conservative causes are unworthy of support. In particular, anticlerical liberals object to the charitable status granted to religious institutions. However that may be, Brooks found that conservatives also give more than liberals to non-religious charities. They also volunteer more hours to non-religious charities, and give 50 percent more blood.

Conservative states are also more likely to provide volunteers for the military. Of the different regions of the country, only the south provides more recruits than its share of the 18–24-year-old population, according to the Defense Department.[19] The class division is particularly noticeable in college ROTC programs, which were banned in most Ivy League colleges until the "Don't Ask, Don't Tell" policy on gays in the military was repealed in 2010. All this is new. As we saw, Jefferson feared that the Society of the Cincinnati would bring the aristocratic government of an officer class to America. He needn't have worried. Today few of the children of the New Class can be found in the services, and the officer class Jefferson so feared is composed of members of the lower and middle classes.

We members of the New Class see social justice as political, not personal, and requited by espousing the correct political and social views about wealth redistribution, affirmative action, same-sex marriage, and the like. Nothing much beyond that is required, no sense of honor not captured by the minimal standards of the American Bar Association's Canon of Legal Ethics, no charitable contributions (unless one plans to run for office), no military service (though like Bill Clinton one must register for the draft to maintain one's political viability). In a meritocracy, the privileged feel they have earned their rewards through their merit and need not account for them through personal sacrifice. We have already paid our dues, in seminar rooms and in academic workshops. We have no scars or medals, and instead have publications and blogs.

In the chapters that follow I argue that the New Class supports policies that preserve their privileges and those of their children at the expense of a rising middle class. They seek an aristocratic society, and therefore may fairly be described as Tories. And because they are allied to America's underclass, they are Red Tories.

Sealing the Deal

The New Class, composed of a slender number of voters, can't win elections on its own, but must ally itself with an underclass. But then what's in it for the underclass? In Disraeli's day, lower class Chartists hoped to play off Whigs and Tories in the hope of extending the franchise beyond the middle class, a strategy that paid off in the Disraeli's Second Reform Act of 1867. But what of today's underclass, locked in to failing schools, competition from immigrants, and other barriers to advancement?

That's not a hard one. The underclass is composed of the most fragile members of society, those most endangered by economic storms. To them, the Red Tory offers resilience, in the sense of Nicolas Taleb, a welfare system that does not distinguish between the deserving and undeserving, the meritorious and the unworthy, and where the payments continue whatever the economic conditions. The safety net is not generous, when the payments to the poor are compared to what the one percent earns. However, Taleb's resilience does not require great wealth, but only protection from change in times of economic stress.

In 2012 Romney offered voters a promise of economic opportunity, but the underclass did not regard this as directed their way. Handicapped by all the obstacles that an immobile society could put before them, they saw their choice as one between the fragility of unfavorable market processes and the resilience of a welfare state. And so, in the Great Recession's crisis of fragility, they allied themselves with the Red Tories and the promise of wealth redistribution and resilience.

There might not even have been a Great Recession without a Red Tory alliance of the highest and lowest classes against the middle. Since the Second World War the Tax Code has subsidized home ownership by permitting taxpayers to deduct interest payments on their mortgages. The bigger the mortgage, the greater the deduction, and home mortgage interest deductibility has therefore been a great deal for the one percent. It left lower class Americans out in the cold, however, and Washington responded with taxpayer-subsidized housing finance through Government Sponsored Entities (GSEs) such as Fannie Mae and Freddie Mac, which by 2008 guaranteed three-quarters of U.S. home mortgages. With the strong backing of politicians, the GSE's total balance sheet exposure ballooned from $1.7 trillion in 1994 to nearly $6 trillion by 2007, nearly half of the country's annual GDP. At no charge from the Treasury, the GSEs deployed the public credit of the United States in guaranteeing subprime housing loans that would not otherwise have passed muster with private lenders.

The government's home ownership policies were plausibly the proximate cause of the Great Recession.[20] Federal interest rates were set very low (the "Greenspan put"), and the GSEs promoted home loans to borrowers who couldn't meet market risk standards. That led to a glaringly obvious housing bubble, and the crash in home prices should have been foreseen, but until the recession every attempt to rein in the GSEs was successfully countered by populist politicians, mortgage bankers, and government-funded community action groups such as the roguish Association of Community Organizations for Reform Now (ACORN). Amongst the banks, there were unscrupulous start-up lenders like such as New Century Ameriquest that approved mortgage applications on a volume basis, with the assistance of brokers who massaged borrower credit scores, and appraisers who kept the loan-to-value ratio low by inflating home values.[21] But for the subsidy the FDIC provides their borrowers through deposit insurance, such banks wouldn't have existed, and they poisoned the well by degrading the risk standards for all financial institutions.[22] Forced to compete with shady lenders, even long-established banks were pressured into accepting more risk. For the most part, however, honest lenders simply reacted to the open spigot of money from the Federal Reserve and the political pressure to provide improvident loans.

Karl Marx observed a similar alliance between bankers and the poor when the French underclass, seemingly against its interests, supported a dictatorial Napoleon III who was allied to high finance. For the underclass, which had betrayed its revolutionary calling, Marx employed all his powers of vituperation and contempt for what he described as the "offal and wreck of all classes." In the *Eighteenth Brumaire*, he called them the *lumpenproletariat*, the passively rotting masses, the "vagabonds, dismissed soldiers, discharged convicts, runaway galley slaves, sharpers, jugglers, lazzaroni, pick-pockets, sleight-of-hand performers, gamblers, procurers, keepers of disorderly houses, porters, literati, organ grinders, rag pickers, scissors grinders, tinkers, beggars."[23] Marx had a way with words, but his description of how an underclass had allied itself with a "finance aristocracy" to elect a plebiscitary president bears some parallel to the Great Recession and the 2012 American election.

As in Marx's day, it is not particularly difficult to persuade the leaders of America's underclass to tug at their forelock and support Red Tory policies that do little to better its lives. America's poor are harmed by bad schools, competition for jobs from immigrants and departures from the rule of law which impose costs on employers and weaken the job market. African-Americans, whose unemployment rate is double that of white Americans, are the principal victims here, and one would therefore expect the NAACP to support charter schools, oppose amnesty for undocumented aliens, and support the tort reform movement. But that's not what happens. Instead, the country's principal black civil rights group lines up with America's upper class on all these issues, opposing charter schools, supporting amnesty, and opposing efforts to rein in job-killing tort awards.[24] The NAACP also weighs in on overclass issues that have little to do with African-Americans as a group: filibuster reform, same-sex marriage, and "climate justice." Then there's abortion. The abortion rates for black women are four times higher than those for white women, and in the past African-American leaders such as Jesse Jackson were pro-life. Perhaps they had detected the whiff of eugenics from the pro-abortion crowd, as expressed by Justice Ruth Bader Ginsberg. Asked about government subsidies for abortion, she told a *New York Times Magazine* reporter "Frankly I had thought that at the time *Roe* was decided, there was concern about population growth and particularly growth in populations that we don't want to have too many of."[25] The "we" in question presumably didn't include African-Americans, but that hasn't prevented the NAACP from taking a pro-abortion stance.

Doubtless, there is some logrolling going on, in which the NAACP is given something in return for its servitude, in the form of better welfare benefits perhaps. Nevertheless, the organization's policies represent a kowtow to America's Red Tories and a repudiation of Booker T. Washington's entrepreneurial vision for the advancement of his race. For the NAACP, that's a complete turnaround, since its founders had thought that Washington was too accommodating to the white overclass. George Fitzhugh would have been amused at the irony, Lincoln less so.

PART V

Things We Can Change

===============

We have…areas of left right convergence where if we set aside our disagreement we could finally get something done.

—RALPH NADER, ReasonTV

Keep on rockin' in the Free World.

—NEIL YOUNG

CHAPTER

16

Education

AMERICA'S FOUNDERS WERE RIGHT TO FEAR HEREDITARY aristocracies. Not merely were they the order of their day, but they seem coded in our DNA. We wish our children to do well, and better still than their peers, and that's all that's needed to produce the kind of aristocracy Jefferson dreaded. If that didn't happen for a time, it was because his America was an open country and slow to adopt wasteful barriers to advancement. The country permitted the Ragged Dicks to rise from the streets and welcomed the immigrant who arrived with nothing in his pocket, fulfilling Jefferson's promise, repeated by Lincoln, that how people would fare would depend primarily on their own talents and efforts.

Since then we've become a country of inequality, where wealth differences persist over generations. That spells aristocracy, and most of the quick fixes we've been offered aren't up to the job. By themselves, skill-based technological changes don't account for the rise of inequality, and we're not going to give them up in any event. When free trade and globalization are added to the mix, it becomes easier to understand the run-up in inequality, but then we wouldn't want to change that either. Nor does this seem like anything more than a piece of the puzzle. As for the welfare system, it's already generous, and the tax rates are already high. Then there are all of the advantages rich kids get from their parents—money, a fostering environment, perhaps even good genes. We can do something about that—but not a whole lot.

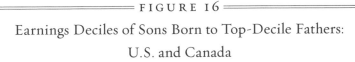

Earnings Deciles of Sons Born to Top-Decile Fathers:
U.S. and Canada

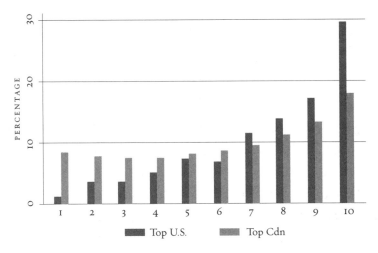

SOURCES: Corak, Curtis and Phipps (2011); Hertz (2005).

There are other things we can do, however, and the easiest way of identifying them is to compare America with other, more mobile countries, particularly the one it most closely resembles. As we saw in Chapter 4, Canada is much more mobile than America, and the differences come from the top and the bottom of the earnings stream, from the Red Tory alliance between the American New Class and the underclass we saw in the last chapter. In the bottom ten percent, children born to low earning parents are far more likely to emerge from poverty in Canada, as we saw in Figure 12. And in Figure 16 we observe the same cross-border differences at the top end. American sons born to top decile fathers are much more likely to remain in the top deciles themselves, and less likely to move down to the bottom ones, when compared to top Canadian sons.

The striking—even shocking—cross-border differences go a long ways towards explaining American income immobility. Take away the lowest and the top deciles, and there isn't much difference between the United States and its much more mobile northern neighbor. The story, then, is one of barriers to advancement that trap the poorest of Americans in poverty, and of the special advantages enjoyed by the richest of Americans, the members of the New Class.

To some extent, this reflects cultural differences between Americans and Canadians which resist reform, but then there are other differences too, notably the superior Canadian K–12 and higher education systems. The typical grade and high school student in Canada knows more than his American counterpart, and the average Canadian university would seem superior to the average American one. But that's just the average. In America, the spread between the best and the worst schools is far greater than in Canada. The worst schools are far worse than the worst Canadian ones, and the best schools far better, just as we'd expect in an aristocracy. The products of top schools go on to earn more than their Canadian counterparts, and their children do so too.

That's how it is now. But it didn't start out that way.

The Promise Made

Lincoln's ideal of a mobile society became the idea of America, as expressed in Horatio Alger novels and countless stump speeches. In Lincoln's time, however, not everyone shared his faith in upward mobility, and not just the southern slaveholders. For John Adams' great-grandson, Henry Adams, the progression from George Washington to the rumpled Ulysses S. Grant seemed inconsistent with Darwin's new theory of evolution.[1] Settling down in Washington, where the Hay-Adams Hotel now stands, Adams was dismayed by the limited choice of dinner guests, and Henry James imagined him saying "hang it,...let us be vulgar and have some fun—let us invite the President."[2]

When Adams looked at what had happened to his country, he saw what he called *The Degradation of the Democratic Dogma*,[3] the descent from a Jeffersonian natural aristocracy and his great-grandfather's aristocracy of birth and beauty to a beastly new world of ignoble usurpers; and he found an explanation for this in Lord Kelvin's Second Law of Thermodynamics: entropy. Energy tended to dissipate and turn order into disorder, in political affairs as well as physical science. That is what had happened to America, he thought, from the time of Washington, John Adams, and John Quincy Adams. In a better age Henry Adams might have been asked to follow his ancestors into politics, but as it was he withdrew into academic life and the company of close friends such as John Hay, Lincoln's biographer and Theodore Roosevelt's Secretary of State. Henry James took his own distaste for America to the next level by joining James McNeill Whistler in England, one of a long line of aesthetic expatriates that included T.S. Eliot, Ezra Pound, and Gertrude Stein.

If that's what Adams saw of America, he should have gotten out more. America's population in 1910, the year he developed his theory of entropy, was 92 million, double that of Great Britain and a 20 percent increase from ten years before. Per capita GDP was $5,000, more than that of Britain and up from $4,000 in 1900. America's economy was the *stupor mundi*, constituting 48 percent of the world's wealth in 1910, up from 16 percent in 1870. By 1920 this would rise to 62 percent.[4]

Culturally, the country was scarcely a backwater, with major poets such as Walt Whitman and Emily Dickinson; novelists such as Willa Cather and Edith Wharton; and painters such as Winslow Homer and John Singer Sargent. In architecture, there was H.H. Richardson and Richard Morris Hunt; in philosophy, Charles Sanders Peirce and William James; in political theory, Herbert Croly and Thorsten Veblen; in music, W.C. Handy and Scott Joplin; in sculpture, Augustus Saint-Gaudens; in psychology, John Dewey; in history, Henry Adams. In 1907 Albert Michelson won the first American Nobel Prize in science, and in California Hollywood was beginning to cut down its orange groves for movie studios.

In a few short years, moreover, American arts would enjoy a renaissance, driven by writers such as Ernest Hemingway, F. Scott Fitzgerald, and William Faulkner; and composers such as Charles Ives and George Gershwin. A second-class military power in 1900, the United States bestrode a unipolar world like a colossus by 2000. The century belonged to America, and as we saw in Chapter 9 Claudia Goldin and Lawrence Katz attributed this to America's education system. The twentieth century was a human capital century, when government investment in education paid extraordinary dividends. Lincoln had made a bet on the American dream and the power of education, and this had paid off better than anyone could have imagined.

While Lincoln is remembered for abolishing slavery, he was not a libertarian. He was a Whig in his economic policies, and more than willing to employ the power of the state on works for the common good. This included, along with roads and canals, public education. Lincoln had become highly educated on his own and was a self-made man, but not by choice. He greatly regretted the absence of public schooling when he was young, and never forgave his illiterate father for his lack of interest in education. As his father lay dying, Lincoln refused to see him, saying both would find the visit painful.

In his first political speech in 1832, the 23-year-old Lincoln described the public works that Sangamon County, Illinois should undertake, and these prominently included schools. Education was the most important subject for the public, he said, and he would be happy to contribute to its spread.[5] That was a major theme of his entire political career, and at the Wisconsin Agricultural Fair twenty-seven years later he spoke of how farmers would benefit from an education in new methods of farming. He was therefore only too happy, as president, to sign into law the Land-Grant Act of 1862 that Congressman Morrill had sponsored. Three years earlier President Buchanan had thought a similar measure constitutionally suspect and vetoed it, but a disciple of Henry Clay had no such scruples about internal improvements.

The Morrill Act deeded 30,000 acres of federal land to every state that wished to create a public university for the study of "agriculture and the mechanic arts" (without excluding the sciences and humanities). The state could then sell the land to pay for the university. The Act and succeeding land-grant statutes transformed American higher education, and universities founded in this way include M.I.T., Cornell, Rutgers, Ohio State, Penn State, Texas A&M, and the universities of California, Florida, Illinois, Iowa, Maryland, and Minnesota, amongst many others, 106 universities in all. It would be difficult to imagine what American higher education would look like without them.

As a child, Lincoln had had little more than a year of schooling in all, just enough to pick up reading, writing, and mathematics to the rule of three. For most Americans, public education came along later, through the efforts of people such as Horace Mann, Lincoln's fellow Whig. Mann served in Congress and the Massachusetts Legislature, but his gaunt appearance, solemn New England rectitude, and demand for moral certainty ill-suited him for the rough-and-tumble of politics. One day he found his brother-in-law, Nathaniel

Hawthorne, smoking a cigar. "Mr. Hawthorne," he snapped, "I am sorry to say that I can no longer entertain the same respect for you that I once had."[6] But if he hated tobacco, Mann had several loves, including phrenology and public education. The first led him to observe closely the heads of fellow train passengers; the second took him from the Berkshires to Cape Cod as his state's Secretary of Education, to argue for tax-funded elementary public schools. He busied himself with the design of children's desks, school bells, and school curricula (which would include courses on the shape of the human head), and his missionary zeal inspired people in other states. By 1870, all states had free elementary schools, and by 1910 education had become compulsory in most states and nearly three-quarters of children attended school.

By all accounts, public schools were more rigorous 100 years ago than they are today, as seen in the kinds of test questions given back then. Here is the 1912 Eighth Grade examination for Bullitt County, Kentucky.

> *Spell*: bequeath, monotony, rhinoceros, synopsis.
> *Mathematics*: Find the amount of $50.30 for 3 years, 3 months and 3 days at 8 percent.
> *Geography*: What waters would a ship pass through going from England though the Suez Canal to Manila?
> *Civil Government*: Define three rights given Congress by the Constitution and two rights denied Congress.
> *History*: Name the last battle of the Civil War; War of 1812; French and Indian War, and the commanders in each battle.[7]

And that was just to get into high school. One wonders how many American college graduates could answer such questions correctly today.

With a reformer's zeal and an impatience with ambiguity, Mann wanted a school system that promoted social uniformity and turned out students formed according to the highest moral precepts and trained in the principles of American government. His timing, as it turned out, was perfect. The rapid industrialization of America hastened the movement from country to city and made mass public education suddenly more feasible. Across America, inner-city P.S. 16 and 63's opened their doors to the children of factory workers, George Fitzhugh's wage slaves. In addition, the rapid waves of immigration after the Civil War filled the cities with children who first learned to speak English and the ways of their new country in public school. Assimilation to American customs and institutions was accepted as a desirable goal, and nothing did the job better than Mann's public schools. "The free common school system," said Adlai Stevenson, "is the most American thing about America."[8]

While Mann meant his public schools to be non-denominational, what this meant was non-denominationally Protestant. Readings were from the King James Version of the Bible and distinctly Protestant prayers were offered. In the public schools of New York City, with its large Irish population, Catholics were stigmatized as deceitful, bigoted, and intolerant by teachers who were often Protestant clerics.[9] In response, Catholics demanded state funds for their own schools, which they receive today in Canada, Britain, France, Germany, and most other First World nations, and which provide a needed competition to the government monopoly on K–12 education.

That wasn't going to happen in America. After the Civil War, many states enshrined barriers to parochial schools in their constitutions, through "Blaine Amendments" that have been condemned as expressions of religious bigotry.[10] In other states, the question of state support for parochial schools ended up, inevitably, before the courts, which worked out a messy compromise. Direct state aid to parochial schools was prohibited, but indirect aid was just fine. Justice Hugo Black, who was not without his own anti-Catholic prejudices,[11] argued for a "high and impregnable wall of separation" between church and state, one which banned direct subventions but nevertheless permitted state funding for bus transportation to and from parochial schools.[12] More recently, the Supreme Court has given qualified approval to state-funded vouchers that parents may use to pay for parochial school education, provided there are adequate non-religious schools for parents to choose.[13]

One can easily forget the sectarian animosities that informed nineteenth century politics. The anti-Catholic American (Know-Nothing) Party won eight electoral votes and more than a fifth of the ballots for their candidate for president (Millard Fillmore) in the 1856 election. His support came principally from Southern states, but anti-Catholicism was also popular amongst Northern intellectuals. In Massachusetts, with its highly educated voters, the Know-Nothings won the governorship and every state-wide election in 1854, as well as 379 out of 381 seats in the state House of Representatives. The newly elected governor pledged to "Americanize America" by banning naturalized citizens from public office and imposing a 21-year residency requirement before they were allowed to vote. A legislative committee raided parochial schools and convents, frightening the nuns, in a search for signs of depravity.[14]

As it turned out, fears of parochial schools turned out to be wildly excessive. One of the best portrayals of how they instilled American values came from Catholic film producer, director and writer, Leo McCarey. For many American Protestants, drawn to a 1945 Bing Crosby comedy, *The Bells of St. Mary's* was their first look at what Catholic education was like. Recognizing this, McCarey toyed with Protestant apprehensions at the beginning of the film, when Crosby, as Father Chuck O'Malley, arrives at St. Mary's to replace his predecessor. "Poor man," says the housekeeper (like all such figures, of minimal seductiveness), "they took him away, mumbling to himself, in a wheelchair."

> *O'Malley*: That's strange. I don't anticipate any trouble.
> *Housekeeper*: Ye don't, eh? Ye've never been pastor of a paro-
> chial school, then?
> *O'Malley*: No. It's my first experience.
> *Housekeeper*: Oh…well…I can see ye don't know what it
> means to be up to yer neck in nuns.

St. Mary's is a decrepit, inner-city school, to which O'Malley has been sent with the idea that it might be closed and its children sent to a larger school. As the housekeeper warned, it is dominated by the sisters, in their pre-Vatican II habit of coif and veil, who quickly learn their way around O'Malley. In every respect, however, the school would have seemed familiar to all Americans. The flag is prominently displayed, along with a portrait of George Washington, and the nuns lead the children in the Pledge of Allegiance. There's a Christmas pageant, and at recess the boys and girls play baseball and basketball. A sissified boy is taught how to box by a nun, and a Grade 8 girl from a troubled family who confesses her desire to become a nun is told that she mustn't think of that until she has had her fill of parties and dances. While O'Malley leads the children in O *Sanctissima* and *Adeste Fidelis*, the Protestant viewer would have found the film entirely inclusive, down to the name of one of the students.

> *Sister* (to the students): I want you to read what you have
> written, so Father O'Malley may hear it. Luther?
> *O'Malley* (aside to sister): Luther? How'd he get in here?
> *Sister*: We never knew.

The film was the most popular in the history of the RKO studio, and earned even more than the McCarey-Crosby film of the year be-fore, *Going my Way*. However, the earlier picture won seven Academy

Awards, including Best Picture, Best Director, and Best Actor. In this picture, Crosby introduced the character of Father O'Malley as a kind of clerical asset manager, charged with turning around run-down parishes. There is no parochial school in the movie, but there are schoolchildren, in a Dead End Kids kind of gang. O'Malley observes their leader stealing a turkey, and persuades him and his fellows to form a church choir. In both McCarey movies, O'Malley wins people over to goodness and virtue simply by placing faith in them and giving them the opportunity to behave well.

Films about Dead End Kids were an important genre in the 1940s, with their own B-movie stars in people like Huntz Hall and Leo Gorcy. A decade later a different kind of teenager appeared in *Blackboard Jungle*: the leather-jacketed juvenile delinquent of the inner city public schools, also seen in *West Side Story*, first the musical, then the film. These were the white slaves of George Fitzhugh, and they appealed to a more cynical theatre audience. Cynicism was always present in McCarey's sentimental comedies, but there it was laughed away by Father O'Malley or prayed away by the nuns. McCarey's optimism and faith in ordinary people had captured the essence of Lincoln's response to George Fitzhugh at the Wisconsin Agricultural Fair.

The Promise Broken

Back in Bing Crosby's day, an American high school diploma was a badge of quality that signaled that graduates were sufficiently educated for most of the jobs then available. Students were equipped with basic math skills and knew how to use the English language, and this powered the country's extraordinary economic growth during Goldin-Katz's human capital century. But that was then. Today math skills have fallen and the job of teaching students how to construct a sentence has been passed on to college instructors.

=========================== TABLE 16.1 ===========================

PISA Student Performance Scores (2009)

	MATH	SCIENCE	READING
Australia	514	527	515
Canada	527	529	524
Norway	498	500	503
Netherlands	526	522	508
Germany	513	520	497
Japan	529	539	520
Sweden	494	495	497
U.K.	492	514	494
Singapore	562	542	526
Italy	483	489	486
France	497	498	496
U.S.	487	502	500

SOURCES: OECD Program for International Student Assessment; U.S. Statistical Abstract, Doing Better for Families, OECD 2011.

As America's public education system has declined, that of other countries has improved, and our relative human capital advantage has vanished. In the most recent OECD Program for International Student Assessment (PISA) rankings, which provide a snapshot of a 15-year-old's knowledge and skills in math, science, and reading in 65 countries, the United States placed 30th in math and 23rd in science. In reading it placed 15th, well below Canada.

The decline in public education helps explain the rise in income immobility. If one wants to see people get ahead, as Lincoln did, a good place to start is with the public school system. Contrariwise, if the goal is to ensconce an aristocracy, one could scarcely do better than to weaken the public schools. That's the message from a study that mapped the dispersion of literacy scores against a measure of cross-country earnings inequality. What the study found was a nearly one-to-one relationship between the two, with the United States leading the pack: highest earnings inequality and highest test score inequality.[15]

Along with perpetuating American inequality and immobility, America's dysfunctional education system imposes a tremendous financial burden on the country. One study concluded that the gain to the U.S. economy, if American public school students were somehow raised to Canadian levels, would be enough to resolve America's projected debt crisis and amount to a 20 percent annual pay increase

=== TABLE 16.2 ===

OECD Proficiency Levels, Literary (Native Language) and Numeracy

	LITERARY MEAN	LITERARY 95TH PERCENTILE	LITERARY PERCENT IN LEVEL 5	NUMERACY MEAN	NUMERACY 95TH PERCENTILE	NUMERACY PERCENT IN LEVEL 5
Australia	280.4	354.6	1.3	267.6	351.6	1.5
Canada	273.5	348	0.9	265.5	349.3	1.3
Denmark	270.8	338.9	0.4	278.3	355	1.7
France	262.1	333.9	0.3	253.2	336.5	0.5
Germany	269.8	341.4	0.5	271.1	350.5	1.2
Japan	296.2	355.3	1.2	288.2	355.4	1.5
Netherlands	284	354.6	1.3	280.3	354.2	1.3
Norway	278.4	346.6	0.6	278.3	356.8	1.7
Sweden	279.2	351.2	1.2	279.1	358.4	1.9
England	272.6	346.7	0.8	261.8	345.5	0.9
U.S.	269.8	344.3	0.6	252.8	340	0.7
Average	272.6	342.1	0.7	268.7	345.6	1.1

SOURCE: OECD Skills Outlook 2013: First Results from the Survey of Adult Skills, Tables A2.4, A2.1, A2.8, A2.5 (2013).

for the average American worker.[16] Call it the price of aristocracy.

Americans who express optimism about their country's future often point to its higher education system, where the country remains the world's leader. Its elite institutions are the best anywhere, and American research and development leads the world. For example, half the science Nobel laureates since 1955 have hailed from the United States. One reason for this is money, of course. Top American universities pay premium salaries to superstars and import talent from other countries. That's been of enormous benefit for America as a whole, for its ability to attract star scientists has substantial spillover benefits for the economy.[17] But that's not to say that the benefits of superstar academics have rubbed off on the average American university student. In the OECD report of student ability seen in Table 16.2, America's top five percent come in at just a little above the average First World country in literary proficiency and second from the bottom in numerical proficiency. The OECD also ranked people according to their level of skills. For the top level of literary skills (level 5), where one could search for and integrate information across dense texts, synthesize ideas and make high-level inferences, Americans were below average. For the top level of numeracy skills, Americans were near the bottom. This evidences the Goldin-Katz findings we saw in Chapter 9 which tied the rise of income inequality to the decline of U.S. higher education.

The Enemies of Promise

I once told a friend of mine, an African-American federal judge, that I had attended a public school run by nuns in Canada. He was taken aback. "Didn't anyone object?" he asked. "Yes," I told him. "There was one group, back when. Its motto was 'One country, One language, One school system.' It was the Ku Klux Klan."

My friend's surprise was quite understandable. The kind of public school I attended wouldn't be found in a country with America's strict First Amendment barriers against religious establishments. Not that anyone thought that my province was establishing Catholicism when it hired nuns (on the cheap) to teach English in a town that was 95 percent French-Canadian. Canada didn't have an established religion, as England does, but then its constitutional traditions lacked Hugo Black's understanding of the Catholic menace. The right to publicly-supported education for religious minorities (Catholics in Ontario, Protestants in Quebec) was guaranteed in the country's founding constitution, the British North America Act, and was a necessary compromise without which Canada would never have been existed. So far from dividing the country, the right to religious school systems was a condition for its unification.[18]

In time, as religious allegiances weakened, the separate confessional school boards gave Canadian parents a range of educational choices and a competition to provide them. When it came time to register my daughter for school, she might have gone to an English or French Catholic or an English or French Protestant school without paying tuition. She might also have gone to an extremely good Jewish school, where the tuition was heavily subsidized by the state and came to about $2,000 a year.

As it happened, those kinds of choices weren't available to us, since we moved to the United States the summer before my daughter began kindergarten. In Canada, we wouldn't have worried overmuch about our daughter's education. The schools are good and it's not a struggle to get into a good university. And as the universities are all about the same, the choice amongst them doesn't much matter. It's very different in the United States, of course, where there are enormous differences in quality between the best and the worst college, and in our area parents begin to worry about college choices around the second month of pregnancy.

American parents who seek to place their children in a good college must choose between two tracks. The first is legacy admissions, the priority given to children of alumni who've made major donations to the college. At elite institutions, legacy children enjoy a tremendous edge over less wealthy children.[19] There really isn't anything much like this in other countries, and legacy admissions help explain why America fares so poorly on measures of social and income mobility.

Daniel Golden's *The Price of Admission* provides a tell-all account of just how unfair legacy admissions are,[20] and deliciously names names. There's Albert Gore III (Harvard) and Harrison Frist (son of Sen. Bill Frist, Princeton), the undistinguished sons of powerful men. For that matter, there's Al Gore II, son of a U.S. Senator and a mediocre student. Not to mention George W. Bush and John Kerry, all of whom took places at elite universities that otherwise would have gone to the more qualified children of the middle class. Conservatives bemoan the affirmative action admission standards that advantage minority students, but turn a blind eye to the most unfair affirmative action standards of all. Whatever one might say about giving a preference to minority students, at least it doesn't perpetuate the class structure the way legacy admissions do.[21]

It would have been nice, but the legacy game wasn't going to work for us. We weren't wealthy enough to play it, and therefore adopted the second admissions strategy: meritocracy. We would work to match, or even exceed, the kind of education our daughter would receive in Canada, and in so doing we saw at first hand the workings of American K–12 education. We learned how to play the game, how to lobby schools for the best possible education for our child. We knew which buttons to push, how to sweetly nag the guidance counselor, how to flatter the vice-principal; and discovered the kinds of teachers who were devoted to their pupils, as well as the burnt-out cases. We also learned how to deal with the school's bureaucracy.

The local elementary school with 200 students had more administrators—principals, guidance counselors, psychologists, technology specialists, "inclusion specialists," occupational therapists, registrars, social workers, and the like—than it had actual teachers.

We were lucky in where we lived, since Northern Virginia is one of the richest and best-educated areas of the country, ground-zero for the New Class, the southern flank of the Acela Corridor. Fully half of the country's ten richest counties are in Northern Virginia. Four of these are amongst the country's ten best-educated counties, and my Alexandria is the country's top book purchaser according to Amazon, ahead of Cambridge MA and Berkeley CA. From friends and colleagues we learned of educational resources we would not have discovered had we lived elsewhere. And so we sent our daughter to academic summer camps at the Johns Hopkins Center for Talented Youth ("CTY") and the University of Chicago (where, curiously, she had fun). By the time she entered high school, she was ready for the kind of math courses that weren't even offered in Grade XII when we were kids.

That didn't free us from the need to provide after-school teaching on our own. Math was a particular problem, and my wife ordered up a series of basic arithmetic texts, which over the years were replaced with books on fractions, decimals, pre-calculus, and finally advanced calculus. Math was not my wife's strong suit, and after her work as an attorney by day she'd bone up by night on the material she'd have to teach our daughter the next day. On top of this, there was religious school to study Hebrew for her bat mitzvah. Did I mention her piano lessons and her crew team? In all of this, our daughter was given advantages that neither of her parents had had when young.

What we had done became the subject of a book by Amy Chua, *Battle Hymn of the Tiger Mother*. Not that we adopted the kind of bullying Chua seemed to enjoy. We never threatened to burn our daughter's stuffed animals if she didn't play her violin. All the same, Chua's book was old news for members of the New Class. We knew about the preparation classes that would boost our daughter's SAT scores. We knew how to supplement school with after-school lessons with specialized tutors. We knew all the things that poor parents never know to do. We could even have taught the Tiger Mother a thing or two about college preparation: calculus is for MIT, Tocqueville is for Chicago, and crew is for Princeton. Forget the damn violin—that's for Julliard.

We didn't think about it, but what we had done contributed to American inequality and immobility. We lived amongst other members of the New Class, and learned from them how to use every trick in the book to give our daughter the kind of boost that children of lower class parents would never get. Ours was a meritocratic society, but it was a self-perpetuating one, and not Ragged Dick's kind of meritocracy. While legacy college admissions perpetuate social immobility in America, so too do meritocratic admissions.

For college admissions, merit is importantly identified through the student's Scholastic Aptitude Test (SAT) score. That's how students are ranked, and colleges too. If the only alternative were legacy admissions, then SAT scores would indeed be more democratic, and that was the idea when they were introduced. It hasn't worked out quite that way, however, for student scores are strongly correlated with parental income. For the poor, those with a family income of $0 to $20,000, the average SAT score is a lowly 1326 (out of 2400). For members of the middle class (family income of $40,000–60,000), this rises to 1461. But for those with a family income of more than $200,000, the average score is 1714.[22] The playing field isn't level. It's tilted towards rich parents, and especially towards the members of the New Class.

Then there's the cost of a college education, which has risen dramatically. That might not be a problem for the very rich, but for others the prospect of graduating with hundreds of thousands of dollars in debt is chilling indeed, and Cornell professor Suzanne Mettler reports that this has heightened American class distinctions.[23] So too has the rot in American higher education. Richard Arum and Josipa Roksa provide startling evidence of the limited educational value of a university degree in *Academically Adrift: Limited Learning on College Campuses*.[24] What they found was that 36 percent of students showed no improvement in analytic abilities and writing skills after four years in college. Bear in mind that we're talking about students tested between the ages of 17 and 21, and that we'd expect some improvement in problem-solving skills for everyone over that period, whether they're in college or not, just because they're older.

Bernie Sanders has proposed that public universities offer free tuition, as a way of reviving the American dream for low-income parents. That's not going to fix the decline of academic standards, and might make it worse. A cheaper solution might be to encourage the kind of on-line or blended educational experience offered by for-profit colleges, which are now under attack by Obama's education department. There is, however, something to be said for capping tuition at colleges that qualify for government-backed student loans. After students were given access to government loans, colleges simply jacked up their tuition, and invested the money in grandiose buildings, frivolous offerings, and deep ranks of sustainability officers. None of that did the students any favors.

As for public schools, it's not as if American K–12 teachers are poorly paid. Indeed, they're amongst the best-paid in the world.[25] There are sizable differences in per-pupil expenditures between U.S. states, but spending increases by themselves don't affect test scores.[26] Immigrant children represent a special challenge for teachers, but then Canada has a higher immigrant population. Some have offered other demographic explanations for the poor U.S. performance. When African-Americans and Latinos are taken out of the mix, the remaining two-thirds of U.S. students are sometimes said to perform at Canadian levels. Even were that true, it wouldn't be fair to compare two-thirds of American children with 100 percent of Canadian children (especially given higher immigration figures for Canada). But it's not true either. Only 41.8 percent of white American 15-year-olds are proficient in math, compared to 49.5 of *all* Canadians.[27] Quite apart from that, it's a little disquieting to hear suggestions that one-third of American students—the minorities— are less than fully American. These are arguments better suited to racist groups such as Stormfront.org (motto: *Every* month is white history month).[28]

The one thing that can be done to fix America's schools is no great secret: educational choice of the kind we might have had in Canada, vouchers, charter schools, state aid for parochial schools. State monopolies, which aren't very good when it comes to making cars, aren't much good either when it comes to K–12 schools. In the most sophisticated econometric analysis of the determinants of school quality, the authors conclude that school choice matters greatly.

> The effect is huge: Going from a system without any private school operation to a system where half the schools are privately operated increases the achievement level by substantially more than the equivalent of one year's average learning in mathematics (three quarters of a grade-level equivalent in science).[29]

The achievement advantage is especially striking when private schools receive public financing, since subsidized tuition gives middle class and poor parents a greater choice of schools. In private schools, their children will be better educated, and even the children left behind in public school will benefit from the competition, since their schools will find it harder to ignore the needs of students.[30] In Washington D.C., where federally-mandated charter schools enroll nearly half the city's public school students, non-charter public school principals now go door-to-door to sell their schools to parents.[31]

If American public schools leave something to be desired, then, one doesn't have far to look to see the entrenched interests that mean to keep things that way. Chief amongst these are the teachers' unions, which wage fierce battles to protect incompetent teachers from dismissal and whose contracts block sensible educational reforms.[32] In elections, they can bring their members to the polls, and are the largest single unaffiliated donors in American politics. Together, the National Education Association and the American Federation of Teachers made $91 million in political contributions between 1989 and 2012, and of this virtually all went to the Democratic Party.[33] For her opposition to school reform, NEA president Randi Weingarten was the villain of *Waiting for Superman*, the 2010 film about America's shoddy public schools. Nevertheless, she is a respected guest on National Public Radio and a board member of Priorities USA Action, the Democratic political action committee with the deepest pockets. Barack Obama talked a good game about school choice when he was a senator, but once he was elected as president one of his administration's first acts was a move to shut down a D.C. program that provides $7,500 vouchers to disadvantaged kids.

That's only the teachers, however. What about everyone else? At one time, religious bigotry explained why voters opposed state aid to parochial schools. Americans United for Separation of Church and State was founded in 1947 by the anti-Catholic liberal intellectual Paul Blanshard as *Protestants* and other Americans United for Separation of Church and State, just in case anyone forgot which side he was on. There's possibly a tiny bit of that still around, but the deeper issue today is the culture wars, and the idea that parochial schools foster conservative beliefs about abortion and same-sex marriage. Still, that's a long way from explaining why American voters are indifferent to the fall of their public schools, and to their country's decline.

There's evidently something else going on, and that's the desire of upper class parents for an aristocracy. They themselves won't be sending their children to the dysfunctional schools in which poor and middle class kids are trapped. As a candidate, Bill Clinton had spoken up for public schools and against school vouchers, but after the election he sent Chelsea to the tony, private Sidwell Friends school (to which the Obamas sent their daughters 16 years later). Not that there's anything wrong with wanting good schools for one's children, but then the New Class doesn't want good schools for anyone else. As John Miller noted, surveying voting patterns on a school choice referendum in California, "vouchers become less popular as one moves up the socioeconomic ladder."[34]

Fixing public schools wouldn't harm upper class children in absolute terms. In relative terms, however, they'd be worse off, as they'd be faced with increased competition from below. That accounts for the New Class' apparently pathological desire to ensure that other people's children enjoy the dubious blessings of a public school education, why it opposes vouchers, hobbles charter schools, and fears a St. Mary's "up to yer neck in nuns." This might seem paradoxical, since even the bird of prey knows not to foul its own nest. But that's the point. It's not their own nest, for the New Class. It's the nest of the Other, the rival.

CHAPTER

17

Immigration

AMERICA ISN'T THE ONLY 'NATION OF IMMIGRANTS,' EVEN if it sees itself that way. Thirteen percent of American residents (legal and undocumented) are foreign born, as compared to 20 percent in Canada and 26 percent in Australia—the true nation of immigrants. America is only a little ahead of Great Britain (11 percent).[1] Nevertheless, Americans take pride in they way in which their country has welcomed immigrants and the country's open door legacy that stretches back to its earliest days and to Abraham Lincoln.

Colonial America welcomed new arrivals as a source of economic growth, and the Declaration of Independence denounced George III for limiting the colonies' population through restrictions on immigration. By Lincoln's day, however, immigration had become a contentious issue. The Know-Nothing Party sought to bar entrants from Catholic Ireland, and after the Party's decline in 1856 its anti-slavery members drifted into the Republican Party. As a rising Republican, Lincoln wanted Know-Nothing votes. What he didn't

want in his Party was Know-Nothing's bigotry and its knee-jerk opposition to immigration. "Of their principles," he wrote:

> I think little better than I do those of the slavery extension-
> ists. Indeed I do not perceive how any one professing to be
> sensitive to the wrongs of the negroes, can join in a league to
> degrade a class of white man.[2]

In his campaign for the Senate in 1858, Lincoln made his sentiments publicly known. The new arrivals—German, Irish, French
and Scandinavian—could not trace their ancestry back to the
America of 1776, but that didn't matter. They had a right to claim
Jefferson's principles for themselves, as the inheritance of all patri-
otic and liberty-loving men.[3] Then, in the 1860 election, the Republican platform decisively rejected immigration barriers and any
effort to restrict the rights of naturalized Americans.

A Nation of Immigrants

Lincoln's faith in the power of American ideals came to define
the country as a nation of immigrants, where the new arrival became American simply by his allegiance to Jeffersonian principles.
In other countries, membership in a common church, participation in a particular culture or a common ancestry provided the
sense of belonging. That wasn't America, whose welcoming attitude was nowhere better expressed than in Hollywood, which itself was importantly the creation of immigrants—Mack Sennett,
Samuel Goldwyn, Louis B. Mayer, the Warner Brothers, Charlie
Chaplin, and Mary Pickford. A later generation of immigrants—
Frank Capra, Billy Wilder, Alfred Hitchcock, Fritz Lang, Ernst
Lubitsch, Otto Preminger, Dimitri Tiomkin, Bob Hope, and Cary

Grant—helped make Hollywood the synonym for the film industry.

One of the most pro-immigrant films was the 1935 Leo McCarey comedy, *Ruggles of Red Gap*, where an English manservant (Charles Laughton) quiets a rowdy cowboy bar by reciting the Gettysburg Address, and in the process discovers that he wants to become a citizen. The same Lincolnian message about immigration can be seen in *The Man Who Shot Liberty Valance*, the masterpiece of John Ford, who himself was the child of Irish-born parents. A newly-arrived Eastern lawyer, Ransom Stoddard (Jimmy Stewart), decides to open a school in territorial Arizona. Below pictures of George Washington and Abraham Lincoln, he begins by telling a mostly adult class about the principles of American government, and poses a question to a Scandinavian immigrant who runs the town's restaurant.

> *Stoddard*: For those of you who have just started, I might explain to you that we've begun the school by studying about our country, and how it's governed. Now, let's see. Well, Nora, would you tell the class what you've learned about the United States?
>
> *Nora*: The United States is a republic,...and a republic is a state in which the people are the boss....That means us! And if the big shots in Washington don't do like we want, we don't vote for them, by golly, no more.
>
> *Stoddard*: Any more.
>
> *Nora*: Any more.

What had made Nora American was neither her birth nor her grammar but rather her defense of American ideals, and that was how Lincoln had thought it should be. Another immigrant, this time from far away, became an American in just the same way. The most positive story and film about the immigrant experience, co-written by an immigrant about the ultimate immigrant, describes how a refugee is adopted as a child by a loving Kansas couple and grows up to defend truth, justice, and the American way. The refugee, of course, is Superman.

The celebration of immigration reinforced the idea of American Exceptionalism, since a country must be exceptionally attractive if immigrants want to come here, and pretty terrible if it requires a Berlin Wall to keep them from leaving. For politicians, however, immigration means something else: a potential source of new votes. In Lincoln's day, the Republican Party's support for immigration did not cost it votes. The massive wave of Irish Catholic immigration, beginning in the 1840s, had swelled the ranks of Democratic voters; but by Lincoln's time new sources of immigration from Germany and the Scandinavian countries had evened things up. This had changed by 1900, however, when new immigrants from southern and eastern Europe supported Democrats much more than Republicans. Not surprisingly, the Republican Party abandoned its support for open borders and provided the decisive support for restrictive immigration legislation in the 1920s.[4] These statutes imposed national origins quotas, based on the origins of native Americans at the time. If a third of Americans were of British origin, then a third of the immigrants would be British. This had the effect of favoring immigrants from countries such as Britain, Germany, and Canada over those from Russia, Italy, and Latin America who had begun to swell the immigrant rolls, and these policies continued in force until 1965, when they were swept aside by the Immigration Act of that year.

The 1965 Immigration Act

The new Act profoundly changed America's immigration intake. Under the old regime, legal emigrants from Europe and Canada had constituted 70 percent of the total over 1950–59, and legal emigrants from Mexico only 11 percent. After the 1965 Act, however, emigration from Europe and Canada declined to 9 percent in 2012.[5] Their places were taken by immigrants from mostly Third World countries in Latin America, Asia, Africa, and the Caribbean, who provided 90 percent of the 2012 intake. If one includes the estimated 11.4 million unauthorized immigrants, approximately 30 percent of the 2000–09 immigrants were from Mexico alone.[6]

As this happened, the benefits of immigration came to be redefined. For Lincoln and John Ford, immigrants became American by subscribing to its founding principles. After 1965, however, immigrants were increasingly seen as different from Americans, and it was the differences that were celebrated when people defended immigration, as Bill Clinton did in a 1998 speech:

> More than any other nation on Earth, America has constantly drawn strength and spirit from wave after wave of immigrants. In each generation they have proved to be the most restless, the most adventurous, the most innovative, the most industrious of people. Bearing different memories, honoring different heritages, they have strengthened our economy, enriched our culture, renewed our promise of freedom and opportunity for all.[7]

The new arrivals might be as industrious and entrepreneurial as Clinton claimed, but not everyone celebrates diversity in so exuberant a way and today immigration is highly controversial again.

The faith in American Exceptionalism and the country's special promise has also diminished, and the superiority of the country's republican principles, as presented in *Liberty Valance*, is little taught in classrooms today if current textbooks are any guide. Classes that expose students to some of the more shameful moments in the country's past, without celebrating what is good in America, pitilessly tear asunder the mystic chords of memory to which Lincoln appealed in his First Inaugural. In doing so, they diminish what Ernest Renan thought defined a nation, the sense that fellow citizens not only share a glorious history but also that they have forgotten many unpleasant things.[8]

The loss of national pride and self-confidence has seemingly rubbed off on immigrants, who are less likely to assimilate today than *Liberty Valance*'s Nora and an earlier cohort of immigrants, according to scholars such as Samuel Huntington and Arthur M. Schlesinger, Jr.[9] The country's largest Hispanic student group, the Movimiento Estudiantil Chicano de Aztlán is openly secessionist, Aztlán referring to a would-be Aztec nation that would stretch from Texas to Oregon. The principal Hispanic group, the National Council of La Raza, defends members of "the Race," but also weakens the feeling of national identity through its support for bilingual education and its celebration of the racial solidarity of its members. There is less of a sense that, like Nora, the new arrival should master American ways and assimilate to their new country's culture,[10] and the metaphor that the country is a melting pot that transforms the immigrant into an American begins to look a little tarnished. All this is reflected in today's popular culture. More recent films about a shady set of immigrants, notably *The Godfather* and *Gangs of New York*, portray the American government as corrupt and don't offer much of an argument for open borders. As for Superman, he gave up his citizenship in 2011. It was just too limiting.

Supporters of the 1965 Act condemn the "closed door" immigration policies that prevailed from 1924 to 1965 as racist, but they did have something going for them. The quota system, based on the national origins of native-born Americans, was designed to produce an intake of immigrants which "looked like America," and that was thought to be an admirable principle when Bill Clinton proclaimed it his criterion for choosing cabinet members. One can do better, however, whether it's designing an immigration system or picking a cabinet, by simply choosing the best and most deserving candidates.

That turns out to be harder than one might think. There's firstly the question of whose welfare counts—native-born Americans, the emigration country, the immigrant himself. Even if the focus is restricted to native-born Americans, it's less than clear whether the 1965 Act conferred a benefit or imposed a cost. The new arrival might create new jobs that hire natives, or might take jobs away from them. He'll also provide cheaper goods and services to the native-born, and he might make some native-born more productive, some less so. The most respected immigration scholar, George Borjas, concludes that the empirical data doesn't support firm conclusions either way.[11]

One thing seems clear, however. Amongst the native-born, current immigration policies create winners and losers. Consumers, particularly wealthy Americans, are better off when their goods and services are produced more cheaply by immigrants, but these gains aren't a blessing for the native-born employees who are displaced or whose wages are competed away by immigrant labor. That's Economics 101, with supply and (downward-sloping) demand curves. Adding new employees increases the supply of labor and lowers employee wages. Segregating by skill group, Borjas found that increasing the immigrant flow by 10 percent depressed the earnings of native-born Americans by 4 percent between 1960–2010.[12] These costs are most heavily felt by African-Americans, the most fragile group of natives, whose unemployment rate is nearly double that of whites, and a 10 percent increase in immigration resulted in a 5.9 percent reduction in the black employment rate. The loss of jobs also breaks up families and results in other social pathologies, especially crime, and a 10 percent increase in immigration was associated with an increased African-American incarceration rate of 1.3 percent.[13]

Opportunity Costs

Those who defend the current immigration system tend to skip over the question of winners and losers, and look instead at the effect on the economy as a whole. That leaves room for both sides in the debate. There's another way of looking at immigration, however, by contrasting the immigrants we receive with those we might have received with a different set of immigration policies. Suppose that on net our present set of immigrants were no better or worse than American natives, when it comes to such things as education and skills. The problem is that that's not the highest of bars, as we saw in the previous chapter, and it's not difficult to imagine how we might admit a superior set of immigrants. By turning away the large number of skilled immigrants awaiting permanent residency,[14] we're incurring the *opportunity costs* of rejecting immigrants who would confer greater benefits on American natives. If we required better educational or skills credentials from immigrants, for example, we'd significantly lower the tax burden of natives.[15] We might also find it easier to adopt generous policies to admit refugees.

That's why critics of American immigration policies point to the Canadian immigration system as an example to be emulated.[16] Most importantly, the Canadian system is geared towards economic entrants likely to benefit native-born Canadians, either through special business categories or through a "skilled worker" points system that gives preference to people according to their language skills, education and work experience. While two-thirds of the Canadian intake is comprised of economic migrants, about two-thirds of American legal permanent resident (green card) admissions are for people who arrive under family preference categories, where they aren't screened for their skills.[17] Canada actually admits as many or more economic immigrants than the U.S., in absolute numbers.

In 2012, Canada welcomed 160,000 people as economic migrants, 16,000 more than America did in all. Remarkably, a country one-tenth the size of the U.S. admitted more people on the basis that they would add to the host country's wealth.

Economic criteria provide an eminently reasonable basis for admission. If all you knew about a potential entrant was that he had a science or technology Ph.D., you'd want to take him over the high school dropout. Given a choice between an unemployed laborer on welfare and a person with a job and a solid employment record, you'd prefer the latter. With American citizens, such distinctions are invidious, and Mitt Romney didn't help his campaign in 2012 when he compared America's welfare "takers" to its taxpaying "givers." Whether a citizen is on net a giver or a taker, he's still an American, and at different points of our lives we're going to be both. When it comes to non-Americans who seek to come here, however, there's nothing wrong with preferring givers to takers. The former will confer a benefit on native-born Americans, the latter a burden. The unemployed Oberlin grad, the slacker with a high school equivalency G.E.D., what sensible country would want to admit them? Not Canada, whose points system is designed to keep them out. The Oberlin grad would have 46 points, 21 points short of the minimum; the slacker only 31 points. Canada has a generous welfare system and refugee policy, but charity to natives requires a constrained sympathy for foreigners.

Canada does have family preference immigrants, but they constitute only a quarter of the total, not two-thirds as in the U.S. There is a moral case to be made for family reunification policies, of course, but such arguments are far weaker today than in the past. In the nineteenth century, when emigrants left their native countries it was often the long good-bye. They didn't expect they'd ever again see or talk to the parents they had left behind, which was why the reunion between the elderly Father Fitzgibbon (Barry Fitzgerald) and his even more aged mother at the end of *Going My Way* was so moving. But that was then. Today, plane tickets are cheap, as are calling cards and Skype.

By rejecting more qualified immigrants, the 1965 Act increases inequality and immobility as well as imposing substantial costs on native-born Americans.[18] Immigrants earn less than native Americans, and these differences persist beyond the first generation. George Borjas reports that U.S. immigrants earn 20 percent less than native Americans and that half of the difference in economic status persists from one generation to the next. In other words, we'd expect second generation Americans to earn 10 percent less and third generation Americans to earn 5 percent less than the native-born.[19] By contrast, Canadian immigrants are more skilled than their American counterparts, and assimilate more quickly into the national economy.[20] As compared to Canadians whose parents were born in Canada, second generation Canadians are as well educated and as likely to be employed.[21]

Canada is a more successful melting pot than the U.S. in social as well as economic terms. What retards economic assimilation in the U.S., argues George Borjas, is the clustering of immigrants in ethnic enclaves and the absence of social assimilation.[22] The largest ethnic groups, primarily from Latin America, develop their own separate economies and social structures and interact little with the economic mainstream. That happens in Canada too, but not nearly to the same extent as in the U.S., with its Hispanic communities, legal and undocumented.

The Canadian system also offers greater certainty to legal immigrants, who may quickly determine whether they qualify for admission. By contrast, American immigrants are generally admitted under a temporary visa and must wait several years for a Labor Department certification showing that there aren't enough U.S. workers to do the job. For a professional asked to give up a good job in the emigration state to move to the U.S., the added uncertainty makes Canada a more attractive destination. For the unemployed or underemployed, however, it won't make a difference. As a consequence, U.S. labor certification requirements create a bias in favor of unskilled or low-skilled immigrants.

As broken as the 1965 Act might be, it's easy to see why efforts at immigration reform have gone nowhere. The Act has proven a game-changer in American politics. Immigrants from Latin America comprised 30 percent of all legal immigration over 2000–09, and Latinos preferred Obama over Romney by 71 to 27 percent in 2012. Latino support was especially important in battleground states such as Florida and Colorado,[23] and an American electorate that resembled the America of 1960 would likely have elected Romney as president in 2012.[24]

Then there are interest groups, immigrant groups and employers. The immigration cohort, principally Hispanic, is well organized and vociferously opposes anything which would lessen the inflow from Latin American countries. For employers, immigrant labor, especially undocumented immigrants, is particularly a bargain. Unsurprisingly, the U.S. Chamber of Commerce supports the regularization of undocumented aliens, with a possible pathway to full citizenship.[25]

Finally, there's one other special constituency, and that is the New Class. For the richest Americans, the 0.1 percent, immigration won't make much of a difference, but the professional class one step down has a stake in maintaining the country's broken immigration system and its barriers to professionals, entrepreneurs and other economic immigrants. An entrepreneur who comes to America to start a business or to invest in an existing business will enrich the country. He's also likely to possess the personal virtues that would make him an admirable citizen. The problem, however, is that he is more likely to compete with America's aristocrats. They wouldn't want to see their jobs lost to the foreign-born. Let them go to Canada, which seems to want them. Or let them stay home. What our aristocrats will want instead are maids and gardeners for their homes and lawns, people who'll work cheaply, and these the 1965 law supplies wonderfully. Should they take jobs from American maids and gardeners, why that's their lookout.

America's immigration system harms low-skilled natives while benefiting high-skilled natives who are members of the New Class. That's a wonderful example of social justice, said no one ever. As compared to the Canadian system, America's immigration laws increase economic inequalities and impose a substantial burden on the American economy. That the current regime persists can in part be attributed to the New Class' ability to frame the political debate and determine the available outcomes.

CHAPTER 18

Crony Nation

THE ONE PERCENT MOVEMENT OF 2011 ARGUED THAT GAINS to the wealthiest of Americans come off the hides of the poorest Americans in a *zero sum* society. In other words, one more dollar for the rich means one less dollar for the poor. Some politicians would have you think that that's always how it works, that there is a finite amount of money in the world, that my gain is inevitably another's loss. In that case, we'd never have seen any economic progress, and the enormous wealth gains of the last 200 years would not have happened. That's nonsense, of course. We live in a *positive sum*, not a zero sum world, a world in which bargains freely entered into make both parties better off, and in which my gains from productive behavior needn't harm anyone. But there's another kind of world, one that interests me more, the *negative sum* world of Beggar Thy Neighbor and dog-in-the-manger, in which losses to one party exceed gains to the other.

In part, that is what has become of America, a country of crony capitalism in which the wealthy persuade their friends in office to erect legal barriers to chill competition from upstart competitors. A courtier-class of favored recipients enriches itself, but the country buys inequality with inefficiency and trades away wealth for corruption.

Benign Neglect

The leading novel about American immigration is Abraham Cahan's *The Rise of David Levinsky*. Cahan was an immigrant himself, and like his David Levinsky a Talmudic scholar who had fled anti-Semitic persecutions in Russia. In America, Cahan founded the *Forward* newspaper, where he defended socialism and mentored a generation of Jewish-American writers, including Isaac Bashevis Singer. Levinsky, by contrast, becomes a garment industry millionaire who abandons his once-intense scholarly interests along the way. At the end of his life Levinsky thinks himself a failure, misses Russia, and regrets that he gave up the chance to study at City College.

David Levinsky is, along with Willa Cather's *My Ántonia* and Henry Roth's *Call It Sleep*, a novel seemingly written to discourage immigration. (Russia wasn't really so bad: Look, they even threw a pogrom in your honor!) For many foreign readers, however, it must have had the opposite effect, since what is gripping is David Levinsky's *rise*, from the time he arrives in New York with four cents in his pocket. He begins as a "greenhorn," unable to speak English, but soon finds himself selling hardware from a pushcart on the lower East Side. When that falls apart he becomes a garment worker, where he soon sees where the business opportunities lie. He operates sweatshops, undercuts his competitors and fights off unions along the way. He also loses a business partner; and later, when his business has wonderfully succeeded and that of his former partner has failed, the ex-partner's wife comes to demand a piece of the action. When he gently makes her leave she threatens litigation, but no lawsuit is ever filed.

Levinsky wouldn't have it so easy today. There are no longer any pushcarts, and so the new arrival might seek to open a convenience store. Before he does so, however, there'll be a few forms to fill out. Today's Levinsky will need a certificate of assumed name from the city and an employer ID number from the IRS. Then he'll need to comply with the city's fire extinguisher, recycling, and waste removal requirements, and fill in the sales tax paperwork. He'll also need to think about employee disability coverage and unemployment insurance for the kid behind the counter. He'll want a lottery agent license from the state and a cigarette retail dealer license from the city, and he'll also want to read up on city policies about commercial vehicle parking, smoke-free air, and pest control, as well as state consumer protection laws. Then there are tax forms: the city unincorporated business tax and payroll tax and federal and state taxes.

Fighting off unions would also be a lot harder for today's Levinsky. And then there's the threat of litigation. When someone comes into one's shop to warn of legal difficulties, it's less likely to prove an empty threat than it was in Levinsky's day. In America's litigation-mad culture, procedural and substantive legal rules seem to assume that one of life's chief joys is spending time talking to and paying a lawyer.

Sometimes the best thing a government can do is back off. That was an insight Daniel Patrick Moynihan brought to the civil rights debate in 1968. Looking at the riots that took place after the assassination of Martin Luther King, when everyone else demanded a strong federal response, Moynihan said that racial questions needed a period of "benign neglect." Moynihan thought he was quoting from the 1839 Durham Report, which had recommended that Britain grant self-government to the Canadian colonies, but the phrase was Moynihan's, not Durham's. It was Moynihan's way of summarizing what Durham thought British policy to Canada should be: Let the colony go its own way.

Perhaps that wasn't the right response to the riots. Moynihan's comment certainly aroused a storm of controversy. But benign neglect served David Levinsky well, permitting him to flourish. There is much less of that today, and most people would be puzzled by the idea that government neglect might be benign. Yet the best method of legislating the American Dream is often not to legislate at all.

Whatever the level of safety regulations, some people will find them excessive. More safety requirements will raise the unit cost of each product, which in turn will raise its price for consumers, and that's going to impose a burden on the less well-off. Where the same product is offered to a mix of people, the poor won't find the additional safety features worth the increased product price. By mandating safety standards only the rich desire, then, we're not doing the poor any favors. In particular, a government agency that seeks to squeeze out every last ounce of safety protection through its regulations is going to make nearly all consumers pay more than they'd want for the product.

These kinds of wealth transfers are inevitable, where governments prescribe safety standards and consumers don't have uniform preferences as to risk. Uniform standards aren't necessarily wasteful, however, since the alternative of no safety standards might be worse still. But there's a second kind of government policy that might be wasteful, in the sense that the losses to losers exceed the gains to winners. Such laws are sometimes called state capitalism, sometimes crony capitalism.

When government regulation establishes neutral safety standards, it doesn't take sides with one company against another. Under *state capitalism*, however, the government tries to second-guess the stock market and pick winners. State capitalism gets rediscovered every generation or so, but it's never had a good economic record, as demonstrated by the spectacular failure of some of the Obama administration's green energy subsidies, such as the $570 million loan guarantee to Solyndra. The company manufactured solar panels and lost money on every panel it sold. It was like the old garment industry joke where the boss' son wonders how they stay afloat when they lose money on every suit they sell. "That's okay," says the boss. "We make it up on volume." For Solyndra, making it up on volume meant passing the loss on to the American taxpayer.

When the Solyndra loan guarantee began to look foolish, Larry Summers famously observed that, "government makes a lousy venture capitalist." That's hardly surprising. There's no reason to expect politicians to outperform investors in identifying profitable opportunities. The investors have skin in the game—it's their own money at risk. When a Solyndra crashes, however, the politician can brush the speck of dust from his shoulder and walk away. It's not his money, and it's not even going to touch his political capital. Unlike the investor, he's not going to worry overmuch about picking profitable projects.

State capitalism imposes another kind of cost. It's not just the subsidy for dumb projects—Solyndra—but also the time and money the firm devotes in lobbying to cajole politicians for favors. Solyndra didn't just happen. For firm executives there was also the constant effort at wooing Washington to back loan guarantees, even as the firm was imploding. The time would have been better spent trying to keep the company afloat, or doing what businessmen should be doing—finding profitable investments.

Politicians will of course receive something in return for their favors, in the form of campaign contributions, donations to presidential libraries, and the like. From this, settled patterns of cooperation develop, and state capitalism morphs easily into a *crony capitalism* in which favored firms pay for protection against business rivals. With the aid of their friends in Washington, established firms will do fine, but new firms will find the entry barriers too high to compete. Being unsubsidized, they won't be able to undercut crony, subsidized firms, and the regulatory requirements which established firms can handle because of economies of scale will impose forbidding entry barriers for start-ups. When that happens, a large firm may find the government's rule-maker more a friend than an enemy.

For large established firms, even a fine can turn out to be a benefit, when it deters competition and permits a firm to reap anti-competitive profits. The 1998 Master Settlement Agreement (MSA) that tobacco companies reached with state attorneys-general was an example of this. After years of litigation over the health hazards of smoking, the four largest U.S. tobacco firms agreed to pay forty-six states $200 billion over twenty-five years. The fine amounted to a 40-cent increase in a pack of cigarettes and a 7–13% decrease in cigarette demand, but for the tobacco companies it also meant an end to the risk of competition from new tobacco companies as well as an end to state litigation. Under the MSA, the industry agreed to restrict advertising in order to reduce consumer demand for cigarettes. The tobacco companies wouldn't have liked that, but at the same time they realized that advertising barriers deter new competitors from entering the market.[1] For established tobacco companies, the MSA turned out to be a license to print money.

A recent paper by Sutirtha Bagchi and Jan Svejnar evidences the costs that crony capitalism imposes on the economy.[2] The authors reported that wealth inequality reduced economic growth, but when they looked more closely at the source of the inequality they found that crony capitalism explained this. They first took the *Forbes* magazine list of world-wide billionaires, and distinguished non-cronies from the cronies who had acquired their wealth through political connections. In a regression equation, they then found that crony wealth reduced economic growth, but not non-crony wealth.

The first person to offer a detailed economic analysis of crony capitalism was my colleague, Gordon Tullock, and it came to be called *rent-seeking*.[3] People rent seek when they try to obtain economic benefits through political leverage. They might seek tariffs on for-eign-produced goods, business subsidies, accelerated depreciation allowances, or regulations to hamper their rivals. Rent seeking does not create new wealth but instead redistributes it from those who lack to those who have access to the rule-maker.

What the well-connected members of the New Class won't do is rent-seek in an obvious way, by reducing marginal tax rates for ex-ample. Instead, they'll employ their influence interstitially, through the cracks in broad rules, the holes in general principles. They'll weigh in through their lawyers and lobbyists, and their leverage is applied in the dead of night when thousand-page bills are crafted, or away from the sunlight when donors talk to politicians who'll send private letters to regulators.

All this makes a country less just as well as less wealthy, and if the game has been rigged in this way it cries out for reform and Moyni-han's benign neglect. Rent seeking should thus be as much an issue for the Left as it is for the Right. The Right will condemn the ineffi-cient laws and regulations that reward those with political clout; the Left will denounce the economic inequalities to which rent seeking gives rise. The diagnosis might be different, but the prescription is the same: end crony capitalism. In both cases, the enemy is Rous-seau's political inequality and the appeal is for an economy shorn of insidious influence and corrupt politicians.

Licensing Entrepreneurs

One in fifteen Americans enjoys the physical and emotional bene-fits of a yoga workout.[4] That's not surprising. Regular yoga exercise promotes flexibility and strengthens muscles, and its devotees claim that it relieves stress and relaxes the mind. New Age guru Deepak Chopra takes it further still, claiming that yoga practitioners experience love, abundance, and true fulfillment in their lives.[5] Perhaps that's a little speculative, but it helps explain why the Obama administration released suspected terrorist Ghaleb Nasser al Bihani from Guantanamo prison. Al Bihani had told a parole board that he's a self-help enthusiast and practices yoga,[6] which at a minimum meant that he had assimilated to life in America.

Inevitably, the growing popularity of yoga led to calls that its teachers be licensed. That's basic consumer protection, for just think how the ill-taught, unlicensed yogi might harm her students when, attempting to align their chakras through meditative suggestion, she confuses the sahasrara (crown) with the svadhishthana (sacrum). That's got to hurt. Virginia therefore required its yoga studios to be licensed, sending them loads of paperwork to fill out and imposing a $2,500 application fee to weed out the charlatans. The state licensing body was the State Council for Higher Education for Virginia (SCHEV), which as its name implies normally concerns itself with university affairs. It wasn't clear how the expertise SCHEV had gained from overseeing law schools was going to help it evaluate downward dog poses. Nevertheless, the licensing movement has spread across the country in the last few years, and there's almost no stopping it. "If you're going to start a school and take people's money, you should play by a set of rules," said a Wisconsin licensing official.[7]

That's the mindset of regulators everywhere, for whom the unlicensed David Levinsky is the enemy. It's especially a problem in America, which devotes resources to a burdensome regulatory apparatus which other countries cannot afford. In the case of yoga studios, however, the regulator overreached, for within a few years the licensing requirement was withdrawn. It was seemingly a logical extension of the regulator's "you should play by a set of rules" philosophy, but it suffered for an embarrassing flaw: it was right out of cloud-cuckoo-land. SCHEV began to look like the Academy of

Lagado in *Gulliver's Travels*, with its project for extracting sunbeams from cucumbers. We were asked to imagine regulators measuring the spiritual benefits offered by ladies in see-through Lululemon stretch pants. And so the licensing requirement was laughed out of existence. Sometimes that still happens.

In spite of the odd setback, licensing requirements have become ubiquitous. The libertarian Institute for Justice, which litigates to set them aside, reports that today one in three U.S. workers requires a license, up from one in twenty sixty years ago.[8] Some of the blame can be attributed to regulators on auto-pilot, for whom every business needs a set of rules. That would explain yoga studio licenses, and perhaps also Washington D.C.'s tourist guide licenses. Until recently it was illegal for an unlicensed tour guide to carry on business, lest he fail to identify the Washington Monument. There's likely something else going on, however. There's a local Guild of Professional Tour Guides, which found the requirement a useful method of chilling the upstart David Levinskys on their Segways. There's usually a cartel of insiders behind the regulations, protecting their turf from new competitors who can't afford the licensing fee. That suspicion helps explain why the requirement was held an unconstitutional restriction of free speech rights by the District of Columbia Court of Appeals, which found that the City's arguments were not "validated by studies, anecdotal evidence, history, consensus, or common sense."[9]

These are the exceptions, however. Today, the list of licensed trades includes strippers, masseuses, hair stylists, florists, interior designers, milk samplers, manicurists, animal breeders, makeup artists, painters, and tree trimmers. The regulator always pleads that he's protecting the public, but it's often easy to see the naked self-interest behind this, and one example was Louisiana's rules about selling funeral caskets. Louisiana did more than mandate a licensing fee. Before selling a casket, one had to have a funeral parlor with a layout for 30 people, a display room for six caskets, embalming facilities, and a full-time funeral director. None of this had anything to do with building a casket, and the regulations effectively restricted their sale to highly priced funeral homes. What got people's attention was the identity of the rule-breaking casket-maker: the Benedictine monks in St. Benedict, Louisiana.

For generations the Abbey had made simple wooden caskets to bury its monks, and sensing a market they began to offer them to the public, for either $1,500 or $2,000. When they did so, the huge mark-up charged by funeral homes for their caskets became apparent. The funeral homes responded by refusing to use the cheaper caskets unless they were paid a $3,000 to $4,000 "casket-handling fee." The fee served no purpose, apart from protecting the funeral homes from competition, and was struck down by the Federal Trade Commission, which noted that the state funeral board was dominated by a cartel of funeral homes. The state board then ordered the monks to stop selling caskets to the public, and the case was taken to the federal Fifth Circuit Court of Appeals, which found no rational basis for the rule in terms of consumer protection or public health. The federal court noted that it was loath to set aside a state law, but in this case federalism had to take a back seat. "The principle we protect from the hand of the State today protects an equally vital core principle – the taking of wealth and handing it to others when it comes not as economic protectionism in service of the public good but as 'economic' protection of the rule-makers' pockets."[10]

Licensing requirements are especially burdensome for the David Levinskys who seek to rise in the world. They're less of a burden for the New Class, whose members are adept at complying with burdensome regulations and setting aside inconvenient rules. That's one reason why Virginia's licensing requirements for yoga studios went nowhere: yoga is popular with members of the New Class, particularly women. Similarly, a recent Food and Drug Administration proposal to ban the use of wood shelving for expensive artisanal cheeses was almost immediately withdrawn. The regulator had picked on the wrong kind of consumer, and should have stuck to Cheez-Whiz and its lower class customer base. The New Class is also key to Uber's marketing strategy. Uber brings a taxi quickly to its customers, who call for rides from apps on their iPhones or BlackBerries. Uber doesn't try to comply with taxi licensing requirements, and instead simply moves into a city and waits to be fined after it has built up its client base. After the fine is imposed, Uber announces that it's withdrawing its services from they city, and waits for its well-heeled clients to storm city hall.[11] So far the strategy has proven highly successful.

Romancing Wall Street

Macroeconomics is the Queen of the social sciences, since its pronouncements are pregnant of import, demand to be heeded, and cannot be contradicted by inconvenient evidence. After the Great Recession of 2008–09, the smartest of Keynesian macroeconomists, led by Federal Reserve Chairman Ben Bernanke, argued that printing more money was the best way back to prosperity. The money would end up in the hands of consumers who would use it to make purchases. This in turn would increase the demand for goods and services, and lead firms to hire more workers to meet the increased demand. And so the Fed lowered short-term interest rates, first to 0.5 percent and thereafter to a range of 0 to 0.25 percent. That was a straight-out gift to the banks, which could then turn around and lend the money to commercial borrowers at a higher interest rate.

The Fed's near-zero interest rates amount to printing more money, and when that didn't produce the desired turn-around, the

Fed embarked on a quantitative easing program of buying long-term government bonds, an even more obvious way of priming the monetary pump and stimulating the economy. This had the effect of artificially creating a demand for government securities, since one branch of the government (the Fed) was buying securities issued by another branch of the government (the Treasury Department). The proximate cause of the recession was the collapse of the housing market, which had been overheated by government-sponsored enterprises such as Fannie Mae and Freddie Mac. And so the Fed also purchased their toxic mortgage-backed real estate securities. The flood of cheap money has been great for wealthy investors, but it's actually worsened American income inequality.

The Fed is an independent agency that sets its own macroeconomic policies. Separately, the U.S. government pumped nearly $1 trillion into the economy through the Troubled Asset Relief Program (TARP). The money went to bankers and their (frequently foreign) investors, green energy companies such as Solyndra, and car manufacturers and their union employees. All this followed a Keynesian playbook that prescribed demand-side responses to recessions, flooding the market with money in order to get people buying and restart the economy. Indeed, it was Keynesianism on steroids, for the U.S. government and the Fed experimented with every demand-side mechanism they could think of, including near zero interest rates, cash for clunkers, home buyer tax credits, and mortgage relief plans.

What they reaped was a stalled economy, and not the recovery that followed past downturns. In the five years following the onslaught of the 1982 recession, the average annual increase in U.S GDP was 3.54 percent; and after the 9-11 recession the five-year average was 2.54. But after 2008 it was only 1.16 percent. Get used to it, we've been told. Annual growth rates of one to two percent are a "new normal," or what Christine Lagarde, the managing director of the International Monetary Fund, calls the "new mediocre."[12]

The Keynesian tool-box didn't seem to do the trick. In focusing solely on the demand side and government spending, the Keynesians had ignored the importance of the supply-side, of entrepreneurs who raise capital, innovate, and create jobs. Over six short years, stimulus spending increased the public debt by 80 percent, from 10 to 18 trillion dollars, this at a time when the economy (GDP) grew by only eight percent. Seeing where things were headed, the Simpson-Bowles commission in 2010 predicted that this would curtail economic growth by crowding out private investment.[13] People would be spending their money on higher taxes to fund the government's public debt, or salting it away to do so, rather than investing it in the economy.

Conspiracy theorists are apt to point to the ties between the White House and prominent bankers at institutions such as Goldman Sachs and Citigroup. The list of people includes Robert Rubin, Larry Summers, Rahm Emanuel, Jack Lew, and Peter Orszag, and while that sort of thing is catnip to the blogosphere it's better seen as the natural consequence of a White House with a major macroeconomic agenda and the desire to enlist the smartest bankers and Keynesians around for advice. Still, politically connected banks received larger bailouts from the Fed than financial institutions that spent less on lobbying or political contributions.[14] Elizabeth Warren also points to a too-cozy relationship between major banks such as Goldman Sachs and the Federal Reserve which is supposed to monitor them.[15] That's a familiar phenomenon, one which economists beginning with George Stigler have called "regulatory capture." Like the Louisiana Funeral Board we saw in the last section, the regulated industry tends to "capture" the regulator, who then sides with the industry more than with the public he's supposed to protect.[16]

Regulatory capture seems to be built into the American system of banking. In what Charles Calomiris and Stephen Haber call the "game of bank bargains," populist politicians and major banks collaborated in drafting banking regulations.[17] To satisfy their political constituencies, the politicians leaned on the banks to make improvident loans to risky, low-income home borrowers. Then, to make up for the banks' added risk, the government eased up on their capital requirements which had been designed to limit the ability of banks to take on risk. The underclass got cheap home mortgages and the bankers went into partnership with the government. When times were good, the banks borrowed interest-free moneys from the Fed which they lent at interest; and when times were bad, after the improvident loans came home to roost in 2008, they were bailed out by the government. It was win-win, except for the ordinary taxpayer who was stuck with the bill.[18]

The game of bank bargains is an example of the Red Tory alliance between an overclass and underclass. During the Great Recession, Canada experienced a housing bubble, not a bust. Canada's home mortgage policies are much more conservative than those of the U.S., but the same percent of people own homes in the two countries. There were no bank failures in Canada during the recession (although several banks required an infusion of support from the Bank of Canada in 2008).

No doubt it could have been worse. Ben Bernanke is credited with saving the U.S. economy, and preventing the Great Recession from turning into another Great Depression. It's hard to argue with that, either for or against, since that would put us into the counterfactual world in which something else had been done.

What is more clear are the distributional effects of the policies of the Fed and the U.S. government. The Fed's near-zero interest rates made banks less willing to make loans, especially to middle class small businessmen. The low interest rates were also bad news for people, particularly retirees, who looked to interest from government bonds for their income. "In this way," noted Joseph

Stiglitz, "there was a large transfer of wealth from the elderly to the government, and from the government to the bankers."[19] Then there's the stock market surge, fueled by the money the Fed has poured into the economy, which has been a tremendous benefit for wealthy Americans. They disproportionately own stock, and the bull market has been especially great for asset fund managers such as Mitt Romney and corporate executives whose compensation is tied to the firm's stock price. But the new money and the bailouts haven't provided much by way of observable benefits for the middle class. Only one in seven employed workers say that the market affects them a lot. For half, the market has little impact on them.[20] Monetary policies that produced the stock bull market have therefore increased income inequality.

Tax Subsidies for the Rich

If the New Class has tried to lower marginal tax rates, it's done a miserable job. As we saw in Chapter 11, America's marginal income and corporate tax rates are amongst the highest in the world. But then one wouldn't expect the rich to win too many battles over highly visible issues such as marginal taxes. Instead, they're much more likely to be successful in tailoring legal minutiae, the *arcana imperii*, to their advantage. The marginal rates of the Tax Code are easily understood, but the American Tax Code is an animal of incredible complexity. Its details are hidden from view and that is where one would look for the special payoffs to which Obama alluded in his Osawatomie speech. Fareed Zakaria minces no words about the Tax Code's culture of corruption.

> The American tax code is a monstrosity, cumbersome and inefficient. It is 16,000 pages long and riddled with

exemptions and loopholes, specific favors to special interests. As such, it represents the deep, institutionalized corruption at the heart of the American political process, in
which it is now considered routine to buy a member of Congress's support for a particular, narrow provision that will
be advantageous for your business.[21]

In 1952 corporate taxes generated 32.1% of all federal tax revenues, but this had fallen to 8.9% in 2010.[22] What brought the figure
down were loopholes or "tax expenditures," the scores of deductions
and tax credits the federal Tax Code provides firms to induce them
to engage in activities the government wishes to promote: oil and
gas extraction, green energy, scientific research, and so on. Taking
tax expenditures into account reduced the effective federal corporate tax rate (taxes paid divided by corporate income) down to 13
percent in 2010, reports the Government Accountability Office.[23]

As shameful as America's corporate tax loopholes might be, they
enjoy bipartisan political support and Bill Clinton was responsible
for many of them. They represent government's attempt to nudge
corporations in what is alleged to be a more socially responsible
or efficient direction, and if one makes the heroic assumption
that the state will get it right one might think this desirable. The
likelihood that the state can intelligently tell businessmen how to
make money is vanishingly small, however, and the possibility of
obtaining a tax break has made companies rent seek by investing
heavily in lobbyists and tax planners. An object lesson is provided
by General Electric, the country's sixth largest company in terms
of revenue, which earned profits of $14.2 billion in 2010 but nev-
ertheless paid no taxes. In part this was because it kept the earnings of foreign subsidiaries offshore, but it also sheltered $5 billion
in U.S. earnings through tax breaks for investments in property
depreciation, low-income housing, green energy, and research and

development, with a tax return that came to 57,000 pages.[24] As we saw, GE's CEO is the chairman of the President's Council on Jobs and Competitiveness, and that's what it takes to be competitive in America today.

Apart from its corporate tax loopholes, the Tax Code has also inflated the after-tax compensation for corporate executives. It's not their regular salaries, however, which are not much greater than what college presidents receive at top universities, and which are taxed as income. Instead, it's their "performance-based" pay, stock options and other forms of executive compensation tied to firm earnings, which are taxed at the much lower rate for capital gains, and which today form a bigger share of the total compensation package as a consequence of a 1993 change in the Tax Code. Prior to then, firms could deduct corporate salaries as a business expense, but thereafter they couldn't do so for salaries above $1 million a year. That led firms to cap executive salaries at $1 million and shift the rest of the compensation to performance-based pay which the firm could deduct as an expense. During the bull market years that followed, some executives received enormous rewards. Ironically, a tax rule meant to reduce executive pay has had precisely the opposite effect.[25]

The move to performance-based pay is more than a tax dodge, however. It's also a way to align the incentives of firm managers with those of the shareholders. It puts the executives "on commission," like salesmen at a car dealer, and gives them stronger incentives to advance stock price. For this reason, the University of Chicago's Michael Jensen argued that compensating executives with a mix of salary and stock options would usefully address a managerial myopia problem.[26] Managers, he argued, had inadequate incentives to focus on long-term gains. They'd be around for a few years, and had no reason to care about the fate of the firm after they left it. They'd overinvest in short-term prospects and underinvest in long-term ones. If they became shareholders, however, by exercising their stock options, they'd have a greater concern for the long-run, and stock options would correct their myopic misincentives.

Whether this worked out in practice as well as it did in theory has been doubted, by Michael Jensen amongst others, for management's single-minded desire to advance stock price can also sacrifice long-term growth to high-risk gambles on present opportunities.[27] In addition, few stock option plans distinguish between stock price increases that result from market-wide trends and those attributable to management's efforts. For example, the high-tech bubble of the 1990s boosted executive pay across the board, but most CEOs were about as responsible for it as my dog Leah, who was around at the same time.

Congressman Chris Van Hollen (D-MD) has proposed that top executives share their performance-based pay increases with all of their firm's employees. His proposed legislation would deprive the firm of the business deduction for the executive's increase unless the employees got a cost of living increase. "Look, you can pay your CEO whatever you want," says Van Hollen. "Just don't ask taxpayers to subsidize that pay if you don't reward workers, as you reward your CEO, for their increases in productivity."[28] That's not a crazy idea, but it's over-general. It would require the firm to offer the same increase to all employees, the slackers as well as the hard workers. Firms should have the discretion to distinguish between the two in their pay decisions. There is a simpler solution, however, that would serve the same goals, without interfering in management decisions or pandering to populist instincts. Simply require all executive compensation, whether performance-based or not, to be treated as income in the hands of the executive. This would include realized capital gains from the executive's sale of stock, which he received as compensation by the company for which he works or has worked.[29] Free market conservatives should like this, because the government shouldn't be in the business of telling firms how to compensate employees by giving them an incentive to adopt performance-based pay. Conservatives generally should also recognize that Obama was right when he complained that secretaries shouldn't have to pay a higher tax rate than their bosses.

Corporate Law Malfunctions

The rise of the one percent has been blamed on the failure of American corporate law to prevent greedy executives from over-paying themselves. As we saw, performance-based compensation packages may reward managers for things for which they weren't responsible. For example, oil company executives were paid more when oil prices increased, even though they had nothing to do with this.[30] When OPEC reduced the supply of oil and prices went up, they simply cleaned up.

Whether firm managers do in fact overpay themselves is a matter of debate.[31] But even if they do, that can't explain more than a fraction of the one percent's rise. The one percent mostly work for financial institutions, not for non-financial firms. When Steven Kaplan and Joshua Rauh broke down the categories of people in the top brackets, they found that non-financial executives comprised less than a quarter of the top 0.5 and 0.1 percent. There were more than twice as many Wall Street people (financial top executives, investment bankers, hedge funds, venture capitalist investors, and private equity investors) as non-Wall Street executives.[32]

Wall Street people earn vastly more money than non-Wall Street business executives. Still, CEO pay is nothing to sneeze at, and this has led to calls to fine-tune compensation packages. If they're excessive, that might point to a more fundamental problem of corporate governance, with a failure of oversight by the boards of directors and the shareholders of publicly-held firms. Corporate boards are supposed to constrain over-reaching managers, who must also report to shareholders at annual meetings. But if executives can expect their pay decisions to be approved by a complaisant board and rubber-stamped at shareholder meetings, that's not going to happen.

These are not new complaints. They were forcefully made in 1932 by Adolf Berle and Gardiner Means in *The Modern Corporation and Private Property*.[33] Berle and Means argued that a new managerial elite had slipped the bonds of board and shareholder control. The older model of capitalism, in which majority shareholder capitalists ran the show through their ownership of company stock, had given way to a separation of ownership (shareholders) and control (managers). In large public companies, said Berle and Means, shareholders were powerless because none of them owned more than a small percent of the company's shares, and this left managers free to do as they liked. There were still boards of directors, but these were puppets in the hands of management. The board didn't appoint managers; instead it was the other way around. Management chose the board.

As a description of American capitalism, the Berle-Means thesis has been widely discredited, at least for the time in which the two authors wrote. However, they had identified a problem of management accountability, which we subsequently saw in the American conglomerization movement of the 1960s and 1970s, where enormous firms were formed through mergers amongst companies in unrelated lines of business. That didn't work out so well, and by the 1980s it was recognized that the parts of a conglomerate were separately worth more than the whole.[34]

On a conglomerization merger, the larger firm that made the acquisition always claimed that this would create synergistic gains, where $2 + 2 = 5$. The market was having none of it, however, and the acquiring firm's stock price fell when the take-over was announced. Nevertheless, the conglomerization movement went ahead, since it was great for the acquiring firm's managers. The combined firm was bigger after the acquisition, and with bigger size went higher pay for the executives. In addition, mergers with unrelated businesses reduced the firm's risk. When Guns Inc. acquired Butter Co., the combined entity was less likely to fail than its separate parts. That didn't help the shareholders, who could more cheaply diversify risk through their own investments. They could buy stock in Guns Inc. and Butter Co. themselves, without the need for an oversized corporate behemoth to diversify for them. But if the merger was inefficient, it nevertheless helped firm managers since it reduced the probability of firm bankruptcy and the loss of their jobs.

The conglomerization movement is a nice example of how inefficient rules might be clothed in a rhetoric of fairness. Firms were less likely to conglomerize when it was easy to launch a take-over bid, but in 1968 corporate "reformers" erected barriers to take-overs in the 1968 Williams Act. The Act required tender offerors to hold their offers open for 20 days, instead of a few days only. It also prohibited them from acquiring more than a 5 percent toehold in the offeree's shares without public disclosure. This was done in the name of shareholder protection, but it also made it harder to bust up an oversized offeree conglomerate. The 1968 Act's principal beneficiaries were therefore the offeree's incumbent managers. The big losers were the conglomerate's shareholders, for whom it meant continued conglomerization and the foregone premium offers for their shares.

What Congress had done chilled what Henry Manne described as the "market for corporate control," the way in which managers of underperforming firms may be displaced in a take-over bid.[35] Berle and Means' separation of ownership and control disappears when a take-over offeror buys up a majority of shares and puts his people in charge, as offerors were able to do with a minimum of fuss prior to the Williams Act.[36] All these changes, which were piously said to benefit offeree shareholders, in reality immunized target managers.

If you want to understand excessive executive pay, argued Henry Manne, that's the reason.[37]

Through licensing requirements, financial and business regulations, tax loopholes, and wasteful corporate law rules, the wealthiest of Americans are protected from competition from below. Similar barriers can be found in other First World nations, but only on a lesser scale. One study reports that American businesses have 165,000 pages of federal regulations with which to comply.[38] Foreign regulators will look with awe on their American counterparts, and those who move here will recognize that America has a special genius, inherited perhaps from the Puritans, for telling other people what to do, as well as thousands upon thousands of government lawyers charged with putting it on the books. If America is less mobile than similar countries, we shouldn't be surprised.

Criminalizing Entrepreneurship

'PROSPERITY IS THE RESULT OF MATCHING BRAINS WITH capital and holding both sides accountable," writes McGill's University's Reuven Brenner.[1] Prosperous though it is, America might do better still by Brenner's standards. The problem isn't with matching brains with capital, which is what the finance industry does with stunning efficiency, but with accountability. There's too little of it in American corporate law, as we saw in the last chapter, since incumbent managers are insulated from take-over bids. American criminal law errs on the other side, however, for there's too much criminal accountability and there are too many prosecutions.

That's something the anti-corporate Occupy Wall Street movement would dispute, for it yearns for Wall Street perp walks, where police parade bankers in handcuffs before the television cameras. There were 1100 criminal prosecutions after the savings-and-loan scandals of the 1980s, but only one banker did jail time after the Great Recession.[2] There's certainly been enough public outrage of late, and for populists of the Left that's enough to make a case for criminal prosecutions.

The United States of Crime

If there haven't been prosecutions, however, it's not because American criminal law is too soft on defendants, whether white- or blue-collar. Compared to the rest of the First World, America has an extraordinarily punitive criminal justice system. With 5 percent of the world's population, America holds nearly 25 percent of its prisoners. In addition to the 2.3 million prisoners, an additional 5 million people are on parole or probation, about 3 percent of American adults. That's more than any other country, and it's not something to be proud of.[3]

Many of the prisoners were convicted of drug crimes. The U.S. Sentencing Guidelines recommends harsh penalties for drug offenders, including up to five years for possession of marijuana and a life sentence for third-time meth dealers. Drugs aside, there are also an untold number of regulatory crimes that businessmen might unknowingly commit. Consider, for example, the plight of Krister Evertson:

> Evertson never had so much as a parking ticket prior to his arrest.... An Eagle Scout, National Honor Society member, science whiz, clean energy inventor, and small business entrepreneur, Krister is now a felon. The nightmare that took two years of his freedom and hundreds of thousands of dollars...began when he made a simple error: he failed to put a "ground" sticker on a package that he shipped. Despite his clear intention to ship by ground—as evidenced by his selection of "ground" on the shipment form and payment for "ground" shipping—the government prosecuted him for his error anyways.
>
> When the jury acquitted Krister, the government turned around and charged him again, this time for alleged

abandonment of toxic materials. Krister had securely and safely stored his valuable research materials in stainless steel drums, at a storage facility, while he fought for his freedom in trial over the missing shipping sticker. He ultimately spent two years in a federal prison for his mistake.[4]

The licensing requirements we saw in the previous chapter have been turned into licenses for heavily armed policemen to raid honest businesses and treat entrepreneurs like criminals. In 2010 two inspectors from the Florida Department of Business and Professional Regulation (DBPR) visited the Strictly Skillz Barbershop in Orlando and confirmed that all of the barbers were properly licensed. The DBPR is authorized to conduct such visits only once every two years, but two days later the inspectors called again with eight to ten heavily armed and masked policemen, who handcuffed the barbers and told the customers to leave. The police didn't have search warrants, and claimed that they didn't need one when investigating licensing laws. When a barber said he had done nothing wrong, the officer responded, "It's a pretty big book, I'm pretty sure I can find something in here to take you to jail for." All that was too much for a panel of federal judges, who noted that they had twice before admonished the police for conducting illegal searches. "We hope that the third time will be the charm."[5]

A "federal criminal code" would indeed be a pretty big book. No one knows just how many federal criminal offences there are, and trying to assemble them all in one place would be a daunting task. One commentator described federal criminal law as "an incomprehensible, random and incoherent, duplicative, incomplete, and organizationally nonsensical mass of federal legislation."[6] Here are some of the evils that are proscribed: transporting alligator grass across a state line, unauthorized use of the slogan "Give a Hoot, Don't

Pollute," and wearing a postal worker's uniform in a theatrical production that tends to discredit the postal service.[7]

What makes it worse is that the crimes often dispense with the requirement of a criminal intention or guilty mind (the lawyer's *mens rea*). That's a throwback to the strict liability of the Anglo-Saxon period, when the act (*actus reus*) alone was enough to convict. If one serf killed another, it didn't matter whether he did it on purpose or whether it was a sheer accident. In the Middle Ages, however, mens rea was imported into the criminal law through the influence of Canon lawyers who argued that criminal wrongdoing, like sin, assumed moral guilt. "God considers not the action, but the spirit of the action," said Peter Abélard,[8] which meant there was no place for Anglo-Saxon strict liability criminal offences.

That was a signal advance in personal and political liberty, but more recently strict liability has made a comeback, in the form of "public welfare crimes." These are regulatory offences that seek to protect the public's welfare by dispensing with the accused's defense that he didn't mean any harm. Very early on, Oliver Wendell Holmes foresaw the new direction the law would take. "[W]hile the terminology of morals is still retaine...the law..., by the very necessity of its nature, is continually transmuting those moral standards into external and objective ones, from which the actual guilt of the party concerned is wholly eliminated."[9] In other words, *mens rea* was getting in the way of securing convictions, when public welfare was at issue. The problem, however, was that the return to strict liability puts well-meaning people such as Krister Evertson at risk of the most severe restrictions on liberty the state can impose. With a *mens rea* requirement, a person knows when he's doing wrong, but not when intention is irrelevant and the criminal offences are technical and numberless. That's today's America, where the law on the books can make every American a felon according to a leading criminal law academic.[10]

A System Designed to Convict

American criminal procedure tilts the balance of power even more strongly towards the prosecution. A criminal case might begin with a grand jury, where the prosecutor makes his case in secret in the absence of a judge. The normal courtroom rules of evidence, meant to protect the accused, don't apply and the prosecutor can present almost any evidence he wants, including hearsay. Prosecutors can call witnesses (including the target of the investigation) without revealing the nature of the case, and the proceedings can last for years. Not surprisingly, the grand jury seldom fails to provide an indictment. In the famous phrase of Judge Sol Wachtler, a grand jury would indict a ham sandwich, if that's what you wanted."[11]

More than other First World countries, America tries corporations as criminals.[12] Ordinarily, firms are quick to settle, since they suffer an enormous reputational loss when charged with crime. For example, a grand jury's indictment effectively destroyed the Arthur Anderson accounting firm and left its 28,000 employees jobless. Three years later the Supreme Court overturned the conviction, but at that point the firm was dead as a doornail. The trial judge had improperly instructed the jury that it could convict even if Arthur Anderson honestly and sincerely believed its conduct was lawful, and that was too much for the Supreme Court.[13] But if the indictment is the death sentence, a posthumous finding of innocence comes too late.

More often than not, the real target is the firm's top executives, for the mere hint of a prosecution is enough to bring the firm to its knees and to cooperate in going after its managers. Under the "Holder memorandum" (named after Eric Holder), federal prosecutors are encouraged to base their discretion on the degree to which the target firm cooperates with the investigation. The firm can thus be expected to sign a "deferred prosecution agreement" in which it agrees to help convict its executives. This might include waiving the attorney-client privilege and letting the Justice Department see the correspondence with their lawyers; and what that means is that firms can't assume they can get confidential legal advice. Until the Supreme Court stepped in, prosecutors also asked firms not to pay for their executive's defense lawyers, even where the firm was obligated by contract to do so.

When pursuing the executives, prosecutors have an enormous bargaining leverage. They can buy favorable testimony by selectively granting or threatening to deny immunity from prosecution, and can coerce a guilty plea to a lesser charge by threatening to indict on a more serious one. Prosecutors can also bring multiple charges, under different theories of criminal liability. The prosecutor need win a conviction on only one count, while the defense must win them all. A jury, minded to split the difference, might easily acquit on 99 counts and convict on one. For sentencing purposes, however, there is generally no difference between a conviction on one count or many. The inequality in bargaining power is magnified by the "trial penalty" courts impose, in the harsher sentences they impose on defendants who refuse to plead, go to trial and are convicted.

As a consequence, nearly everyone caught in the maw of the federal criminal system pleads guilty. In recent years, prosecutors have secured guilty pleas from 96 percent of the defendants and for the remaining four percent who went to trial prosecutors won convictions against three percent. Less than one percent were acquitted, and that was only after they had spent years fighting the case, seen their reputation tarnished and their business damaged or destroyed.[14] These are staggering numbers, when one considers that a third of Canadian criminal defendants are either acquitted or emerge victorious after Crown Attorneys decide to abandon the prosecution.[15]

Once convicted of a white-collar crime, a corporate executive is often looking at a lengthy prison term. The U.S. Sentencing Guidelines asks judges to take into account the amount of the financial loss in computing the sentence. For crimes that result in a large firm's bankruptcy, then, the jail time for a first offender might easily exceed that given multiple offenders for rape or murder. For Enron CEO Jeffrey Skilling, for example, it was 24 year (later reduced on appeal to 14 years).[16]

Then there's the matter of prosecutorial ethics, or the lack thereof. There is enormous pressure on American prosecutors to rack up convictions, and little by way of sanctions should they cut corners to do so. Prosecutors are said to rely on notoriously unreliable jailhouse snitches and routinely to withhold evidence that might assist the defendant (as they did when they charged Republican Senator Ted Stevens).[17] They can also cut highly favorable plea bargains with lower-down rogues in order to secure the conviction of their higher-up bosses. That rarely happens in other First World countries, where most prosecutors are lifetime civil servants who are not pressured to secure convictions and who are expected to abandon a prosecution when the interests of justice so demand. They're not aspiring politicians and have no interest in trying a case before the press or playing to the television cameras, in the manner of a Rudy Giuliani or Eliot Spitzer.

With the extraordinary expansion in the number of federal crimes, and with the enormous discretion and threat advantages of prosecutors, American criminal law poses a serious threat to liberty. If we all commit "three felonies a day," as Harvey Silverglate claims,[18] and if prosecutors can indict almost anyone they want, we've taken a step toward the country that Soviet NKVD head Lavrentiy Beria described when he said "Show me the man, and I'll show you the crime." The threat is particularly serious to business executives, in a country with politically ambitious prosecutors.

Enemies of the People

Honoré de Balzac wasn't the only person to think that great fortunes that come out of nowhere are built on crime. That's almost the only explanation for the five months Martha Stewart spend in federal prison. Born Martha Kostyra in Jersey City, she became a model and then a cook and caterer. She branched out from cookbooks to write books about homemaking, house décor, and entertainment, and within a few years her *Martha Stewart Living* magazine reached a circulation of 2,000,000. Her company went public in 1999, and she became America's first self-made female billionaire and, worse still, an omnipresent celebrity on television. A parody of her magazine, *Martha Stewart's Better than you at Entertaining*, told readers how to prepare when the Pope drops in for a visit, with photos of the Supreme Pontiff kneeling before Martha. To every woman who prided herself on her Bertazzoni dual fuel range, her hand-printed seating cards, and her floral garlands, she was a standing rebuke, the symbol of an impossibly unattainable perfection in good living. It's no wonder she was hated.

In 2001 Stewart learned from her broker that a friend of hers, the ImClone CEO Samuel Waskal, was about to sell shares in his company. That signaled bad news about ImClone, and Steward sold all 4,000 of her own shares in the company. Waskal was subsequently prosecuted for insider trading, but then he was an ImClone "insider" and Stewart wasn't. That should have meant that she hadn't broken the law, but then she did something stupid. She talked to federal investigators in the absence of her lawyers. What she told them was a false story about why she sold the shares. She wasn't under oath, and she hadn't committed a crime, but it was nevertheless a crime to lie to the Feds about non-crimes. She was convicted of obstruction of justice and making false statements about something which, had she told the truth, would not have been an admission of guilt.[19]

Entrepreneurs like Stewart are risk-takers and innovators, and when the criminal law is as extensive and vague as that of America, and its prosecutions as politicized, they make a big fat target. Another such person was Michael Milken, a dynamo of industry and a poster boy for Nicholas Taleb's antifragiles. What Milken had recognized was that U.S. capital markets had failed to finance upstart firms that were considered too risky by Wall Street. In doing so, an old boys club of mostly WASP New York bankers had ignored the way in which the risk of one borrower's default could be neutralized with a portfolio of investments in other high-risk borrowers. When the returns of the different firms in the basket are well-diversified (i.e., not correlated with each other), the risk of the portfolio as a whole is less than that of any individual borrower. That's simply an application of the maxim "don't put all your eggs in one basket," but one that finance economists had only recently rediscovered, and Milken was ahead of the pack. In the 1970s he had found an investment opportunity that others had missed, and as his lenders could charge borrowers a high yield premium for the higher risk, this turned out to be wildly profitable.

Milken had done more than recognize the gains to be made through diversification. Though a partner of the Philadelphia-based Drexel Burnham investment firm, he ran his operations through a Wilshire Boulevard office in Beverly Hills, California as an quasi-independent firm, arriving at work at 4:00 am to be ready for the New York markets when they opened at 6:00 am Pacific time. With his extraordinary work habits, Milken simply beat the competition in picking undervalued companies. Back East, rating agencies such as Standard & Poor's had focused of a firm's historical earnings and physical assets and ignored better predictors of future earnings, such as the quality of management and prospects for growth, things

Milken saw as more important. As his reputation grew, Milken attracted some of the wealthiest venture capitalists as clients, people such as T. Boone Pickens and Carl Icahn, and Drexel became known as a firm that could raise billions of dollars to finance a takeover of a company within a matter of hours.

Like Pickens and Icahn, Milken came from a humble background. As a nerdy Jewish teen-ager, he had attended a public high school in Encino, Ca., and his rise was a splendid example of the American Dream of income mobility. He wasn't a member of the club, and the high risk, high yield bonds he was peddling didn't win him any friends back East, on Wall Street, in the legal academy, or on the Securities and Exchange Commission. The high yield securities he was pushing were called "junk bonds," and his annual meeting for investors was labeled the "predators' ball." Worse still, he wasn't sharing his profits with Wall Street underwriters. There had been a tradition that lead underwriters on a deal would pass on part of the securities to be sold to other underwriters, but Milken wasn't having any of that. Drexel found it could raise billions of dollars to finance a takeover all by itself, and it did just that.

What really made Milken an Enemy of the People, however, was the leading role he took in financing "leveraged buy-outs." As we saw in the last chapter, the 1960s and 1970s had seen a wave of conglomerization in which large, public corporations acquired new firms in unrelated lines of business. Broken up, they'd be worth more, and what was needed was some way to exploit the gains from deconglomerization. Corporate managers realized they could do so themselves by making a take-over bid for control (a "buy-out") and selling off the pieces of the firm at a profit (in a "bust-up merger"). Because the remaining entity would be financed mainly by borrowing, this would be a "leveraged" buy-out. Management needed someone to lend the money to finance this, however, and that's where Milken came in, with high yield "junk" bonds.

None of this went down well, with the country's opinion leaders, in *Time*, the *New York Times*, the *New York Review of Books*, and other journals. Milken's junk bonds and leveraged buyouts were portrayed as a plague that every decent person should condemn. The "excesses in the financial community," the "unsound financial structures," the "dangerous levels of corporate borrowing," the excessive greed epitomized by Drexel Burnham, threatened the very foundations of the economy.[20] Milkin's critics noted that, after a bust-up merger, the remaining firm was highly leveraged, with a small slice of equity shares held by the new firm managers, and massive amounts of debt held by lenders. Inevitably, some of the firms were unable to meet their loan obligations, and the investors had to take a haircut in a reorganization under Chapter 11 of the Bankruptcy Code. But the firms were still worth more than they had been before the bust-up, and by taking the lead in financing leveraged buy-outs Milken had helped create the business revival of the 1980s. The conglomerates had inefficiently sat on piles of money, and breaking them apart released many billions of dollars into the economy.

It's easy enough to ignore the *New York Review of Books*, the Manhattan charity balls, the Georgetown soirées. It's harder for a businessman to ignore America's populist criminal law and the grandstanding, politically ambitious prosecutors who leak their stories to a plutophobic press. Milken had revitalized the country's economy, but for his pains was fined $600 million, sentenced to ten years (later reduced to two) in prison, and required to perform three years of community service. An eminent scholar took a look at the proceedings and concluded that, "to achieve these results, the government changed the rules in the middle of the game, radically expanded the scope of the criminal law to include harmless and even beneficial practices, and routinely engaged in questionable ethical practices as it pursued victory at any cost."[21]

The state had used all the pressure at its command to force Milken to plead guilty to victimless offenses that had previously not been thought criminal. It offered very lenient plea bargains to notorious liars such as Ivan Boesky ("greed is good") in exchange for their promises to implicate Milken. Further, it threatened to prosecute Milken's brother and sent FBI agents to visit his 93-year-old grandfather, using them as bargaining chips to get Milken to plea guilty. The state also waved the prospect of a Racketeer Influenced and Corrupt Organization Act (RICO) order at Drexel Burham, securing a guilty plea from it as well as the firm's cooperation in the prosecution's pursuit of Milken. RICO was passed in 1970 as a vaguely defined federal statute aimed at the Mafia and organized crime, but by Milken's time it had been used against investment firms for nothing more than technical violations of the Securities and Exchange Act. For federal prosecutors, RICO is a Big Bertha since it empowers the government to seek an order to freeze a defendant's assets at the time of indictment, and that's an immediate death sentence for a securities firm. Remarkably, the federal government can destroy a company without any proof of wrongdoing, and without alleging anything resembling organized crime. And having done all that, the state can pressure a person to plead guilty and provide a groveling confession designed to produce a lenient sentence, in a scene right out of the Soviet show trials in Arthur Koestler's *Darkness at Noon*.

Michael Milken had fought the financial establishment, and the establishment won. For the lead prosecutor, Rudy Giuliani, who had pursued Milken with the intensity of Victor Hugo's Inspector Javert, it led to a successful campaign to become the Mayor of New York. For Kimba Wood, the judge who had imposed an extraordinarily harsh sentence on Milken, it meant a request from Bill Clinton to serve as the country's Attorney-General. Amusingly, the nomination went nowhere, brought down by that scourge of the New Class, a nannygate scandal in which high-powered moms dump their kids on undocumented aliens.

Administrative sanctions, though not as threatening as a prosecution, can also cripple an entrepreneur. When Catherine Engelbrecht, a Texas businesswoman, formed a Tea Party group in 2009 to investigate voter fraud by Democrats, the group's request for tax-exempt status was held up by Lois Lerner's IRS. Given how politicized the IRS has become, that's not surprising, but then Engelbrecht, her husband and their company were all audited by the IRS. In short order the business was visited by other federal agencies: the FBI, the Bureau of Alcohol, Tobacco and Firearms (BATF), and the Occupational Safety and Health Administration (OSHA).

Since Engelbrecht was an opponent of the administration, that was perhaps to be expected in today's America, but even a proudly apolitical executive can find himself rapped sternly on the knuckles. Michael Milken thought that, in his splendid isolation at the corner of Wilshire and Rodeo Drive, he didn't need allies back East. Bill Gates was similarly misinformed. Out in Redmond WA he thought Microsoft immune from attack and he himself more important than the politicians in Washington. That changed when Microsoft's success invited an antitrust prosecution and Gates' display of arrogance at trial led to an order that the company be split in two. That decision was reversed on appeal, but since then Microsoft has assembled one of the biggest government relations offices in Washington, and a chastened Gates has retreated into the world of philanthropy. That was good news for the activities supported by the Gates Foundation, but less good for Microsoft shareholders, for the company has fallen flat in every one of its projects since then. It was worse still for the American economy, if the lesson to be taken is that, in a crony nation, every business is in partnership with the federal government, and woe to those who forget it. That's something the New Class already knows, but some people have to learn the hard way.

It's difficult to measure the cost that overzealous prosecutors impose on the economy. The target will always be the rule-breaker, the innovator, the antifragile, the person who bucks the trend and leaves the protective shell of a comfortable and well-connected establishment. Such people were once seen as heroes, but now they're potential criminal defendants. They're the engines of growth in the economy, but they're asked to navigate the shoals of a million laws and regulations. Somehow that can't be a good way to run a railroad.

There is one winner, however, and that is the legal profession. The number of regulatory crimes is so great, and the penalties are so severe, that firms must invest heavily in regulatory compliance experts. Often these are the same people who drafted the rules while working for government, and now are cashing in in the private sector. The rules can actually get in the way of safety, for at some point more regulations makes them harder to process. For regulatory lawyers, however, more is always better.

The Rule of Lawyers

THIS IS THE CENTURY OF THE RULE OF LAW. TWENTY years ago, Milton Friedman offered a simple prescription for economic growth. All that a country need do, he thought, was shrink the state by privatization. With the benefit of hindsight he subsequently changed his mind.

> Just after the Berlin Wall fell and the Soviet Union collapsed, I used to be asked a lot: "What do these ex-communist states have to do in order to become market economies?" And I used to say: "You can describe that in three words: privatize, privatize, privatize." But, I was wrong.... Privatization is meaningless if you don't have the rule of law.[1]

Russia is a good example of what Friedman meant. After the fall of communism, the country privatized by selling off state assets at bargain basement prices to political cronies. What that led to was today's Russia, where businessmen cannot oppose Vladimir

Putin without risking prison, at a cost to the entire economy.

Corrupt countries such as Russia may be rich in natural assets such as farmland, oil, and minerals, and in capital assets such as plant and machinery, but these are not the most important sources of wealth. The World Bank estimates that natural and capital assets amount to only 23 percent of a country's wealth. The rest is intangible assets, of which the most important element is adherence to the rule of law: the absence of corruption and an efficient and honest judicial system. Remarkably, that accounts for 44 percent of a country's total wealth according to the World Bank.[2]

America isn't Russia, not by a long shot, but it still doesn't rank very highly on the World Justice Project's Rule of Law Index, coming in at 19 out of 99 countries and thirteenth amongst 24 First World nations. By way of comparison, Canada ranks eleventh out of 99 countries and eighth amongst First World countries. Denmark comes in first in both categories.[3] One reason for America's poor showing is the perception of government corruption on Transparency International surveys of business leaders.[4] That's going to hurt, since public corruption makes a country poorer,[5] favoring well-placed cronies at the expense of the Ragged Dicks.

On the Rule of Law Index, America is also dragged down by its civil justice system, in its enforcement of contract and tort claims, and in its rules of civil procedure. Without enforceable contracts, bargainers are left in the state of nature, in which strangers cannot easily rely on each other's promises. Between members of the same family, W.D. Hamilton's kin selection may promote the necessary degree of trust; and beyond that the New Class' old boy network may also foster Robert Trivers' patterns of reciprocal altruism, in which no one has an incentive to defect in a settled relationship of cooperation. But none of this will help the Ragged Dicks get their start. They're not in the same family as the powerful, and not even in the same tribe. They didn't go to the right schools, and they're in no one's posh club. What they need are enforceable contracts.

Dick made his way through his personal efforts and the relationships he created for himself. In doing so, he bore witness to what Sir Henry Maine called the defining characteristic of modernity, the move from status to contract, from immobility to mobility.[6] Status meant the ancient positions of peasant and peer, serf and thane, slave and freeman, where one's position was fixed for life. When all that was swept away, what remained was contract, the law the parties made for themselves through their bargains, and by which the new man might form his own bonds and advance in a hostile world. Today, however, the movement is from contract to status, for where we are born is increasingly where we'll end up.

Compared to other first world countries, America poorly enforces contracts.[7] Its courts are much more ready to strike aside a bargain that didn't turn out the way one of the parties wanted, under a rich doctrine of excuses: mistake, frustration, impracticability. Courts are also more willing to admit oral evidence and ignore the written terms of a contract, and to enforce amending agreements written when one of the parties enjoys a threat advantage over the other and can use its clout to rewrite the contract in its favor. Because of this, American bargainers will charge a higher risk premium against the possibility that their contracts won't be enforced, or that they'll have to incur substantial litigation costs. They'll have a weaker incentive to invest in the contractual relationship, and that's highly wasteful since the very purpose of contract law is to permit the parties to exploit the bargaining gains facilitated by mutual trust. All this results in a less equal and more aristocratic society, since it favors the members of the same family or club who don't need contract law to trust each other.

One case makes the point well. In *Trident Center v. Connecticut General Insurance*,[8] two of Los Angeles's largest and most sophisticated law firms financed their new office building with a $56 million loan from the insurance company. That was in 1983, when Federal Reserve Chairman Paul Volcker was trying to squeeze out inflation with sky-high interest rates, and the insurance company was able to obtain a 12.14 percent rate over a 15-year period. To lock in the parties, the agreement further provided that the law firms "shall not have the right to prepay the principal amount in whole or in part" for the first 12 years of the loan. Within a few years, however, interest rates had plummeted and the two law firms sought to refinance, even though the agreement had provided that they were locked in at the higher rate. While the written agreement clearly barred prepayment, the law firms argued that, under California law, they were permitted to introduce oral evidence of a 1983 conversation that varied the written terms of the contract. Judge Alex Kozinski wasn't very impressed. Such arguments, he thundered, "chip away at the foundation of our legal system. . . . If we are unwilling to say that the parties, dealing face to face, can come up with language that binds them, how can we send anyone to jail for violating statutes consisting of mere words?" But that was the law of California, he concluded, and he remanded the case to permit the plaintiffs to introduce the oral evidence they wanted. The two law firms, by the way, boast of their expertise in commercial real estate financing.

Parties to a contract may choose to have it governed by the law of another, more sensible jurisdiction,[9] and increasingly that's Britain. But then there's also American tort law, which is much harder to escape, and which at times resembles a demented slot machine of judicially sanctioned theft, with enormous awards for what seem like trivial faults.[10] Through contingency fees, trial lawyers share in the recovery, and this has served to make many of them enormously wealthy. After deducting exorbitant legal fees, the injured parties are often left with a tiny fraction of the award.

The defendants are deep-pocketed corporations, not middle class individuals. Amongst them, however, entrepreneurial firms are more likely to be sued. The entrepreneur is going to be a risk-taker, and it is an easy matter to ask a jury to infer that a departure from standard business practices was negligent. The stick-in-the-mud can defend himself by arguing that he was only doing what everyone else does. It's the innovator, who creates better products but with novel risks, who is more likely to find himself in court.[11] That's a highly effective way of weakening an economy.

Entrepreneurial firms will also experience more volatile stock price swings, and when they are publicly held this invites lawsuits which assert that the firm failed to disclose material information under U.S. securities law. With no evidence to back up their claims, but with an enormously costly demand for documents under the discovery rules of civil procedure, plaintiff's lawyers may commence an action in the expectation of a handsome settlement agreement. The burden of discovery falls entirely upon the defendant, which means that plaintiff's lawyers can ask for discovery that would cost the defendant many millions of dollars to produce, and then propose a settlement for a lesser amount of money. This has made discovery rules a court-sanctioned form of blackmail, and effects a wealth transfer from the firm's shareholders (including middle class pension fund holders) to the plaintiff's bar.

In almost every respect, the American rules of civil procedure are tilted towards plaintiffs, as compared to the civil procedure rules of other countries. In Canada, courts routinely deny demands for discovery when this would impose disproportionate costs on the defendant. Unlike America, Canada and other countries also rely on a system of "fact pleading," which means that plaintiffs must plead sufficient facts to sustain their claim, failing which it can be dismissed on summary judgment. In the U.S. fact pleading isn't required, which encourages plaintiff's lawyers to embark on a fishing expedition, with the expectation that they'll find something on discovery upon which to base a claim. As well, in America, almost alone in the world, the losing party is not required to pay court costs. In other countries, a "loser pays" rule of courts discourages frivolous claims. Other countries also dispense with civil juries in non-criminal trials. As a matter of federal and state constitutional law, that doesn't happen in the U.S. That matters, because civil juries appear to be more susceptible to populist appeals to "teach the defendant a lesson," particularly when awarding punitive damages that exceed whatever would be required to compensate a plaintiff for his loss. Punitive damages are far less likely to be awarded elsewhere, and class action lawsuits brought on behalf of millions of alleged victims that magnify damages are relatively rare.[12] Further, American trial lawyers bringing a class action have enjoyed a broad discretion to choose the state in which to sue, which permits them to shop for the courts most friendly to plaintiffs.[13]

One such state is Mississippi. In 1995, O'Keefe, a local funeral home, sued Loewen group, a Canadian competitor, in a contract dispute that at the very most that might have justified an award of $5–8 million in damages. After inflammatory racial and xenophobic appeals by the plaintiff's lawyer, however, the Mississippi jury awarded damages of $500 million, including an absurd award of $75 million for emotional distress, and $400 million in punitive damages. Loewen moved to appeal the damages award, but was met with a Mississippi procedural rule that would have required it to post a "supersedeas" bond of $625 million with the court. Loewen couldn't afford to do this, and the Mississippi Supreme Court refused to lower the amount. With its back to the wall, Loewen was forced to settle the claim for $130 million.[14]

Supersedeas bonds are a uniquely American procedural device, and one final cross-country difference should be noted. Canada is a federal state, but basic contract and tort disputes are resolved by judges appointed by the national government. In the U.S., however, they are handled by state-appointed judges, and that results in a systemic bias in favor of in-state plaintiffs and against out-of-state defendants, whether foreign like Loewen or simply from another U.S. state.[15] These pathologies are exacerbated by another feature of American law. As in Mississippi, many states choose their judges by popular ballot, which increases their incentive to favor in-state plaintiffs. West Virginia Supreme Court Justice Richard Neely offered a very candid confession about his biases.

> As long as I am allowed to redistribute wealth from out-of-state companies to in-state plaintiffs, I shall continue to do so. Not only is my sleep enhanced when I give someone else's money away, but so is my job security, because the in-state plaintiffs, their families and their friends will re-elect me.[16]

All this helps account for why litigation is so much more a feature of American life than it is in other countries, why Americans are four times more likely to be sued than the average Canadian.[17] That might be an acceptable trade-off, if Canadians were more likely to suffer actionable injuries than Americans, but that doesn't seem to be the case either. As for litigation costs, Towers Perrin Tillinghast (TPT) estimates that litigation consumes 2.2 percent of the American economy, about three times more than France or Britain. That's mostly money into the pockets of lawyers, and while the accuracy of the TPT study has been challenged there's little doubt that the burden of litigation falls more heavily on the U.S. than other First World countries. All of this has vastly enriched American trial lawyers; and at the same time it's made middle class consumers pay more for their goods and services, since the extra litigation costs are passed on to them. If America is less mobile than other First World countries, its civil justice rules help explain why.

The Way Back

ARISTOCRACIES ARISE NATURALLY, BUT WHAT IS NATURAL to man is seldom benign and never necessary. "Nature, Mr. Allnut, is what we were put in this world to rise above," observed Katharine Hepburn in *The African Queen*. An American aristocracy, in the form of a New Class, might be natural and faithful to its selfish genes, but it weakens the economy and frays social bonds; and, while deeply entrenched, might nevertheless be humbled. That was the project of the Occupy movement of 2011, with all its incoherent rage, and it is one in which Americans of every political stripe might join, provided the means be just and the goals desirable.

Sadly, those who loudly decry income disparities often support policies which make things worse, and Senator Bernie Sanders (I–VT), is a good example. School choice would give lower and middle-class children a better education, but Sanders has sided with the teachers' unions to vote against charter school vouchers. Our immigration system is tilted towards low-skilled entrants who increase income inequalities, but Sanders has opposed immigration reforms that would admit more highly skilled people. Then there's Senator Elizabeth Warren (D–MA), who has made her name as a middle-class champion, but who supports the Export-Import Bank's corporate subsidies that many see as a glaring example of crony capitalism. Of course it's unfair to demand consistency from a politician, but the point is that politicians are to be judged on their record and not on their rhetoric. What is needed, more than professions of outrage about inequality, is the reversal of policies that promote aristocracy.

A Wish List

It is easy to assemble a wish list of federal and state legislation that would help to undermine entrenched hierarchies and assist everyone except America's aristocrats. Here's my list, five easy pieces of useful and efficient legislation, in the pursuit of socialist ends through capitalist means.

- Top marginal tax rates for capital gains and corporate taxes should be lowered to Canadian levels. In return, every corporate tax incentive or loophole should be withdrawn. It's not the business of government to tell businesses how to make money, nor should it be the business of business to rent-seek. Instead the business of business is to produce value by satisfying consumers. And while we're at it, executives should not be permitted to shelter their remuneration as something other than income in order to pay lower marginal taxes than their secretaries.

- The Immigration Act should be remodeled on Canadian lines, greatly reducing the intake of family preference immigrants while expanding the number of economic immigrants, in a vastly simplified system. This would increase tax revenues, reduce the welfare burden and admit more job creators.

· The number of people in American jails is shamefully large. Criminal sanctions should largely be restricted to crimes of violence, and to end the war on business, a guilty mind (mens rea) should be required before anyone is convicted of a criminal offense.[1]

· Let all civil cases, tort or contract, in which any of the defendants is in a different state from any of the plaintiffs be removable by the defendant from state to federal courts.[2] This would eliminate judicial incentives to shift money from out-of-state defendants to in-state plaintiffs and their lawyers. It would also address problems of bias created by a system of elected state court judges who must raise campaign funds from donors. Like Canadian judges, U.S. federal judges are appointed and not elected, and the change would remove the baneful influence of money in justice.

· States should permit parents to choose the schools their children attend through generous voucher programs. This would help place all children on an equal footing with the children of the New Class.

The goal, Francis Fukuyama tells us, is "getting to Denmark." Doing so would give us a richer and fairer country, as well as a more mobile one. I know little of Denmark, but for anyone seriously interested in restoring the idea of America, for anyone who has seen

Figures 12 and 16, the way back is simple indeed. Begin by admitting a problem. And then emulate Canada.

Endless History

But that won't be easy. It won't be handed to us, as readers of Fukuyama's *The End of History* might have been led to believe. In a brilliant essay, then a book, Fukuyama argued that the modern liberal democracies of America and other First World nations represent the highest possible form of political development. By implication, any departures from this would be self-correcting; and were that the case the pathologies I described in the previous five chapters would in time wither away.

For Fukuyama, history had ended in two ways. First, the fall of communism, both as an economic and a moral project, had left the free market principles of liberal democracies in command of the field. Fukuyama wrote in 1989, and back then his note of triumphalism was shared by many on both the Right and Left in America. There was room for debate about the size of the state's welfare burden, but the fall of the Berlin Wall and the break-up of the Soviet Union had put paid to the idea that the state should guide the economy, picking winners and losers. Or so we had thought.

History had also ended in a second way, in the success of the egalitarian ideals of the modern state. This, said Fukuyama, was implicit in Hegel's idea of *recognition* as a crucial element in self-consciousness. Hegel thought that we are less than entirely conscious unless others recognize that we are conscious, an idea about as dense and difficult to follow as anything ever written by a German philosopher.[3] As explained by Alexandre Kojève, however, recognition was nothing more than the human need to be fully respected by others, a need which could only be achieved in a classless, egalitarian society.[4] A country's economy might give us the material welfare needed to keep body and soul together, but that won't be enough for those who feel they are treated like second-class citizens. We'll demand an equality of respect, of the kind that African-Americans seek through antidiscrimination laws or that gays seek through the legal recognition of same-sex marriages. Having gotten there, with a modern state, we'll not go back; and in that sense too history will have ended.

That was Fukuyama's story in *The End of History*. "The universal and homogenous state that appears at the end of history can thus be seen as resting on the twin pillars of economics and recognition."[5] But since then Fukuyama has backed away from this in two recent books which describe a sclerotic society of special interests that enact wealth-destroying laws.[6] This might happen in two ways, says Fukuyama. In Third World countries, political leaders hide their support for friends and relatives behind the outward form of a modern state, a system which Fukuyama describes as "neopatrimonialism." In America, on the other hand, large parts of the government have been captured by well-organized interest groups, which he calls "repatrimonialism."

Fukuyama has evidently had second thoughts about the triumph of the West, and of America in particular. Kojève's demand for recognition has never been stronger, but America is increasingly riven by class distinctions, best explained by the sociobiological imperatives of parents who wish well for their children. Economic inequalities have also reopened the debate about free market ideals, and there was never a time when American politicians did not seek to direct the economy through tax breaks, subsidies, and tariffs. Nor do I see a sharp distinction between Fukuyama's Third World neopatrimonialism and his American repatrimonialism, which is simply an extension of the aristocratic rule by the families of the New Class who are determined to preserve their status against a rising middle class.

The Promised Land quickly recedes whenever we approach it.
History is never linear, in the sense of Fukuyama's earlier book,
moving always towards the Heavenly end-state of a modern, liberal economy. Instead, it's cyclical, balanced between the opposing
forces of egalitarianism and aristocracy, efficiency and inefficiency,
and oscillating unevenly between them. History is driven by the
contradictory impulses of the bequest motive and the need to avoid
the waste that social stagnation can impose on an economy. In time,
a hierarchical society invites a social or political revolution that
overthrows its elites, but thereafter a new aristocracy will emerge.

Nor do individual families remain on top. What Joseph Schumpeter called "creative destruction," the way in which once dominant
businesses are replaced by a new set of competitors, has a parallel
amongst families as well.[7] We start with a rough-hewn founder who,
dirt under his fingernails, lifted himself from the lower class. He
gave his children fancy-pants MBAs but they lacked his drive; and
of his grandchildren on Ritalin it is best not to speak. Shirtsleeves to
shirtsleeves in three generations, according to the old Chinese prov-
erb. In part this is a function of what behavioral geneticists call "regression to the mean," the idea that the offspring of brilliant parents
tend to be smart but less smart than their parents, that the children
of very tall parents tend to be tall but shorter than their parents.
Even as Netscape gave way to Google, so too the Adamses of Boston gave way to the Kennedys. Where are the Roosevelts today? As
for the Kennedy clan, which rose to prominence with "Honey Fitz"
Fitzgerald, three generations later they are mostly an embarrassing
reminder of former glories.

America has an aristocracy, to be sure, but its families are begot-
ten, born and die, like Yeats' dying generations in *Sailing to Byzan-
tium*. One family rises, holds court for three of four generations, and
then is replaced by a new aristocracy. So it has always been, an end-
less history of aristocracy after aristocracy. With efficient laws and

egalitarian impulses, they are always in tension, a battle in which neither side will ever claim total victory, but one that *The End of History* could not explain.

Reversing

There's more than one linear theory of history. A dystopian version would have us headed downhill all the way, and for modern Western states this was Mancur Olson's forecast in *The Rise and Decline of Nations*.[8] Olson saw a world in which interest groups would become more and more powerful until they strangled the economy with wasteful laws and red tape that transferred wealth to themselves at the expense of the economy as a whole. We haven't gotten there, of course, but we've moved in that direction, especially America, and this helps explain the greatest puzzle of all, why is our country less mobile than most other First World Countries. Every aristocracy seeks to ensure that its children will stay on top, but somehow that's happened more here than in other countries. Why is that?

As compared to its peers, there are three reasons why America is more likely to descend down Olson's road to Hell. First, the country might be simply too big. Second, it has problems fixing things once they're broken. Finally, it's especially hard to get everyone to agree on projects for the public good as opposed to narrow, wasteful interests.

The Costs of an Extensive Republic. There's an optimal size for a state, but just what is it? Applying the Goldilocks principle, it shouldn't be too big and it shouldn't be too small. It should be just right. What that might be was the subject of a debate at the 1787 Philadelphia Convention that gave us our Constitution.

On June 6, 1787 Roger Sherman of Connecticut told his fellow delegates that what America needed was a decentralized republic with strong state governments. "The people are more happy in small rather than large states," he said.[9] In this, he was merely echoing the received wisdom of the time, as expressed by Montesquieu and Rousseau.[10] Because they were closer to the people, small states would be more likely to reflect their interests. But the small is beautiful theory had not gone unanswered. A larger state would be better, argued David Hume, since private groups that subvert the interests of the whole country would be harder to form in large states. "The parts are so distant and remote, that it is very difficult, either by intrigue, prejudice, or passion, to hurry them into any measures against the public interest."[11] That would take care of Olson's fears of death by interest groups.

As a student at Princeton, James Madison had read Hume, and to answer Sherman he advanced Hume's argument for a large, *extended republic*. Madison had seen corrupt voters back in Orange County, Virginia, and expected something better from a national American government. With Hume, he believed that a large state would prevent a majority from oppressing a minority; and in the Convention, he employed Hume's ideas to respond to Sherman.

> The only remedy is to enlarge the sphere, & thereby divide the community into so great a number of interests & parties, that in the 1st place a majority will not be likely at the same moment to have a common interest separate from that of the whole or of the minority; and in the 2d place, that in case they shd have such an interest, they may not be so apt to unite in the pursuit of it.[12]

Today's political theorists are apt to accept without question the Madisonian claim that large states better protect liberty than small states. But theories are only interesting if they can be tested against real world experience, and on that basis Roger Sherman had the better of the argument. Had Madison been right, we'd see more interest groups in state capitals than at the federal level, and that's not the case. Lobbyists come to Washington because there's more bang for your buck when laws are passed at the national level, and with modern communications and transportation it's a lot easier to organize a national coalition today than in Madison's day.

A large size isn't entirely a bad thing. During the last two centuries it gave America an enormous free trade zone, as we saw in Chapter 10. A merchant could ship goods from California to Maine without paying tariff duties. A large size has also made America the strongest country in the world. But just looking at interest groups, and the way in which they may use their clout to impose wasteful laws and regulations, the country is too big and too centralized.

Reversing. Getting legislation passed or repealed in America is like waiting for three cherries to line up in a Las Vegas slot machine. Absent a supermajority in Congress to override a Presidential veto, one needs the simultaneous concurrence of the President, Senate, and House. In a parliamentary system, by contrast, one needs only one cherry from the one-armed bandit. In Canada, for example, neither the Governor General nor the Senate has a veto power. All that matters is the House of Commons, dominated by the prime minister's party. Gridlock is absent in parliamentary governments.[13]

There is a nevertheless a downside to the ease of legislating in a parliamentary system. Since bills require the concurrence of different branches of government in a presidential system, they might be more closely vetted. This was Hamilton's argument for the separation of powers in *Federalist* 73. "The oftener [a] measure is brought under examination, the greater the diversity in the situations of those who are to examine it, the less must be the danger of those errors which flow from want of due deliberation, or of those missteps which proceed from the contagion of some common passion

or interest." If the government legislates less under the separation of
powers, then, that is no bad thing if good laws survive and bad laws
don't. On the other hand, it's harder to repeal a bad law in a presidential system, which raises the question whether pre-enactment
screening of laws is more desirable than the ability to reverse them.

Posed that way, it's clear that reversibility trumps getting it right
at first instance. First, it's not as if there's much evidence of pre-enactment screening in Washington, not where laws are drafted at
dead of night by twenty-something legislative assistants fueled on
Red Bull and pizzas, and where we are told we have to pass 1,000-
page bills to see what is in them. Second, it is easier to identify bad
laws with the benefit of hindsight. Bad laws, based on bad ideas,
with what are conceded to have bad consequences, are enacted everywhere, but are typically recognized as such only after the fact.
When one Parliament reverses a prior Parliament, it does so with
more information than was available to the prior enacting Parliament. It will know better what works and what doesn't.

Reversibility is particularly important for what might be called
"experience laws." The economist's "experience goods" are goods
whose quality cannot be evaluated until after they are sold. Many a
used car looks good on the lot, only to fall apart after three months.
Similarly, legislation that looks good on paper sometimes results in
unintended consequences that are more costly than the problem it
was meant to remedy. To some extent, all laws are experience laws,
whose effects can only be seen with hindsight. What the separation
of powers has given us, then, is a one-way ratchet in which bad ideas
are adopted and then turned into the inflexible laws of the Medes
and the Persians.

The belief that good legislation will emerge from the separation
of powers in the American constitution, that a reverse gear can be
dispensed with, is an example of what Nobel laureate Friedrich
Hayek called the "fatal conceit."[14] This was the idea that planners

could anticipate all the problems that might arise with a well-drafted statute, prepared according to the most advanced scientific thought of the time. More modestly, parliamentary regimes assume that in a world of human fallibility mistakes will be made, that "experts" are often unreliable, and that dumb laws will be passed; and that what is more important is giving the legislator the ability to bring hindsight wisdom to bear in undoing laws which experience tells us were ill-planned. If American government has gotten too large, if the statutory code and the Code of Federal Regulations have caught a case of elephantiasis, that's not surprising. The know-it-all hubris of the planner was baked into the American constitution from the start.

Why Narrow Interest Groups Dominate in America. In his defense of extensive republics, Madison identified a problem of majoritarian misbehavior, in which a coalition of 51 percent of the voters oppresses the 49 percent. The separation of powers amongst President, Senate, and House was designed to cure this, by making it more difficult for a majority to enact legislation. But then there's the opposite problem of minoritarian misbehavior, where a Congressman pushes for wasteful earmarks that benefit his district at a greater cost to the country as a whole. For examples, think of bridges to nowhere, the John Murtha Airport in Johnstown PA and West Virginia's Robert Byrd Center for this, that, and the other thing. We know that pork barrel projects are bad, but we like how the money ends up next door, and that explains the paradoxical polling figures about Congress and Congressmen. We all hate Congress, pollsters tell us, but love our individual Congressman. We love his ability to bring home the bacon, even if we recognize that the system that permits him to do so is corrupt.

To reverse this, what is needed is a grand coalition, a coalition of the whole of the voters, one that will vote for the general welfare rather than the narrow interest of their Congressional district.

Mancur Olson called this a "superencompassing majority,"[15] one that treats minorities no better or worse than anyone else, and stands in proxy for the nation as a whole. Discovering and empowering such a majority might then be thought the very goal of constitution-making. It was the idea behind Bolingbroke's idealized Patriot King, who governs "like the common father of his people...where the head and all the members are united by one common interest."[16]

That's the coalition Republican lawmakers sought to create in their ban on earmarks after they took control of the House of Representatives in 2010. We're seeing fewer of the kind of obvious earmarks that disfigured legislation in the past, but pork barrel spending continues to this day. In parliamentary systems, by contrast, coalitions of the whole are easier to assemble. National parties are typically stronger, and with a two-party system and a diverse electorate a party requires broad support across the country to be elected. It will therefore have a greater incentive to acquire a reputation that puts what it understands as the common, national good ahead of the wasteful local projects promoted by interest groups. Such a parliament, composed of nobodys but led by party leaders with an eye on the main chance and a national election, more closely resembles the idealized assembly described by Edmund Burke in his Address to the Electors of Bristol, an assembly "of *one* nation, with *one* interest, that of the whole; where, not local purposes, not local prejudices, ought to guide."[17]

All this helps explain why America is more immobile than other countries. The bequest motive, the desire to see one's children on top, is as strong in other countries, and we would therefore have expected to see the same degree of income immobility in the rest of the First World. If we don't, it's because of differences in the systems of government. America is too big, and it's also too hard to undo bad laws and assemble a coalition behind national interests.

This has left us with an inferior education system, problematic immigration policies, and a weakened rule of law.

Can this be turned around? Mancur Olson didn't think that history led inevitably to a sclerotic government ruled by powerful families and interest groups. After the Second World War, Japan and Germany had quickly rebounded, and from that Olsen concluded that a cataclysmic event, such as the destruction that befell the two countries after their defeat, could sweep away entrenched interest groups and lead to an enormous growth spurt. For Americans, that happened in 1776 and again in 1861–65, but it's not something one would ordinarily wish on any country. On a smaller scale, however, First World countries may experience peaceful and profitable economic revolutions if they aren't hampered by an American-style separation of powers. With its reverse gear, the Canadian government drastically shrank the size of its public debt in the 1990s, simply because a majority Liberal government decided it had its back to the wall. Parliaments can do that, presidential systems not so much, particularly when a country is riven by bitter partisanship.

Must America remain immobile, then? Parliamentary countries have a way of dealing with small problems before they become large. Given the gridlock built into the separation of powers, however, presidential countries must normally wait until their problems reach crisis levels before they can act. But then income immobility has become a large problem now, one upon which elections turn, and so the time is ripe to tackle it. Which Party will do so is very much an open question, however. Until now, voters have been asked to choose between a Party that feels your pain and does nothing about it and a Party that doesn't even feel your pain. The Democrats have made income immobility their issue, but when elected are beholden to a New Class which wishes well for its children and blocks attempts at reform. And so one is left to wonder whether anything will change, whether the promise of America is irretrievably lost.

That need not be our fate. Within the folds of both Parties, there are voices which oppose wasteful interest groups and the rise of aristocracy, and which appeal to individual liberty and a common humanity. They refuse to employ the cronies on one side in order to oppose the cronies on the other side, and scorn them both. Theirs is an uphill battle, for they are ridiculed and condemned by every well-thinking member of the New Class. But then, two hundred years ago, a democratic poet looked at what must have seemed even longer odds. After hearing news of the Peterloo massacre, in which the yeomen cavalry attacked a peaceful crowd of reformers, Shelley charged the British aristocracy with brutality in *The Mask of Anarchy*. The aristocrats had power on their side, but their opponents had liberty and justice on theirs. And they had one thing more:

YE ARE MANY—THEY ARE FEW.

Appendices

INCOME INEQUALITY

How to Measure Income. Measuring inequality requires making choices about how to measure income. In the United States, there are two principal sources of information about people's income: Internal Revenue Service (IRS) administrative records and the Current Population Survey (CPS) from the U.S. Census Bureau. Of these, the IRS data is more reliable, and that's what I use. It's a crime to misrepresent one's income to the IRS, but there's no crime in lying on a survey. Second, many people won't have a good idea about their income when someone comes knocking on their door, especially when asked to specify what they paid in taxes or received as in-kind benefits. Third, the CPS survey has too small a sample of top earners to be representative and tell us much about them. In general, therefore, IRS data are to be preferred.

The Effect of Government Policies. Richard Burkhauser and his co-authors report that government tax and welfare policies have reduced income inequalities.[1] Pre-tax and pre-welfare benefits, income gains did in fact go to people at the top end, but when the authors tweaked the income numbers to account for the effects of tax and welfare policies they reported much lower inequality levels.[2] So adjusted, the top 5 percent saw a 63 percent gain from 1979 to 2007, the middle quintile a 36.9 percent gain and the bottom quintile a 26.4 percent gain.

In two respects, however, the Burkhauser study failed to address concerns about income inequality. First, it took the top five percent of earners as the measure of the top end, when the real story was how the top one or two percent made out. There wasn't much Burkhauser and his colleagues could do about this, as the sample size for the top one percent in the Current Population Survey (CPS) survey was too small to be reliable. The other problem was the study's exclusion of capital gains from its definition of income. This followed from the use of CPS data, since the CPS questionnaire does not ask about capital gains. This omission biased the findings, since capital gains go disproportionately to the people at the top of the economic pyramid, who increasingly remunerate themselves with stock options to take advantage of lower marginal tax rates for capital gains as opposed to regular income. In 2007, capital gains accounted for 1 percent of the income for the middle quintile of earners and 31.7 percent of the earnings of the top one percent.[3] The top 0.1 percent—Fortune 500 CEOs, hedge fund mangers, and asset managers such as Romney—account for half of the country's capital gains, and leaving capital gains out of the mix substantially understates the earnings of top earners.

More recently, Burkhauser and his co-authors have returned to the fray with a study of 1989–2007 earnings that incorporated capital gains. Instead of using realized capital gains, however, they used unrealized capital gains, and after doing so reported that income inequality between the quintiles disappeared. In fact, they found that the poor and middle classes had done better, on a percentage basis, than the rich.[4] There are several difficulties with the study, however. First, unrealized capital gains are the paper gains when the value of my assets goes up, whether or not I plan to sell them, and don't really change my spending behavior. I'm happy when Trulia.com tells me it's increased its estimate of my home value, but I don't feel that my standard of living has changed.

Second, data limitations required the authors to cut off the survey at 2007, at the height of the housing boom, and this artificially increased middle class wealth. People in the middle quintile of earnings have a relatively small stock portfolio, but they do own houses and home values were at an all-time peak in 2007. If account had been taken of unrealized capital gains over 2007–09, when housing prices fell, many middle class households would have had negative earnings.

Burkhauser and his colleagues are serious and well-respected researchers, but a third problem with their study is the artificial assumptions that they had to make about unrealized capital gains. Because of data limitations, their studies focused on the top five percent of earners and not the one percent. It's difficult to estimate just what the latter's gains were, but Harvard economist Lawrence Katz suggests that Burkhauser et al. might have made it look as thought the top earners received smaller gains than they really got.[5] Burkhauser et al. assumed that all investments received the ordinary rate of return for investments of that class, and that's simply not how top management sees its stock option plans. Instead, compensation plans featuring company stock has been seen as a sure-thing method of bringing top executives into a lower tax bracket. In addition, as Burkhauser et al. note, their assumptions don't capture the gains to one percent asset managers such as Mitt Romney who purchase entire companies and turn them around at an enormous profit.

B

PIKETTY'S LAW OF ACCUMULATION

In his magisterial *Capital in the Twenty-First Century*,[1] Thomas Piketty paints a still darker picture of income inequality. Capitalism tends inexorably towards inequality, he argues, because of capital's tendency to grow more quickly than the economy as a whole. To those who have more is given, and great fortunes accumulate over time. Piketty's *Capital* has been compred to Marx's *Capital*, and if he's right we're headed towards a patrimonial society of increased income inequality and immobility, one that invites the kind of leveling political revolution that Marx foresaw.

Piketty seeks to persuade us that the inequality problem is greater than we think, and to do this asks us to compare two measures of wealth. The first is r, the annual rate of return on capital investments; the second is g, the annual growth rate of a country's national income. What's going to happen, says Piketty, is that r will outstrip g and the capitalists who own the assets will become richer than the economy as a whole. And that's it: $r > g$, which Jonah Goldberg calls, "already the most famous mathematical formula since $E=MC^2$."[2]

So far so good, but what many will find surprising are Piketty's figures for g, the growth rate for a country's national income. We're apt to think that there's something normal about a 3 percent annual growth rate, but Piketty tells us to be happy with half that much. Over 1913–50, the North American (U.S. and Canada) g was 1.5, down to 1.4 percent over 1990–2012.

Get used to it, Piketty tells us. For countries playing catch-up, such as China today or postwar France during "les trente glorieuses" of 1945–75, there can be a momentary period of exceptional growth, but that doesn't work for countries at the technological edge such as the United States. "There is no historical example of a country at the world's technological frontier whose growth in per capita output exceeded 1.5 percent over a lengthy period of time."[3]

Predicting the future is a mug's game, but were one to do so one might wonder whether we'll do better than the 1.5 and 1.4 percent growth rates for 1913–50 and 1990–2012. There were two world wars over the first period, and major depressions or recessions in both. For the quieter period in-between, from 1950 to 1990, the annual growth rate was 2.25, and that was a period when North America was indeed on the technological frontier. At 2.25 percent growth per year, the economy would double in size over a single generation of 30 years, and that's what Americans have come to expect as normal. There is no particular reason why we should anticipate quiet periods of sustained future growth, however. Of the growth-killing foolishness of politicians there is never an end, nor of wars either, even if John Kerry thought that sort of thing so very 19th century when Russia invaded the Crimea in 2014.

Economist Robert Gordon takes an even more pessimistic view of things, predicting a growth rate of 1 percent or less.[4] The pace of technological improvements has slowed, he argues, and today the United States faces headwinds that will impede future growth. But let's suppose, says Gordon, that I'm wrong about technological decline, and that future innovation will power a 1.8 per cent growth rate. Even then, he tells us, after factoring in the demographic decline of an aging and shrinking population, as well as the relative decline in American education, the growth rate will decline 1.4 per cent. Gordon then subtracts further, to take into account such things as higher energy taxes, the looming crisis in unfunded social security and Medicare payments, and the transfer of American jobs offshore, to arrive at a 0.2 percent growth rate in real disposable income for the bottom 99 percent of Americans.

While Gordon thinks Piketty's 1.5 percent growth rate excessively optimistic, let's assume for the sake of argument that Piketty is right. That's not really so terrible. Compounded annually, a growth rate of 1.5 percent a year will multiply a $10 investment to $15.63 over a single generation of 30 years, and to 44.32 over 100 years. But then what about r, the rate of return on capital? In the novels of Jane Austen and Honoré de Balzac it was 5 percent and that's about what Piketty thinks it is today. With a $100,000 investment, you'd get a return of $5,000 annually, and what that means is that, comparing r and g, wealth will quickly become more concentrated in the wealthy. If a growth rate of 1.5 percent turns a $10 investment into $15.63 over 30 years, at 5 percent it becomes $43.22. Over 100 years the differences are starker still: $44.32 at 1.5 percent and $1,315.01 at 5 percent. That's the magic of compound interest.

What this would leave us with, says Piketty, is the Balzacian world of Eugène de Rastignac. In Balzac's *Le Père Goriot*, Rastingnac is an impoverished provincial noble who comes to Paris to study law. Above all he seeks to make his way in Parisian society, but soon learns that his law studies aren't going to get him there. Talent, drive, mere effort at the bar might give him a modest salary. Were he to marry the unappealing but wealthy Mademoiselle Victorine, however, he would lay his hands on a million francs. At 5 percent, that would immediately give the twenty-year-old Rastignac an annual income of 50,000 francs, as much as the ablest advocate might earn after a lifetime of toil.

If that's what the future holds, we might expect a frontal attack on the institutions of capitalism. But Piketty's numbers have not passed without challenge, and it's by no means clear that we're headed towards an entrenched aristocracy of wealth. Whatever r might be, it will be reduced by the one percent's personal consumption, since what we're really talking about is not the rate of return on capital but the capitalist's savings rate when he reinvests his wealth. The more that wealth is spent in present periods, the less will be saved and passed on to his children. What economist Thorstein Veblen derided as the "conspicuous consumption" of the rich, money thrown away on expensive baubles, therefore serves to increase income mobility. For people such as footballer George Best, the savings rate may even be far less than g. "I spent over 90% of my money on gambling, women, and drink," he said. "The rest I wasted."

Large families, where wealth is passed on to several children, also serve to weaken an aristocracy of wealth, which as we saw in Chapter 2 was Jefferson's point in attacking primogeniture. When everything is left to the eldest son, thought Jefferson, we'd see a concentration of wealth in a family, passed on in its entirety generation after generation. That doesn't seem to happen, however. Instead, wealth gets divided amongst several children, not to mention charitable bequests. For example, Leona Helmsley struck a blow for income equality when she endowed a $12 million trust fund to look after her dog. Then there are divorces and trophy wives, the flip side of marriage to Balzac's Madame Victorine. Nothing breaks up an estate more quickly than a few messy divorces, which is perhaps why we're always on the side of gold diggers such as Anna Nicole Smith.

Piketty's critics also note that we're not likely to head towards a society in which all wealth is held by the capitalists, since the incremental return on an additional unit of capital can be expected to decline as capital accumulates. That is, if we hold everything the same and capital increases by 1 percent, the return on the additional unit of capital would increase by less than 1 percent. Economists call this the law of diminishing returns, and the weight of evidence supports them.

On the other hand, the value of r is tilted strongly towards the rich. The very poor have no capital to speak of, and their r is effectively zero. For the middle class, things are rosier, but the major investment is tied up in one's house, where the historical rate of investment return (shorn of the consumption value of living in it) is only about 1 percent. At greater levels of wealth, equity (stock) investments make up a greater portion of one's assets, and here the average rate of return is closer to 7 or 8 percent. At the highest levels, amongst the venture capitalists and asset fund managers such as Mitt Romney, expected returns are higher still.

Piketty's arguments have given rise to a storm of criticism, and the jury is still out on his findings. A *Financial Times* report has found several problems in the data, although it's not clear to what extent this undermines Piketty's argument.[5] The evidence about where America's super-rich get their money is also inconsistent with Piketty's story. Each year *Forbes* magazine lists the 400 wealthiest Americans, and only a tenth of the people on the 1982 list remained on the list 30 years later. The old money had been replaced by new money, by the Bill Gates and Mark Zuckerbergs, and the new money had come from entrepreneurial labor more than from capital. That's only 400 people, of course, the billionaires in the .0001 percent of Americans, but America's one percent also seem to have earned and not inherited their money. The share they received of total wealth transfers from their parents, through inheritance or gifts, declined over 1989–2007,[6] and that's completely inconsistent with Piketty's law of accumulation. Not surprisingly, Piketty himself has walked back the suggestion that the $r - g$ gap tells us very much about the rise of inequality in America.[7]

Finally, even a theory as elegant as $r > g$ stands or falls on the evidence, and in Piketty's case it's simply not there. As Daron Acemoğlu and James Robinson note:

> The reader may come away from the huge amount of inter-
> esting data presented in *Capital* with the impression that the
> evidence supporting these claims is overwhelming. But Piketty
> does not engage in hypothesis testing, statistical analysis of
> causation or even correlation.[8]

Acemoğlu and Robinson then conducted the kind of empirical test the theory called for, with a sample of 28 countries over 1870–2012, and failed to find the positive correlation between a country's inequality (the top one percent's share of the economy) and the capitalist's premium of r − g (the difference between the rate of return on capital less the country's annual growth rate) that would support Piketty. There was a correlation, but it was negative (i.e., the greater the inequality, the smaller the capitalist's premium). That's just the opposite of what the theory would have predicted. Without the evidence to back him up, Piketty simply offers us a theory. And there are a lot of theories around. They're better when they're backed by evidence.

C

REGRESSION ANALYSIS

Regression analysis is a statistical technique used to estimate the relationship between a *dependent* variable (or outcome) and one or more *independent* (or explanatory) variables. Regression analysis cannot prove that one thing causes something else, but can show how one set of numbers is statistically related to (correlated with) another set of numbers. And that's as good as it gets.

In Figure 4.3, for example, we'll want to understand how inequality is related to immobility. The scatterplot shows how different countries rank on both measures, but that doesn't tell us much about the strength of the relationship. To do that, we'll treat the immobility variable as a dependent variable and the inequality variable as an independent variable, and then employ a statistical model that seeks to explain the extent to which inequality "predicts" immobility.

The immobility measure for each country is y, its position above the x-axis in the Figure, as seen in the dot. Corresponding to each y, on the straight line above or below it, is where the regression model represents the country to be, or ŷ. If there were a perfect relationship between the two variables, then y and ŷ would be identical and every country observation would lie on the straight line. While y and ŷ are not identical in the Figure, they aren't all that far apart either, and the line was drawn to minimize the difference between them. This was done through the canonical Ordinary Least Squares (OLS) procedure, producing the line that minimizes the squared value of the vertical distances between y and ŷ (hence the term "Least Squares").

The *regression equation* at the bottom of the Figure is of the following form:

$$\hat{y} = \alpha + \beta x$$

where α is a constant and β is the fixed number or *coefficient* which is multiplied by the measure of inequality (x) for each country. In Table C.1, the β coefficient is 1.06, which indicates a nearly one-to-one relationship between the immobility and inequality. Why call this *regression analysis?* Because the dependent variable (immobility) is *regressed on* (estimated from) the independent variable (inequality).

In Figure 4.3 the x-axis is truncated at an inequality measure of 20. Imagine extending the x-axis down to 0 on the left, and then mentally draw the regression line till it intercepts the vertical axis at $x = 0$. The number at the intercept is the *constant* of the regression equation, or α. The regression equation reports that this is .93, which as it happens is very close to zero.

The next question is how well the model, as represented by the straight line, explains the relation between immobility and inequality. The .49 Adjusted R^2 which I report at the bottom of the Figure tells us that the model explains 49 percent of the variation between the variables, with 51 percent unexplained. In estimating immobility, there is (unsurprisingly) more going on than simply the inequality ratios.

We'd also like to know to what extent the β coefficient assists in explaining the relationship between the independent and dependent variables. To do so, the model reports on the coefficient's *p-value*, which is the probability that there is, in reality, no relationship between x and y, and that the observed relationship is due to chance, i.e., the probability that the coefficient is zero. The smaller the p-value the better the fit, and by convention anything less than .05 is taken to satisfy the standard of statistical significance. In Table C.1, the inequality coefficient has a p-value of .001 and is thus highly significant.

Table C.1 makes the highly simplifying assumption that the relationship between immobility and inequality can be represented by Figure 4.3's (linear) straight line, and that a single explanatory variable can be employed to explain the dependent variable. Where there is only one explanatory variable we have what is known as a *simple regression*; if there is more than one, we have what is known as *multiple regression*. Table C.2 reports on a multiple regression, where voting shares are regressed on both the one percent share and a second explanatory variable which is the squared value of the one percent share.[1]

$$\hat{y} = \alpha + \beta_1 x + \beta_2 x^2$$

TABLE C.1

The Determinants of Immobility

Inequality	1.06
	(0.001)
Constant	−0.93
	(0.92)
Adjusted R²	0.49

SOURCES: Miles Corak, "Inequality from Generation to Generation: The United States in Comparison," in Robert Rycroft (ed.), The Economics of Inequality, Poverty, and Discrimination in the 21st Century, ABC-CLIO (2013); CIA Fact Book.

TABLE C.2

The Determinants of Voting

	MODEL I	MODEL II
One-percent share	−0.57	−5.25***
	(0.000)	(0.001)
One-percent share, squared	—	0.19*
	—	(0.002)
Constant	62.14***	88.51***
	(0.000)	(0.000)
Adjusted R²	0.20	0.31

SOURCE: CIA World Fact Book. *** significant at the .001 level, * significant at the 0.05 level. Standard errors in parentheses.

What this produces is the curved line in Figure 7, representing the relationship between voting shares and income inequality in (non-linear) quadratic form. Squaring the one percent share magnifies its values, and Model 2 of Table C.2 examines whether the relationship changes with more extreme values of one percent wealth.

D

ALTRUISM AND EVOLUTIONARY FITNESS

After publishing his first papers, evolutionary biologist W.D. Hamilton received a request for offprints from George Price, of whom he had never heard before. Price was an extraordinary gifted American scientist, who had taught in chemistry departments and worked for the Rand Corporation, but had never trained in population genetics. Nevertheless, he had worked through the Hamilton rule and sent its author a much more rigorous formulation, expressed in terms of the covariance between the offspring an individual produced and the genes which affected fitness. Covariance is a statistical term that measures how much two random variables change together. If more of one variable is associated with more of the other, the covariance is positive; if more of one means less of the other the covariance in negative. This formulation could then be employed to measure the fitness of altruistic genes: are altruistic genes associated with a larger or smaller number of altruistic genes in succeeding generations?

For Hamilton, Price's letter was a revelation. Here was Price, who had never studied statistics or even encountered a covariance before, with a proof that united every kind of natural selection. Hamilton described how they first spoke.

> His voice was squeaky and condescending, rather guarded, on the phone.... He spoke of his formula as 'surprising for me too—quite a miracle." I thought this reference to a "miracle" was a mixture of metaphor and modesty but I later realized he was more serious.... He would like some time to take up with me—especially, he said, there was something about spite. ""About what?," I said. "Spitefulness—spiteful behavior." "Oh, but you don't even cover selfishness in the paper you sent me," I said. "That's true. That will all come later...Have you seen how my formula works for group selection" I told him, of course, no, and may have added something like: "So you actually believe in that do you?"[1]

Price's Equation

To see how Price's formula works, let the altruistic gene be represented by z. The number of the altruists' offspring is w, the change in the total population is $\hat{w}$, and the change in the average number of altruists in each generation is Δz. Price recognized that Δz could be expressed in the following covariance equation:[2]

$$\Delta z = \text{cov}(w/\hat{w}, z)$$

We can then express this relation with the least-squares coefficient β we saw in Appendix C.

$$\Delta z = \beta_{w/\hat{w},z}\, z$$

That is, we can multiply the initial frequency of the altruistic gene z by a number β to give us the change in number of altruists in the next generation. Making the assumption that the linear relationship does not begin at the origin, we might then add the intercept α that we saw in Appendix C, where the constant α represents baseline fitness.

$$\Delta z = \alpha + \beta_{w/\hat{w},z}\, z$$

Kin Selection

Recall from Chapter 13 that Hamilton's Rule for the selfish gene was:

Body, be altruistic if rB > C,

where *r* is Sewall Wright's coefficient of relatedness, and B and C are the fitness benefits and costs, respectively, of altruistic genes. Hamilton's Rule can then be derived using the Price equation. Hamilton hypothesized that fitness might be a function of both the individual's genes (z) and also by the genes of an individual's kin (z'). The previous equation can then be rewritten to include both of these effects

$$\Delta \check{z} = \alpha + \beta_{w/\hat{w},z}\, z + \beta_{w/\hat{w},z}\, z'$$

Here the partial effect of altruistic genes on the individual's own fitness is $\beta_{w/\hat{w},z}\, z$, and that is Hamilton's C, the fitness cost of altruism to the individual. The partial effect of altruistic genes on the individual's kin is $\beta_{w/\hat{w},z}\, z'$ or Hamilton's B. Finally, the genetic association between social partners is βz'z, which is the coefficient of relatedness r. What we'd like to know is when altruism is a net fitness benefit for what Richard Dawkins labeled the selfish gene, so as to trigger the command "body, be altruistic." That is given by the following inequality:

$$\beta z'z\, \beta_{w/\hat{w},z}\, z' > \beta_{w/\hat{w},z}\, z$$

which is the same as Hamilton's Rule: be altruistic if

$$rB > C.$$

Kin Selection and Families

Let us abandon the assumption that parents will have more than one child, but now let's suppose that that child will have one child, and he one child, and so on indefinitely. What is the value of r now? Mathematically, it is the sum of .5 plus .25 plus .125 and so on to infinity, and that is a geometric series that converges absolutely on 1.0. The selfish gene will now be indifferent as between its present body and that of its descendants in their entirety. Given $200, he'd consume $100 and spend $100 on his child.

Suppose next that the parent has only one child, but that child has two children himself, and they two each as well, and so on indefinitely. The value of the parent's r ratio in the child is 0.5. For the two grandchildren it is $(2*0.25 =)$ 0.5, and for the four great-grandchildren $(4*0.125 =)$ 0.5, and so on to infinity. With each new generation, the number of descendants increases and the coefficient of relatedness as to each descendent declines. Surprisingly, the value of the parent's r as to all his descendants, on these assumptions, is infinite.[3]

Probability theorists will recognize this as the St. Petersburg Paradox that Daniel Bernoulli identified in 1738. What is the expected value, asked Bernouli, of the following lottery? A fair coin is tossed, and one is paid $1 if it comes up tails. If it comes up heads the game continues and one is paid $2 if it comes up tails on the second toss, and $4 if it's heads on the first two tosses and tails on the third. The first time it comes up tails the game is over. The player has a .5 probability of wining $1, a .25 probability of $2, a .125 probability of wining $4, and so on, with the pot doubled each time; and that is equal to the sum of an infinite series of 50 cent prizes, which is an infinitely large number.

Spite: How 'r' can be less than zero

Imagine three people, x, y, and z, where x incurs a fitness cost C in order to impose a fitness cost on y, with the ultimate goal of conferring a fitness benefit on z with whom y is in competition. Suppose further that z's fitness gain (B) is equal to y's fitness loss (-B). Donor x is wholly unrelated to y (r_Y = 0) but is related to z (r_z > 0). In that case, Hamilton's Rule explains how x might be willing to bear a fitness cost C to inflict a fitness cost $-B$ on y.

$$\text{Be spiteful if } (r_y - r_z)(\text{-}B) > C$$

Note that $r_y - r_z$, is a negative number. The coefficient of relatedness, r, might thus take a value of less than zero, more than 1, or any fraction in between. The cost $-B$ is also negative, so that multiplying it by the coefficient of relatedness $r_y - r_z$ gives us a positive number. Donor x will then be spiteful so long as $(r_y - r_z)(\text{-}B)$ exceeds his fitness cost C.

Group Selection

Price's equation can also be employed to show how altruistic genes might be selected to survive at the level of groups and not of individuals (even though it's the individuals who mate). For each individual, altruism will impose fitness costs and altruistic groups would therefore be expected to decline. Because of this, "group selection" was for many years thought a fallacy. What Price had shown, however, was that the number of altruistic groups might also increase because of the ability of altruists to exploit the gains of cooperation.

From Price's cryptic paper, it was not easy to see just how group selection might be explained, but after Hamilton worked it out several years later he telephoned Price with the news.

I am pleased to say that, amidst all else that I ought to have done and did not do, some months before he died I was on the phone telling him enthusiastically that through a "group-level" extension of his formula I had now a far better understanding of group selection and was possessed of a far better tool for all forms of selection acting at one level or at many that I had ever had before. "I thought you would see that," the squeaky laconic voice said, almost purring with approval for once. "Then why aren't you working on it yourself, George? Why don't you publish it," I asked. "Oh yes…but I have so many other things to do…population genetics is not my main work, as you know. But perhaps I should pray, see if I am mistaken."[4]

Price's main work, as he saw it, was the applied altruism of a devout Christian. After a conversion experience, he devoted his mental energies to a recalculation of the dates of Easter and Holy Week, all the while living in utter poverty. What few possessions he had he gave away to the drug addicts with whom he lived in squatter houses. On January 6, 1975 he killed himself and now lies in an unmarked grave in Saint Pancras cemetery, London.[5]

Endnotes

CHAPTER I

1. For a more technical explanation by a philosopher, see Neven Sesardic, *Making Sense of Heritability* 18–27 (Cambridge U.P., 2005).

2. Deuteronomy 23:20.

3. Charles Murray, *Coming Apart: The State of White America, 1960–2010* (New York: Random House, 2012); *Robert Putnam, Our Kids: The American Dream in Crisis* (New York: Simon & Schuster, 2015).

4. Alain Finkielkraut, *Et si l'amour durait* 12 (Paris: Gallimard, 2011).

CHAPTER 2

1. August 30, 1787, Thomas Jefferson, *Writings* 909 (New York: Library of America, 1984); I *The Adams-Jefferson Letters* 194, 196 (Lester J. Cappon, ed.) (UNC Press, 1959).

2. So his antifederalist colleague Robert Yates heard him say. Max Farrand (ed.), I The Records of the Federal Convention of 1787 301 (Yale U.P., rev. ed. 1937) [hereafter "Farrand"].

3. Farrand I.289.

4. Gordon S. Wood, *Revolutionary Characters: What Made the Founders Different* 50 (New York: Penguin, 2006).

5. Farrand I.288.

6. Farrand I.48 (Gerry).

7. Farrand I.51 (Randolph).

8. George Washington to Alexander Hamilton, July 10, 1787, in Farrand III.56.

9. See F.H. Buckley, *The Once and Future King: The Fall and Rise of Crown Government in America* ch. 2 (New York: Encounter, 2014).

10. Farrand I.363 (William Johnson).

11. Warren M. Billings, John E. Selby, and Thad W. Tate, *Colonial Virginia: A History* 59–65 (White Plains: KTO Press, 1986).

12. Jonathan Daniels, *The Randolphs of Virginia* 135 (Garden City: Doubleday, 1972).

13. Russell Kirk, *John Randolph of Roanoke: A Study in American Politics* 46 (Indianapolis: Liberty Fund, 1997).

14. See generally Rhys Issac, *The Transformation of Virginia 1740–1790* 43–44, 94–114, 131–35 (UNC Press, 1982). For a close account of the life of a prominent planter, see Isaac's *Landon Carter's Uneasy Kingdom: Revolution and Rebellion on a Virginia Plantation* (Oxford U.P., 2004.

15. Gordon S. Wood, *The Radicalism of the American Revolution* 71 (New York: Vintage, 1993).

16. See *Papers of George Washington*, at http://gwpapers.virginia.edu/documents_gw/civility/civility_transcript.html/.

17. Farrand III.85.

18. Which earned them a reproach for laziness from an early historian of the colony. See Robert Beverley, *The History and Present State of Virginia* IV.18 at § 76, IV.22 at § 83 (London: Parker, 1705), at http://docsouth.unc.edu/southlit/beverley/bcverley.html.

19. Isaac Samuel Harrell, *Loyalism in Virginia* (Duke U.P., 1926). See also Timothy Breen, *Tobacco Culture: The Mentality of the Great Tidewater Planters on the Eve of the Revolution* 128 (Princeton U.P., 1985); Emory G. Evans, *"A Topping People": The Rise and Decline of Virginia's Old Political Elite*

1680–1790 114–20 (U. Va. Press, 2009).

20. Robert Rutland (ed.), I *The Papers of George Mason 1725–1792* 287 (UNC Press, 1970).

21. See Jeff Broadwater, *George Mason: Forgotten Founder* 78 (UNC Press, 2006).

22. Before this, James Wilson of Pennsylvania had written in 1774 that, "the happiness of the society is the first law of every government," in his *Considerations on the Nature and Extent of the Legislative Authority of the British Parliament*. It is more likely, however, that Jefferson's reference to the pursuit of happiness was borrowed from his fellow Virginian. Broadwater, *George Mason: Forgotten Founder*, at 81–91. See Pauline Maier, *American Scripture: Making the Declaration of Independence* 133–34, 165–68, 182–83 (New York: Vintage, 1998).

23. Stanley N. Katz, *Republicanism and the Law of Inheritance in the American Revolutionary Era,* 76 Michigan L. Rev. 1 (1977). It had also proven easy to transform the title of lands held in fee tail to fee simple. But see Holly Brewer, "Entailing Aristocracy in Colonial Virginia: 'Ancient Feudal Restraints' and Revolutionary Reform," 54 *Wm. & Mary Q. Third Series* 307 (1997).

24. Thomas Jefferson, "Autobiography," in *Writings* 1, 44 (Library of America (1984).

25. Farrand II.31.

26. Farrand I.50. Other delegates subscribed to the filtration theory: I.133 (Wilson); I.136 (Dickinson); I.152 (Gerry); II.54 (G. Morris). Hamilton subsequently endorsed it in the New York ratifying debates. June 21, 1788, 5 *The Papers of Alexander Hamilton* 41 (Harold C. Syrett and Jacob E. Cooke, eds., Columbia U.P., 1962).

27. "Vices of the Political System of the United States," 9 *Papers of James Madison* 348 (Robert A. Rutland et al., eds., U. Chicago P., 1962–).

28. See F.H. Buckley, *The Once and Future King*, at ch. 2.

29. Farrand I.49.

30. At http://www.fordham.edu/halsall/mod/senecafalls.asp.

CHAPTER 3

1. Farrand IV.111.

2.   Robert A. McGuire, *To Form a More Perfect Union: A New Economic Interpretation of the United States Constitution* 52–53 (Oxford U.P., 2003).

3.   Clinton Rossiter, *1787: The Grand Convention* 146–47 (New York: W.W. Norton, 1966).

4.   Rufus Griswold, *The Republican Court: Or, American Society in the Days of Washington* 98–99 at note (D. Appleton: New York, 1867).

5.   Thomas Jefferson to John Adams, Oct. 28, 1813, in Philip B. Kurland and Ralph Lerner (eds.), I *The Founders' Constitution* 569 (Indianapolis: Liberty Fund, 1987); II *The Adams-Jefferson Letters*, at 387, 388.

6.   John Adams to Thomas Jefferson, Sept. 2, 1813, in Kurland and Lerner, at 568; II *The Adams-Jefferson Letters*, at 370, 372.

7.   John Adams to Thomas Jefferson, Nov. 15, 1813, in Kurland and Lerner, at 572; II *The Adams-Jefferson Letters*, at 397, 402.

8.   Cleveland Amory, *The Proper Bostonians* 11 (New York: E.P. Dutton, 1950).

9.   Farrand I.101. See also Farrand I.215 (Elbridge Gerry); Farrand II.201 (Oliver Ellsworth).

10.   November 14, 1786, at http://founders.archives.gov/documents/Jefferson/01-10-02-0384.

11.   See Newton D. Mereness (ed.), *Travels in the American Colonies* 365, 403, 405 (Journal of Lord Adam Gordon, 1764–65) (New York: Macmillan, 1916).

12 .   I *A Diary in America* 18 (London: Longman, Orme, 1839).

13.   Alexis de Tocqueville, *Democracy in America* 528, at II.ii.19, (U. Chicago P., 2000).

14.   Frances Trollope, *Domestic Manners of the American* ch. 5 (1832).

15.   I Marryat, at 22.

16.   Marryat at Series II, Vol. II, ch. 2, at http://www.gutenberg.org/ebooks/23138.

17.   Jefferson, *Writings*, at 290.

18.   George Fitzhugh, *Sociology for the South, or The Failure of the Free Society* 248 (A. Morris: Richmond, 1854). The term "mud sill" was first employed by Senator James Hammond (D-SC) in a speech on the floor of the U.S. Senate on March 4, 1858. James Hammond, "The Mud-Sill

Speech" in E.L. McKitrick (ed.), *Slavery Defended: The Views of the Old South* 121–25 (Upper Saddle River, N.J.: Prentice Hall, 1963). On Fitzhugh's importance as a thinker, see Eugene Genovese, *The World the Slaveholders Made: Two Essays in Interpretation* 129 (New York: Pantheon, 1969).

19. Fitzhugh, *Sociology for the South*, at 244.

20. George Fitzhugh, "Southern Thought" and "Southern Thought Again" in Drew Gilpin Faust (ed.), *The Ideology of Slavery: Proslavery Thought in the Antebellum South*, 1830–1860 274 ff. (LSU P., 1981).

21. See David M. Levy, *How the Dismal Science Got its Name: Classical Economics and the Ur-text of Racial Politics* (U. Michigan P., 2002).

22. "Lincoln's 1859 Address at Milwaukee," 10 *Wisc. Mag. History* 243 (1927).

23. *Lincoln: Speeches and Writings 1832–1858* 526 (New York: Library of America, 1989).

24. C. Vann Woodward, "George Fitzhugh, Sui Generis," in George Fitzhugh, *Cannibals All! Or Slaves without Masters* vii, xxx (Harvard U.P., 1988).

25. Letter to Henry L. Pierce and Others, April 6, 1859, in *Lincoln: Speeches and Writings 1859–1865* 18, 19 (New York: Library of America, 1989).

26. *Lincoln: Speeches and Writings 1859–1865* 213 (February 22, 1861).

27. Id. at 85 (speech in Cincinnati, Ohio, September 17, 1859).

CHAPTER 4

1. William Kristol, "G.O.P. Dog Days," *N.Y. Times*, Nov. 10, 2008.

2. At http://www.whitehouse.gov/the-press-office/2011/12/06/remarks-president-economy-osawatomie-kansas.

3. Anthony P. Carnevale, Tamara Jayasundera and Ban Cheah, *The College Advantage: Weathering the Economic Storm* (Washington: Georgetown Public Policy Institute).

4. Linda Levine, *The U.S. Income Distribution and Mobility: Trends and International Comparisons*, Congressional Budget Office 7-5700, November 29, 2012.

5. Emmanuel Saez, *Striking it Richer: The Evolution of Top Incomes in the United States*, September 3, 2013, at http://elsa.berkeley.edu/~saez/

saez-UStopincomes-2012.pdf. See generally Facundo Alvaredo, Anthony B. Atkinson, Thomas Piketty, and Emmanuel Saez, *The World Top Incomes Database*, at http://topincomes.g-mond.parisschoolofeconomics. eu/.

6. Levine, op. cit.

7. Emmanuel Saez and Thomas Piketty, "Income Inequality in the United States, 1913–1998," 118 *Q.J. Econ.* 1 (2003), updated at http://elsa. berkeley.edu/~saez/.

8. Emmanuel Saez, *Striking it Richer: The Evolution of Top Incomes in the United States, supra.*

9. Thomas Piketty, *Capital in the Twenty-first Century* 347–49 (Harvard U.P., 2014). That might be too low. Emmanuel Saez and Gabriel Zucman put the figure at over 40 percent, at http://gabriel-zucman.eu/ files/SaezZucman2014Slides.pdf.

10. Edward Wolff reports that the top one percent owned 33–35 percent of the nation's wealth in the 1960s, and 35.4 percent in 2010 after the Great Recession, down from 39 percent in 1998. Edward N. Wolff, "Recent Trends in Household Wealth in the United States: Rising Debt and the Middle Class Squeeze—An Update to 2007," Working Paper 589, Levy Economics Institute of Bard College (2010); Edward N. Wolff, "The Asset Price Meltdown and the Wealth of the Middle Class," NBER Working Paper 18559 (2012).

11. Jobs requiring the lowest level of skills have actually increased between 1980–2005. David H. Autor and David Dorn, "The Growth of Low-Skill Service Jobs and the Polarization of the US Labor Market," 103 *Am. Econ. Rev.* 1553 (2013).

12. Daron Acemoğlu and David Autor, "What Does Human Capital Do? A Review of Goldin and Katz's The Race between Education and Technology," 50 *J. Econ. Lit.* 426 (2012).

13. Steven Pressman, "Cross-national Comparisons of Poverty and Income Inequality," in Robert S. Rycroft (ed.), *The Economics of Inequality, Poverty, and Discrimination in the 21st Century* 17, 23–24, at Tables 2.3 and 2.4 (Santa Barbara: Praeger, 2013).

14. Daniel Aaronson and Bhashkar Mazumder, "Intergenerational

Economic Mobility in the U.S., 1940 to 2000," Federal Reserve Bank of Chicago, WP 2005–12 (February 2007); Katharine Bradbury, "Trends in U.S. Family Income Mobility," 1969–2006, Federal Reserve Bank of Boston, Working Paper 11–10 (Oct. 20, 2011). Researchers report that the United States was considerably more mobile in terms of jobs than Britain in the late 19th century, but that the American lead over Britain had been erased by 1950. Jason Long and Joseph Ferrie, "Intergenerational Occupational Mobility in Great Britain and the United States Since 1850," 103 *Am. Econ. Rev.* 1109 (2013).

15. On the calculation of intergenerational elasticity, see Gary Solon, "Intergenerational Income Mobility," in Steven Durlauf and Lawrence Blume (eds.), *The New Palgrave Dictionary of Economics* (London: Palgrave, 2008); Miles Corak, "Introduction," in Miles Corak (ed.), *Generational Income Mobility in North America and Europe* 1 (Cambridge U.P., 2004).

16. Bhashkar Mazumder, "The Apple Falls even closer to the Tree than We Thought: New and Revised Estimates of the Intergenerational Inheritance of Earnings," in Samuel Bowles, Herbert Gintis, and Melissa O. Groves (eds.), *Unequal Chances: Family Background and Economic Success* 80 (Princeton U.P., 2005) (reporting an immobility ranking of 0.6). This might even understate income immobility for the very rich, since the 0.6 figure is a measure for all parents and Mazumder reports that there is relatively less mobility in top income brackets. See also Bhashkar Mazumder, "Fortunate Sons: New Estimate of Intergenerational Mobility in the United States Using Social Security Earnings Data," 87 *Rev. Econ. Stat.* 235 (2005).

17. Karl Marx, *The Eighteenth Brumaire of Louis Napoleon* 21–22 (trans. Daniel DeLeon) (Chicago: Charles H. Kerr, 3rd ed., 1913). Social mobility was also the answer to Werner Sombart's *Why Is there No Socialism in the United States?* (Armonk NY: M.E. Sharpe, 1979).

18. The Gini data were compiled from the CIA World Fact Book, since other cross-country data sets are problematical. The World Bank data use both income and consumption metrics as well as individual and household methodologies, without clarifying what metric and

methodology is employed. By contrast the CIA data are consistently based on family income. I averaged the data for each country and extrapolated through the entire period. If anything, the CIA data understates income inequality in the U.S. The Congressional Budget Office reports a Gini ratio of .59 for the U.S.in 2007, nearly .15 higher than the CIA does.

19. Raj Chetty, Nathaniel Hendren, Patrick Kline and Emmanuel Saez, "Where is the Land of Opportunity: The Geography of Intergenerational Mobility in the United States," NBER Working Paper 19843, January 2014; Raj Chetty, Nathaniel Hendren, and Laurence Katz, "The Effects of Exposure to Better Neighborhoods on Children: New Evidence from the Moving to Opportunity Experiment," NBER Working Paper 21156, May 2015.

20. Scott Winship, "The Great Gatsby Curve: All Heat, No Light," Brookings Institution, May 20, 1985.

21. Irving Kristol, *Two Cheers for Capitalism* 14–17 (New York: Basic Books, 1978); Christopher Lasch, *The Revolt of the Elites and the Betrayal of Democracy* (New York: W.W. Norton, 1995).

22. Raj Chetty, Nathaniel Hendren, Patrick Kline, Emmanuel Saez and Nicholas Turner, "Is the United States Still a Land of Opportunity? Recent Trends," NBER Working Paper 19844.

23. Charles Murray, *Losing Ground: American Social Policy, 1950–1980* (New York: Basic Books, 1984).

CHAPTER 5

1. Tony Judt, *Ill Fares the Land* (New York: Penguin, 2010).

2. Timothy Noah, *The Great Divergence: America's Growing Inequality Crisis and What We Can Do about It* (New York: Bloomsbury, 2012).

3. Hedrick Smith, *Who Stole the American Dream?* (New York: Random House, 2012); Donald L. Bartlett and James B. Steele, *The Betrayal of the American Dream* (New York: Public Affairs, 2012); Peter Edelman, *So Rich, So Poor: Why It's So Hard To End Poverty in America* (New York: Twenty Years, 2012); Larry M. Bartels, *Unequal Democracy: The Political Economy of the New Gilded Age* (New York: Russell Sage, 2008).

4. Lawrence Lessig, *Republic, Lost: How Money Corrupts Congress—and a*

Plan to Stop It (New York: Twelve, 2011).

5.   Darrell M. West, *Billionaires: Reflections on the Upper Crust* (Washington: Brookings, 2014).

6.   *Nickel and Dimed: On (Not) Getting By in America* (New York: Metropolitan, 2001). See also Jeff Faux, *The Servant Economy: Where America's Elite Is Sending the Middle Class* (New York: John Wiley, 2012).

7.   Teresa A. Sullivan, Elizabeth Warren, and Jay L. Westbrook, *The Fragile Middle Class: Americans in Debt* (Yale U.P., 2000).

8.   Bureau of Labor Statistics, Economic News Release, Table A-15, at http://www.bls.gov/news.release/empsit.t15.htm.

9.   The job losses have been attributed to an aging population, but that's only a small part of what happened. If that were the whole story, we would have expected to see a sharp drop in the 20–64 working age bracket, but instead there was only a 0.3 percent decline between 2008 and 2012. American Fact Finder, U.S. Census, at http://factfinder2.census.gov/faces/tableservices/jsf/pages/productview.xhtml?src=bkmk.

10.   At http://www.economicsecurityindex.org.

11.   Asma Ghribi, "One in Four Americans Has No Emergency Savings," *Wall Street Journal*, June 23, 2014.

12.   Linda Levine, "An Analysis of the Distribution of Wealth Across Households, 1989–2010," Congressional Research Service 7-5700, July 17, 2012.

13.   International Monetary Fund, World Economic Outlook Database, GDP per capita, September 2011.

14.   Amy Sullivan, "The American Dream, Downsized," *National Journal*, April 26, 2013.

15.   Tami Luhby, "The American Dream is Out of Reach." *Money*, June 4, 2014.

16.   Alberto Alesina and George-Marios Angeletos, "Fairness and Redistribution," 95 *Am. Econ. Rev.* 960 (2005).

17.   "Most See Inequality Growing, but Partisans Differ over Solutions," Pew Research Center for People and the Press, Jan. 23, 2014.

18.   *Mother Jones*, September 2012.

19.   It wasn't as though Romney's distinction between "givers" and

"takers" had come out of the blue, for this had become a popular meme on the right, one launched by the president of the American Enterprise Institute. Arthur C. Brooks, *The Battle: How the Fight between Free Enterprise and Big Government Will Shape America's Future* (New York: Basic Books, 2010). See also Nicholas Eberstadt, *A Nation of Takers: America's Entitlement Epidemic* (West Conshohocken PA: Templeton Press, 2012).

20. Suzanne Mettler, *The Submerged State: How Invisible Government Policies Undermine American Democracy* (U. Chicago P., 2011).

21. Dan Balz, *Collision 2012: Obama vs. Romney and the Future of Elections in America* ch. 23 (New York: Viking, 2013).

22. Karlyn Bowman, "Election Results from A to Z," *The American*, November 7, 2012.

23. Teresa Tritch, "Voting their (thin) Wallets," *New York Times*, Nov. 8, 2012.

24. Hart Research Associates, "Hard Work, Hard Lives: America's Low-Wage Workers—Report of Findings from a National Survey among Low-Wage Workers" (August 2013), at http://www.oxfamamerica.org/files/hart-low-wage-workers-survey.

25. AEI Political Report 11.3, March 2015 (Washington: American Enterprise Institute).

26. Nasim Nicholas Taleb, *Antifragile: Things that Gain from Disorder* (New York: Random House, 2012).

27. Billionaire Entrepreneur Mark Cuban: "Failure is part of the Success Equation," *Entrepreneur*, Sept. 25, 2014.

CHAPTER 6

1. See Shanker Satyanath, Nico Voigtlaender, and Hans-Joachim Voth, "Bowling for Fascism: Social Capital and the Rise of the Nazi Party in Weimar Germany, 1919–33," NBER Working Paper No. 19201 (July 2013).

2. Theda Skocpol has noted that the state increasingly does what voluntary associations used to do, and that this has contributed to their decline. Theda Skocpol, "Voice and Inequality: The Transformation of American Civic Democracy," 2 *Perspectives on Politics* 3, 9 (2004).

3. Robert Putnam, *Bowling Alone: The Collapse and Revival of American Community* (New York: Simon and Schuster, 2000).

4. Cary Funk and Greg Smith, "Nones on the Rise: One-in-Five Adults Have No Religious Affiliation," The Pew Forum on Religion and Public Life, October 2012.

5. "Loneliness Among Older Adults: A National Survey of Adults 45+," *AARP The Magazine*, September 2010.

6. Tara Parker-Pope, "Suicide Rates Rise Sharply in U.S.," *New York Times*, May 2, 2013.

7. John T. Cacioppo and William Patrick, *Loneliness* 260 (New York: W.W. Norton, 2008).

8. Marc J. Dunkelman, *The Vanishing Neighbor: The Transformation of American Community* (New York: W.W. Norton, 2014).

9. Miller McPherson, Lynn Smith-Lovin and Matthew E. Brashears, "Social Isolation in America: Changes in Core Discussion Networks over Two Decades," 71 *Am. Soc. Rev.* 353 (2006).

10. Everett C. Ladd, *The Ladd Report* (New York: Free Press, 1999).

11. "Public Trust in Government: 1958–2013," Pew Research Center for the People and the Press, Jan. 31, 2013.

12. Pamela Paxton, "Is Social Capital Declining in the United States? A Multiple Indicator Assessment," 105 *American J. Sociology* 88 (1999).

13. Putnam, at 140.

14. "Millennials in Adulthood," Pew Research Social and Demographic Trends, March 7, 2014.

15. Michael P. McDonald, "United States Elections Project," at http://elections.gmu.edu/voter_turnout.htm.

16. The straight line in Figure 6.3 masks a non-linear relationship, where trust declines sharply for Gini values between 20 and 40 percent. However, there is a negative relationship throughout between inequality and trust.

17. Richard Wilkinson and Kate Pickett, *The Spirit Level: Why Greater Equality Makes Societies Stronger* 53, at Figure 4.2 (New York: Bloomsbury, 2009).

CHAPTER 7

1. Whether Brandeis actually said this is another matter. See Peter S. Campbell, "Concentrated Wealth: In Search of a Louis Brandeis Quote," 16 *Green Bag* 2d. 251 (2013).

2. Quoted in James K. Galbraith, *Inequality and Instability: A Study of the World Economy Just Before the Great Crisis* 147 (Oxford U.P., 2012).

3. See Alberto Alesina and Roberto Perotti, "Income Distribution, Political Instability, and Investment," 40 *European Economic Review* 1203 (1996); Terry Lynn Karl, "Economic Inequality and Democratic Instability," 11 *J. Democracy* 149 (2000); Philip Keefer and Stephen Knack, "Polarization, Politics and Property Rights: Links between Inequality and Growth," 111 *Public Choice* 127 (2002).

4. At http://www.freedomhouse.org/report-types/freedom-world. Freedom House also ranks countries according to personal rights, but these largely track political rights.

5. This assumes that voter preferences are single-peaked, and that outcomes further from the median are always less preferred.

6. See Daron Acemoğlu and James A. Robinson, "Why Did the West Extend the Franchise? Democracy, Inequality, and Growth in Historical Perspective," 115 *Q.J. Econ.* 1167 (2000).

7. New York: Encounter Books, 2014.

8. Citizens United v. Federal Election Commission, 558 U.S. 310 (2010).

9. Joseph E. Stiglitz, *The Price of Inequality: How Today's Divided Society Endangers our Future* (New York: W.W. Norton, 2012).

10. Daron Acemoğlu and James A. Robinson, *Why Nations Fail: The Origins or Power, Prosperity, and Poverty* 364–65 (New York: Crown, 2012).

11. For a review of similar empirical evidence, see Daron Acemoğlu and James A. Robinson, *Economic Origins of Dictatorship and Democracy* 58–61, at Figure 3.15 (Cambridge U.P., 2006). In a dynamic model, Carles Boix found that greater equality increases the chance of a transition to democracy and the stability of a democratic regime. Carles Boix, *Democracy and Redistribution* 71–92 (Cambridge U.P., 2003).

12. For similar findings, see François Bourguignon and Thierry Verdier, "Oligarchy, Democracy, Inequality and Growth," 62 *J. Dev. Econ.* 285 (2000).

13. Acemoğlu and Robinson offer a similar explanation for the lack of democracy in countries with high levels of economic equality. In such cases, they suggest, there is little demand for democracy, as the majority of people already have what they prize. Daron Acemoğlu and James A. Robinson, *Economic Origins of Dictatorship and Democracy* (Cambridge U.P., 2009).

CHAPTER 8

1. Arthur M. Okun, *Equality and Efficiency: The Big Tradeoff* 91 (Washington: Brookings, 1975).

2. See Andrew Berg, Jonathan D. Ostry, and Jeromin Zettelmeyer, "What Makes Growth Sustained?," 98 *J. Development Economics* 149 (2012); Tortsen Persson and Guido Tabellini, "Is Inequality Harmful for Growth?," 84 *Am. Econ. Rev.* 600 (1994); Alberto Alesina and Dani Rodrik, "Distributive Politics and Economic Growth," 109 *Q.J. Econ.* 465 (1994); but see Kristin J. Forbes, "A Reassessment of the Relationship Between Inequality and Growth," 90 *Am. Econ. Rev.* 869 (2000).

3. Gary S. Becker, Tomas J. Philpson, and Rodrigo R. Soares, "The Quantity and Quality of Life and Evolution of World Inequality," 95 *Am. Econ. Rev.* 277 (2005). See also Lyn Squire, "Fighting Poverty," 83 *Am. Econ. Rev.* 377 (1993); Angus Deaton, *The Great Escape: Health, Wealth, and the Origins on Inequality* 152–56 (Princeton U.P., 2013).

4. Paul Krugman, "Viagra and the Wealth of Nations," *N.Y. Times Magazine* 24 (August 23, 1998).

5. For the measure of happiness, Gallup asked samples of people 15 and older over a 2001–06 period to rank themselves on a scale from 0 (worst possible life) to 10 (best possible life), and stronger levels of life satisfaction were reported in richer OECD countries. OECDiLibrary, "Life Satisfaction—Society at a Glance 2009." See also Betsey Stevenson and Justin Wolfers, "Growth and Subjective Well-Being: Reassessing the Easterlin Paradox," National Bureau of Economic Research no. 14282

(2008), at figure 9 (reporting a strong linear relationship between life satisfaction and the logarithm of GDP per capita); Ed Diener, Marissa Diener, and Carol Diener, "Factors Predicting the Subjective Well-being of Nations," 69 *J. Personality & Soc. Pscyh.* 851 (1995); Bruno S. Frey and Alois Stutzer, *Happiness and Economics: How the Economy and Institutions Affect Human Well-being* 19 (Princeton U.P., 2002).

6.   Daniel Kahneman, Jack L. Knetsch, and Richard Thaler, "Fairness and the Assumptions of Economics," 59 *J. Bus.* S285 (1986); Werner Guth, Rolf Schmittberger & Bernd Schwarze, "An Experimental Analysis of Ultimatum Bargaining," 3 *J. Econ. Behav. & Org.* 367 (1982).

7.   Robert H. Frank, *The Darwin Economy: Liberty, Competition, and the Common Good* 68–69 (Princeton U.P., 2011); Robert H. Frank, *Luxury Fever: Why Money Fails To Satisfy in an Era of Excess* (New York: Free Press, 1999).

8.   See also Michael R. Hagerty, "Social Comparisons of Income in One's Community: Evidence from National Surveys of Income and Happiness," 78 *J. Personality and Social Psych.*, 78, 764 (2000); but see Maarten Berg and Ruut Veenhoven, "Income Inequality and Happiness in 119 Nations," in Bent Greve (ed.), *Social Policy and Happiness in Europe* 174 (Cheltenham: Edgar Elgar, 2010).

9.   Richard Layard, *Happiness: Lessons from a New Science* 45 (London: Penguin, 2005).

10.   Shigehiro Oishi, Selin Kesebir, and Ed Diener, "Income Inequality and Happiness," 22 *Psychological Science* 2011 1095 (2011).

CHAPTER 9

1.   See, e.g., David H. Autor, Lawrence F. Katz, and Melisa S. Kearney, "Trends in U.S. Wage Inequality: Revising the Revisionists," 90 *Rev. Econ. & Stat.* 300 (2008); Daron Acemoğlu, "Technical Change, Inequality, and the Labor Market," 40 *J. Econ. Lit.* 7 (2003). The first economists to argue that *skill-based technological change* (SBTC) explains the rise of income inequality were John Bound and George Johnson in "Changes in the Structure of Wages in the 1980's: An Evaluation of Alternative Explanations," 82 *Am. Econ. Rev.* 371 (1992). See also Lawrence F. Katz and Kevin M. Murphy, "Changes in Relative Wages, 1963–1987: Supply and

Demand Factors," 107 *Q.J. Econ.* 35 (1992). Even before this, Zvi Griliches reported that investments were moving to high-skilled industries in the 1950s, in "Capital-Skill Complimentarity," 51 *Rev. Econ. & Stat.* 465 (1969).

2. Tom Vanderbilt, "Unhappy Truckers and Other Algorithmic Problems," 3 *Nautilus* (2013).

3. William J. Cook, *In Pursuit of the Traveling Salesman: Mathematics at the Limits of Computation* (Princeton U.P., 2012).

4. Economic News Release, Bureau of Labor Statistics, Jan. 24, 2014.

5. Robin Abcarian, "President Obama's Self-flogging on the Affordable Care Act," *L.A. Times*, Nov. 14, 2013.

6. OECD Skills Outlook 2013: First Results from the Survey of Adult Skills 3.

7. Employment Projections: 2010–2020 Summary, Bureau of Labor Statistics, USDL-12-0160, February 1, 2012.

8. Angela Moscaritoio, "Google's Self-Driving Car Takes Blind Man for a Ride," *PCMag.com*, March 29, 2012. See also Erik Brynjolfsson and Andrew McAfee, *Race Against the Machine* 13–14 (Lexington, Ma.: Digital Frontier, 2011).

9. William D. Nordhaus, "Two Centuries of Productivity Growth in Computing," 67 *J. Econ. Hist.* 128 (2007).

10. Claudia Goldin and Lawrence F. Katz, *The Race between Education and Technology* (Harvard U.P., 2008); see also Daron Acemoğlu and David Autor, "What Does Human Capital Do? A Review of Goldin and Katz's The Race between Education and Technology," 50 *J. Econ. Lit.* 426 (2012).

11. Jonathan Huebner, "A possible declining trend for worldwide innovation," 72 *Technological Forecasting & Social Change* 980 (2005).

12. Jon Bakija, Adam Cole, and Bradley T. Heim, "Jobs and Income Growth of Top Earners and the Causes of Changing Income Inequality: Evidence from U.S. Tax Return Data," at http://web.williams.edu/Economics/wp/BakijaColeHeimJobsIncomeGrowthTopEarners.pdf (evidence from 2005 tax return data).

13. Anthony B. Atkinson, Thomas Piketty, and Emmanuel Saez,

"Top Incomes in the Long Run of History," 49 *J. Econ. Lit.* 1, 56 (2011).

14. Robert J. Gordon, "Why Innovation Won't Save Us," *Wall Street Journal*, Dec. 21, 2013; Robert J. Gordon, "Is U.S. Economic Growth Over? Faltering Innovation Confronts the Six Headwinds," NBER Working Paper 18315 (August 2012), at http://www.nber.org/papers/w18315.

15. Tyler Cowen, *The Great Stagnation: How America Ate All the Low-Hanging Fruit of Modern History, Got Sick, and Will (Eventually) Get Better* (New York: Dutton, 2011).

16. Henry Siu and Nir Jaimovich, "Jobless Recoveries," *Third Way* (April 8, 2015).

17. Timothy Aeppel, "Economists Debate: Has All the Important Stuff Already Been Invented?," *Wall Street J.*, June 15, 2014.

18. Erik Brynjolfsson and Andrew McAfee, *The Second Machine Age: Work, Progress, and Prosperity in a Time of Brilliant Technologies* (New York: W.W. Norton, 2014).

19. Clarence Day, *Life with Father and Mother* 162 (New York: Knopf, 1943).

20. Brynjolfsson and McAfee, at 96.

21. The Federal Reserve Bank of Chicago also reports a mismatch between what recent students had learned and the skills employers were looking for. R. Jason Faberman and Bhashkar Mazumder, "Is there a Skills Mismatch in the Labor Market?," Chicago Fed Letter, June 2012.

CHAPTER 10

1. A 2006 World Bank study asserted that intangible capital (meaning human and social capital and social institutions) is the largest share of total wealth in most countries. Kirk Hamilton, et. al., *Where is the Wealth of Nations? Measuring Capital for the 21st Century* 87 (2006).

2. John J. Mearsheimer, *The Tragedy of Great Power Politics* 220 (New York: W.W. Norton, 2014).

3. Adam Smith, IV *The Wealth of Nations* ch. 2.

4. David Wessel, "Big U.S. Firms Shift Hiring Abroad," *Wall Street J.*, April 19, 2011.

5. Shahien Nasiripour, "Obama Picks Jeffrey Immelt, GE CEO, To Run New Jobs-Focused Panel As GE Sends Jobs Overseas, Pays Little In Taxes," *Huffington Post*, Jan. 21, 2011.

6. Christoph Lakner and Branko Milanovic, "Global Income Distribution from the Fall of the Berlin Wall to the Great Recession," World Bank Policy Research Working Paper 6719 (December 2013).

7. State of the Poor, World Bank, April 17, 2013; "A Measured Approach to Ending Poverty and Boosting Shared Prosperity," World Bank Group, at https://openknowledge.worldbank.org/bitstream/handle/10986/20384/9781464803611.pdf.

8. The State of the Poor, Word Bank, id. "Extreme poverty" was defined as $1.25 a day in 2005 dollars.

9. Uri Dadush, Kemal Derviş, Sarah Puritz Milsom and Bennett Stancil, *Inequality in America: Facts, Trends, and International Perspectives* 46 (Washington: Brookings, 2012).

10. David H. Autor, David Dorn, and Gordon H. Hanson, "The China Syndrome: Local Labor Market Effects of Import Competition in the United States," 103 *Am. Econ. Rev.* 2121 (2013). See further Michael Spence, *The Next Convergence: The Future of Economic Growth in a Multispeed World* (New York: Farrar, Straus and Giroux, 2011).

11. Robert H. Frank and Philip J. Cook, *The Winner-Take-All Society: Why the Few at the Top Get So Much More Than the Rest of Us* 48 (New York: Free Press, 1995).

12. A thesis advanced by Erik Brynjolfsson and Andrew McAfee, "Race against the Machine," *supra*. See also Xavier Gabaix and Augustin Landier, "Why Has CEO Pay Increased So Much?," 123 *Q.J. Econ.* 49 at Figure 1 (2008).

13. Steven N. Kaplan and Joshua Rauh, "Wall Street and Main Street: What Contributes to the Rise in the Highest Incomes?," 23 *Rev. Fin. Stud.* 1004 (2010); Xavier Gabaiz and Augustin Landler, "Why Has CEO Pay Increased So Much?," 123 *Q.J. Econ.* 49 (2008).

14. Sherwin Rosen, "The Economics of Superstars," 71 *Am. Econ. Rev.* 845 (1981).

15. Institute of Directors, "Offshoring Is Here to Stay," January 23,

2006. See also Alan Binder, "Offshoring: The Next Industrial Revolution," 85 *Foreign Affairs* 113 (March-April, 2006).

16. Michael E. Porter, "Location, Competition, and Economic Development: Local Clusters in a Global Economy," 14 *Econ. Dev. Q.* 15 (2000).

17. Walter Isaacson, *The Innovators* (New York: Simon & Schuster, 2014).

18. Tom C.W. Lin, "The New Investor," 60 *UCLA L. Rev.* 678 (2013). Around 70 per cent of the orders to buy or sell on Wall Street are said to be placed by software programs. Sarfraz Manzoor, "Quants: The Math Geniuses Running Wall Street," *The Telegraph*, July 23, 2013.

19. John Markoff, "Armies of Expensive Lawyers, Replaced by Cheaper Software," *N.Y. Times*, March 4, 2011.

20. See Douglas A. Irwin, *Free Trade under Fire* (3d ed., 2009); Douglas A. Irwin, *Against the Tide: An Intellectual History of Free Trade* (1996). For a review of free trade's effect in alleviating a country's poverty, see Jagdish Bhagwati, *In Defense of Globalization* ch. 5 (2004); David Dollar and Art Kraay, "Growth is Good for the Poor," 1 *J. Econ. Growth* 195 (2002). For more critical studies of free trade, see Paul Krugman, "Trade and Wages Reconsidered," *Brookings Papers on Economic Activity* 3, Spring 2008; Lawrence Summers, "America Needs to Make a New Case for Trade," *Financial Times*, April 27, 2008; Lawrence Summers, "A Strategy to Promote Healthy Globalization," *Financial Times*, May 4, 2008.

CHAPTER II

1. Karen Spar, "Spending for Federal Benefits and Services for People with Low Income," Congressional Research Service, Oct. 16, 2012. See Daniel Halper, "Welfare Spending Now Largest Budget Item," *Weekly Standard*, October 18, 2012.

2. Derrick Morgan, "Reform the Welfare State, Don't Enlarge It with Amnesty," Heritage Foundation, 2013.

3. Price V. Fishback, "Social Welfare Expenditures in the United States and the Nordic Countries: 1900–2003," NBER Working Paper 15982, 2010.

4. Willem Adema, Pauline Fron, and Maxime Ladaique, "Is the

European Welfare State Really More Expensive? Indicators on Social Spending 1980–2012," OECD Social, Employment and Migration Working Papers no. 124 33 at Table I.4, 34 at chart I.11 (2011).

5. Suzanne Mettler, *The Submerged State: How Invisible Government Policies Undermine American Democracy* (U. Chicago P., 2011).

6. Book Review, 52 Harv. L. Rev. 700, 703 (1939).

7. At http://www.scribd.com/doc/190499803/Fed-U-S-Federal-Individual-Income-Tax-Rates-History-1862-2013.

8. A story persuasively told in Robert L. Bartley, *The Seven Fat Years—And How To Do it Again* (New York: Free Press, 1992).

9. Gerald Prante and Austin John, Top Marginal Effective Tax Rates by State and by Source of Income, 2012 Tax Law vs. 2013 Tax Law (as enacted in ATRA) (February 3, 2012), SSRN-id2176526.

10. The Distribution of Household Income and Federal Taxes, 2010, Congressional Budget Office (December 2013).

11. Even when taking account of capital gains, the Tax Code is sharply progressive. The Congressional Budget Office estimates that the 2013 effective tax rate (federal tax liabilities divided by before-tax income *plus* capital gains) is 33.6 percent for the top one percent and only 3.1 percent for the lowest quintile.

12. In addition, the burden of high capital gains taxes weighs especially heavily on start-ups, where entrepreneurs sacrifice their salaries in a safe job for the risks of starting a new business. There's a lively public debate about capital gains, but it's largely a debate about the efficiency losses from higher capital gains. Chris Edwards, "Advantages of Low Capital Gains Tax Rates," Cato Institute (December 2012).

13. Scott Klinger and Sarah Anderson, *Fleecing Uncle Sam* (Washington: Institute for Policy Studies Center for Effective Government, 2014).

14. The *Wall Street Journal* found that sixty large U.S. companies parked a total of $166 billion abroad in 2013, an amount equal to 40 percent of their annual profits. Scott Thurm and Kate Linebaugh, "More U.S. Profits Parked Abroad, Saving on Taxes," *Wall Street J.,* March 10, 2013.

15. Kyle Pomerleau and Andrew Lundeen, International Tax Competitiveness Index 3 (2014).

16. At http://www.transparency.org/country.

17. Reid J. Epstein, "David Brat Pulls off Cantor Upset despite Raising just $231,000," *Wall Street J.*, June 10, 2014.

18. Citizens United v. Federal Election Commission, 558 U.S. 310 (2010).

19. Ramsey Cox, "In First Speech Back, Reid Blasts Koch Brothers," *The Hill*, Sept. 8, 2014.

20. Peter Schweizer, *Extortion: How Politicians Extract Your Money, Buy Votes, and Line Their Own Pockets* (Boston: Houghton, Mifflin, Harcourt, 2013).

21. Wisconsin v. Peterson, ___ Wisc.2d ___ (July 16, 2015).

CHAPTER 12

1. Richard J. Herrstein and Charles Murray, *The Bell Curve: Intelligence and Class Structure in American Life* (New York: Free Press, 1996).

2. Steven N. Kaplan and Joshua Rauh, "It's the Market: The Broad-Based Rise in the Return to Top Talent," 27 *J. Econ. Persp.* 35 (2013).

3. Julissa Cruz, "Marriage: More than a Century of Change, National Center for Family and Marriage Research, Bowling Green State University" (July 2013).

4. National Poverty Center, University of Michigan, at http://www.npc.umich.edu/poverty/. Single-headed families earned a median income of $23,000 in 2007, about half of what the median married-couple family earned. Rebecca M. Blank, *Changing Inequality* 65, 74 (U. Calif. P, 2011). Women who aren't married when they have their first child are subsequently less likely to graduate from high school or to find a job. Lindsay M. Monte and Renee R. Ellis, "Fertility of Women in the United States: June 2012," Current Population Reports P20-575, U.S. Census Bureau (2014).

5. David Popenoe, *Life Without Father: Compelling New Evidence that Fatherhood and Marriage Are Indispensible for the Good of Children and Society* (New York: Free Press, 1996).

6. Chetty, Hendren, Kline, Saez and Turner, "Is the United States Still a Land of Opportunity?" See also Isabel V. Sawhill, *Generation Unbound: Drifting into Sex and Parenthood without Marriage* 151, at Figure 4, Brookings Institution, 2014).

7. Betty Hart and Todd R. Risely, "The Early Catastrophe: The 30 Million Word Gap by Age 3," *American Educator* 4 (Spring 2003).

8. Jeremy Greenwood, Nezih Guner, Georgi Kocharkov, and Cezar Santos, "Marry Your Like: Assortative Mating and Income Inequality," 104 *Am. Econ. Rev. (Papers and Proceedings)* 1 (2014).

9. June Carbone and Naomi Cahn, *Marriage Markets* (Oxford U.P., 2014).

10. Charles Murray, *Coming Apart: The State of White America, 1960–2010* (New York: Random House, 2012).

11. Since welfare benefits are means tested and cut off at higher levels of earnings, they can amount to an implicit marginal tax rate over 100 percent for people who leave welfare to get a job. When that happens, notes University of Chicago economist Casey Mulligan, people can make more money by staying on welfare than by working. Casey B. Mulligan, *The Redistribution Recession: How Labor Market Distortions Contracted the Economy* (Oxford U.P., 2012). See "Effective Marginal Rates for Low- and Moderate-Income Workers," Congressional Budget Office, Pub. No. 4149, November 2012.

12. George A. Akerlof and Janet L. Yellen, "An Analysis of Out-of-Wedlock Births in the United States," *Brookings Policy Briefs* (August 1996); FastStats: "Unmarried Childbearing," Centers for Disease Control and Prevention, at http://www.cdc.gov/nchs/fastats/unmarry.htm.

13. On Canada, see Miles Corak, Lori J. Curtis, and Shelly Phipps, "Economic Mobility, Family Background, and Well-Being of Children in the United States and Canada," in Timothy M. Smeeding, Robert Erikson, and Markus Jäntti (eds.), *Persistence, Priviledge, and Parenting: the Comparative Study of Intergenerational Mobility* 73, 76–78 (New York: Russell Sage, 2011); on the U.S., see Tom Hertz, "Rags, Riches, and Race: The Intergenerational Mobility of Black and White Families in the United States," in Samuel Bowles, Herbert Gintis, and Melissa Osborne Groves

(eds.), *Unequal Chances: Family Background and Economic Success* 165, Table 5.10 (Princeton U.P., 2005).

14. Pew Research Global Attitudes Project, Jan. 14, 2004.

15. Seymour Martin Lipset, *Continental Divide: The Values and Institutions of the United States and Canada* (Toronto: C.D. Howe, 1989).

16. Corak et al., at 84–85.

17. Seymour Martin Lipset, *American Exceptionalism: A Double-Edged Sword* 46–51 (New York: W.W. Norton, 1996).

18. David Hume, "Idea of a Perfect Commonwealth," in *Hume: Political Essays* 222 (Cambridge U.P., 1994).

19. Margaret F. Brinig and F.H. Buckley, "The Price of Virtue," 98 *Public Choice* 111 (1999).

20. See Ewen Callaway, "Economics and Genetics Meet in Uneasy Union," *Nature*, Oct. 10, 2012.

21. David Lykken, *Happiness: The Nature and Nurture of Joy and Contentment* 55–56 New York: St. Martin's Griffin, 1999).

22. Amir Sariaslan, Henrik Larrson, Brian D'Onofrio, Niklas Langstrom, and Paul Lichtenstein, "Childhood Family Income, Adolescent Violent Criminality and Substance Abuse," 205 *Brit. J. Psychiatry* ___ (2015); Thomas Frisell, Paul Lichtenstein, and Niklas Langstrom, "Violent Crime Runs in Families," 41 *Psych. Medicine* 97 (2011).

23. Christopher Jencks, "Heredity, Environment, and Human Policy Reconsidered," 45 *Am. Soc. Rev.* 723 (1980); Richard E. Nisbett et al., "Intelligence: New Findings and Theoretical Developments," 67 *American Psychologist* 130 (2012).

24. Bruce Sacerdote, "What Happens when We randomly Assign Children to Families?," NBER Working Paper No. 10894 (November 2004).

25. Samuel Bowles and Herbert Gintis, "The Inheritance of Inequality," 16 *J. Econ. Persp.* 3 (2002). Higher figures are reported in Daniel J. Benjamin, "The Promises and Pitfalls of Genoeconomics," 4 *Annual Rev. Econ.* 627 (2012).

26. Jonathan P. Beauchamp et al., "Molecular Genetics and Economics," 25 *J. Econ. Persp.* 57 (2011).

27. Amy Chua and Jed Rubenfeld, *The Triple Package: How Three Un·likely Traits Explain the Rise and Fall of Cultural Groups in America* (New York: Penguin, 2014).

28. Melissa Osborne Groves, "Personality and the Intergenerational Transmission of Economic Status," in Samuel Bowles et al., *Unequal Chances* 208.

29. Kurt Vonnegut, *Welcome to the Monkey House* (New York: Dial, 1998).

30. Arthur Goldberger, "Heritability," 46 *Economica* 327 (1979).

CHAPTER 13

1. Albert Ando and Franco Modigliani, "The Life Cycle Hypothesis of Saving: Aggregate Implications and Tests," 53 *Am. Econ. Rev.* 55 (1963); Franco Modigliani and Richard Brumberg, "Utility Analysis and Aggregate Consumption Functions. An Attempt at Integration," in Andrew Abel (ed.), II *The Collected Papers of Franco Modigllani* 128 (MIT Press, 1980).

2. Laurence J. Kotlikoff and Lawrence H. Summers, "The Role of Intergenerational Transfers in Aggregate Capital Accumulation," 89 *J. Pol. Econ.* 706 (1981); Laurence J. Kotlikoff, "Intergenerational Transfers and Savings," 2 *J. Econ. Persp.* 41 (1988). Other studies, while rejecting Modigliani's Life Cycle hypothesis, report smaller thought still large intergenerational transfers. See Willima G. Gale and John K. Scholz, "Intergenerational Transfers and the Accumulation of Wealth," 8 *J. Econ. Pers.* 145 (1994).

3. Thomas Love Peacock, II *Works: Crochet Castle* 253 (London: Richard Bentley, 1875).

4. Richard Dawkins, *The Selfish Gene* (Oxford U.P., 2006). See also Graham Bell, *Selection: The Mechanism of Evolution* 367–69 (Oxford U.P., 2d ed. 2008).

5. Sewall Wright, "Coefficents of Inbreeding and Relationship," 56 *American Naturalist* 330 (1922).

6. Hamilton's breakthrough articles on inclusive fitness may be found in Chapter 2 of volume I of his collected essays, *Narrow Roads of*

Gene Land (Oxford: W.H. Freeman, 1996). For a more extensive version of Hamilton's Rule, in the statistical form proposed by George Price, see W.D. Hamilton, "Selfish and Spiteful Behavior in an Evolutionary Model," 228 *Nature* 1218 (1970), in *Narrow Roads of Greenland*, at 177–82; Oren Harman, *The Price of Altruism* 367–68 (New York: W.W. Norton, 2010).

7. See http://www.huffingtonpost.com/2013/09/13/baby-elephant-cries_n_3920685.html.

8. Robert H. Frank, *The Darwin Economy: Liberty, Competition, and the Common Good* 16 (Princeton U.P., 2011).

9. See Amotz Zahavi and Avishag Zahavi, *The Handicap Principle: A Missing Piece of Darwin's Puzzle* (Oxford U.P., 1997).

10. Ewen Callaway, "Size doesn't always matter for peacocks," *Nature*, April 18, 2011.

11. Amotz Zahavi recognized this as a costly signaling strategy, one which had earlier been identified by economist Michael Spence in "Job Market Signaling," 87 *Q.J. Econ.* 355 (1973).

12. Charles Dickens, *Great Expectations* (London: Penguin Classics, 1996).

13. If the decision to reject an unequal split in an ultimatum game were just about abstract feelings of fairness and not about protecting future players, it wouldn't matter if the sender were entirely anonymous. But it does matter. Senders are more likely to offer one-sided splits when they think their identities are hidden and there's no one to "punish." See Vernon L. Smith, "Constructivist and Ecological Rationality in Economics," 93 *Am. Econ. Rev.* 465 (2003). See also Martjin Egas and Arno Riedl, "The Economics of Altruistic Punishment and the Maintenance of Cooperation," 275 *Proceedings of the Royal Society: Biological Sciences* 871 (2008).

14. This was E.O. Wilson's evolutionary explanation for spite in *Sociobiology: The New Synthesis* 119 (Harvard U.P., 1975). See also Stuart A. West and Andy Gardner, "Altruism, Spite, and Greenbeards," 327 *Science* 1341 (2010).

15. "Business in the Blood," *The Economist*, November 1, 2014.

16. Christopher Lasch, *Haven in a Heartless World: The Family Besieged* (New York: W.W. Norton, 1995).

CHAPTER 14

1. Robert L. Trivers, "The Evolution of Reciprocal Altruism," 46 *Q. Rev. Biology* 35 (1971). Trivers' insight found its way into the analysis of human behavior when political scientist Robert Axelrod and W.D. Hamilton recognized that patterns of reciprocal altruism could also be found amongst people. Robert Axelrod and W.D. Hamilton, "The Evolution of Cooperation," 211 *Science* 1390 (1981). See generally Robert Axelrod, *The Evolution of Cooperation* (New York: Basic, 1984).

2. On gift economies as an alternative to market economies, see Lewis Hyde, *The Gift: Imagination and the Erotic Life of Property* (New York: Vintage, 1983).

3. W.D. Hamilton, *II Narrow Roads of Geneland* 325 (Oxford U.P., 2001).

4. N.A. Christakis and J.H. Fowler, "Friendship and Natural Selection," 111 (Suppl. 3) *Proc. Nat'l. Acad. Sc.* 10796 (2014).

5. Alexander Todorov, Anesu Mandisodza, Amir Goren and Crystal Hall, "Inferences of Competence from Faces Predict Election Outcomes," 308 *Science* 1623 (2005).

6. Jonathan B. Freeman, Ryan M. Stolier, Zachary A. Ingbretsen and Eric A. Hehman, "Amygdala Responsivity to High-Level Social Information from Unseen Faces," 34 J. *Neuroscience* 1 (2014).

7. B. Duchenne, *The Mechanism of Human Facial Expression or an Electrophysiological Analysis of the Expression of the Emotions* (A. Cuthbertson trans.) (Cambridge U.P., 1990) [1862].

8. Charles Darwin, *The Expression of the Emotions in Man and Animals* 202 (New York: Oxford, 1998) [1872]. These findings have been replicated in recent tests. See Paul Ekman, Wallace V. Friesen, and Maureen O'Sullivan, "Smiles when Lying," in Paul Ekman and Erika L. Rosenberg, *What the Face Reveals* 201 (New York: Oxford, 1997). See generally Paul Ekman, *Telling Lies: Clues to Deceit in the Marketplace, Politics, and Marriage* (New York: Norton, 1985).

9. George C. Williams, *Adaptation and Natural Selection: A Critique of Some Current Evolutionary Thought* 94 (Princeton U.P., 1992).

10. *Noblesse Oblige* (London: Hamish Hamilton, 1956).

11. Tom Wolfe, *Mauve Gloves & Madmen, Clutter & Vine* 233 (Toronto: Collins, 1967).

12. Pierre Bourdieu, *Distinction: A Social Critique of the Judgment of Taste* (Harvard U.P., 1984).

13. James K. Galbraith, *Inequality and Instability: A Study of the World Economy Just Before the Great Crisis* 144 (Oxford U.P., 2012).

14. Charles Murray, *Coming Apart: The State of White America, 1960–2010* (New York: Crown Forum, 2012). Before Murray, Christopher Lasch described the emergence of a haughty and déraciné New Class in his last book, *The Revolt of the Elites and the Betrayal of Democracy* (New York: W.W. Norton, 1995).

15. Irving Kristol, *Two Cheers for Capitalism* 14–17 (New York: Basic Books, 1978).

16. Joel Kotkin, *The New Class Conflict* (Candor NY: Telos, 2014).

17. Emily Badger, "Strong Correlation between Politics, Home Prices in U.S.," *Washington Post*, Oct. 28, 2014.

18. Bill Bishop, *The Big Sort* (New York: Houghton Mifflin, 2008.)

19. Robert A. Dahl, *Democracy in the United States: Promise and Performance* 309 (Chicago: Rand McNally, 1972).

20. Bill Clinton, "We Have Only One Remaining Bigotry," *The New Republic*, November 20, 2014.

21. At http://www.foxnews.com/politics/elections/2012-exit-poll.

22. Benjamin I. Page, Larry M. Bartels, and Jason Seawright, "Democracy and the Policy Preferences of Wealthy Americans," 11 *Perspectives on Politics* 51 (2013).

23. Benjamin I. Page and Cari Lynn Hennessy, "What Affluent Americans Want from Politics," at: http://ssrn.com/abstract–1665082 (2010).

24. http://www.ropercenter.uconn.edu/elections/how_groups_voted/voted_12.html.

25. See E.E. Schattschneider, *The Semi-Sovereign People: A Realist's View of Democracy in America* (New York: Holt, Rinehart and Winston, 1960);

George Stigler, "The Theory of Economic Regulation," Bell J. Econ. Management Sc. 3 (1971).

26. Martin Gilens and Benjamin I. Page, "Testing Theories of American Politics: Elites, Interest Groups, and Average Citizens," 12 Perspectives on Politics 564

27. As discussed in F.H. Buckley (ed.), *The American Illness: Essays on the Rule of Law* (Yale U.P., 2013).

28. Amy Mitchell, Jeffrey Gottfried, Jocelyn Kiley, and Katerina Matsa, "Political Polarization & Media Habits," Pew Research Journalism Project, Oct. 21, 2014.

29. At http://www.njdc.org/blog/post/4questions.

30. At http://www.yourrepublicanuncle.com/.

31. Robert Costa and Jose A. Del Real, "GOP's anti-Obamacare Push Gains new Momentum in Wake of Gruber Video," *Washington Post*, November 12, 2014.

32. Pierre Boudieu observed the same ossification of classes in France, another ostensibly meritocratic society. Pierre Bourdieu, "The Forms of Capital," in *Handbook of Theory and Research for the Sociology of Education* (John. G. Richardson, ed.) (New York: Greenwood, 1986).

33. Milovan Djilas, *The New Class: An Analysis of the Communist System* (New York: Praeger, 1957).

34. Gaetano Mosca, *The Ruling Class* 61 (trans. Hannah D. Kahn) (New York: McGraw-Hall, 1939).

CHAPTER 15

1. D.L. Keir, *The Constitutional History of Modern Britain* 414, at n. 5 (London: Adam & Charles Black, 1948). John Cannon, *Parliamentary Reform 1640–1832* 257 (Cambridge U.P., 1973).

2. Benjamin Disraeli, *Sybil, or the Two Nations* 76–77 (London: Longmans, Green, 1871).

3. Mark Girouard, *The Return to Camelot: Chivalry and the English Gentleman* 92–110 (Yale. U.P., 1982).

4. Thomas Carlyle, *Past and Present* 148 (Richard D. Altick, ed.) (NYU Press, 1965).

5.   Charles Whibley, I *Lord John Manners and His Friends* 133–38 (Edinburgh: Blackwood, 1925).

6.   Kenelm Henry Digby, *Broad Stone of Honour* 17 (London: R. Gilbert, 1823).

7.   Karl Marx and Friedrich Engels, *The Communist Manifesto* 97 (New York: Simon and Schuster, 1964).

8.   Whibley, at 153.

9.   Crane Britton, *English Political Thought in the Nineteenth Century* 131 (London: Ernest Benn, 1933).

10.   Shropshire Conservative, Aug. 31, 1844, quoted in William Monypenny, II *The Life of Benjamin Disraeli* 231 (New York: Macmillan, 1913).

11.   Max Weber, *Political Writings* 121–22 (Peter Lassman and Ronald Speirs, eds.) (Cambridge U.P., 1994).

12.   Voltaire, *The History of the War of Seventeen Hundred and Forty One* 224 (London: J. Nourse, 1756) ("The English officers saluted the French by taking off their hats. The count de Chabannes and the duke de Biron advanced forward, and returned the compliment.")

13.   Booker T. Washington, *Up from Slavery: An Autobiography* 1 (New York: Doubleday, Page, 1907). See Robert J. Norrell, *Up from History: The Life of Booker T. Washington* (Harvard U.P., 2011).

14.   Booker T. Washington, at 300.

15.   Nasim Nicholas Taleb, *Antifragile: Things that Gain from Disorder* (New York: Random House, 2012); Charles Murray, *Coming Apart: The State of White America, 1960–2010* (New York: Random House, 2012).

16.   Kenelm Henry Digby, *The Broad Stone of Honor: Godefridus* 116 (London: Joseph Booker, 1824).

17.   "The Politics of Giving," *Philanthropy Magazine*, August 19, 2012. See also "How States Compare and How They Voted in the 2012 Election," *The Chronicle of Philanthropy*, Oct. 5, 2014, at http://philanthropy.com/article/How-States-CompareHow/149169/.

18.   Arthur C. Brooks, *Who Really Cares? The Surprising Truth about Compassionate Conservatism* (New York: Basic Books, 2007).

19.   http://www.defense.gov/news/Dec2005/d20051213mythfact.pdf.

20. See Peter J. Wallison, *Hidden in Plain Sight: What Really Caused the World's Worst Financial Crisis and Why It Could Happen Again* (New York: Encounter Books, 2015).

21. *The Financial Crisis Inquiry Report, Financial Crisis Inquiry Commission* 91 (New York: Public Affairs, 2011); Bethany Mclean and Joe Nocera, *All the Devils Are Here: The Hidden History of the Financial Crisis* (New York: Penguin, 2010).

22. John A. Allison, *The Financial Crisis and the Free Market Cure* 39 (New York: McGraw Hill, 2013).

23. Karl Marx, *The Eighteenth Brumaire of Louis Napoleon* 83 (trans. Daniel deLeon (Chicago: Charles H. Kerr, 1913).

24. See Fernanda Santos, "N.A.A.C.P. on Defensive as Suit on Charter Schools Splits Group's Supporters," *N.Y. Times*, June 10, 2011; http://www.naacp.org/blog/entry/the-immigration-movement-advancing-social-and-economic-justice-for-all; http://www.courts.mo.gov/SUP/index.nsf/0/1d75c81ee711b9238625767800592obe/$FILE/SC90107 Nat'l_Assoc_for_the_Advancement_of_Colored_People_%20Amicus_Brief.pdf.

25. Emily Bazelon, "The Place of Women on the Court," *N.Y. Times Magazine*, July 7, 2009.

CHAPTER 16

1. Henry Adams, "The Education of Henry Adams," in *Adams* 963 (New York: Library of America, 1983).

2. Henry James, "Pandora," *18 Novels and Tales* 95, 131 (New York: Scribner's, 1909).

3. Henry Adams, *The Degradation of the Democratic Dogma,* (New York: Macmillan, 1919).

4. John J. Mearsheimer, *The Tragedy of Great Power Politics* 220 (New York: W.W. Norton, 2014).

5. *Lincoln: Speeches and Writings 1832–1858* 1, 4 (To the People of Sangamo County, March 9, 1832).

6. Paul Bixler, "Horace Mann, —'Mustard Seed,'" 7 *American Scholar* 24, 25 (1938).

7. At http://bullittcountyhistory.org/bullitthistory/bchistory/schoolexam1912.html.

8. Quoted in David Tyack, *Seeking Common Ground: Public Schools in a Diverse Society* (Harvard U.P., 2003).

9. Philip Hamburger, *Separation of Church and State* 22 (Harvard U.P., 2002).

10. See Mitchell v. Helms, 530 U.S. 793, 828–29 (plurality opinion of Thomas, J., joined by Rehnquist, C.J., and Scalia and Kennedy, JJ.) (2000).

11. Id. at 422–34.

12. Everson v. Board of Education, 330 U.S. 1 (1947).

13. Zelman v. Simmons-Harris, 536 U.S. 639 (2002).

14. Jack Beatty, *Rascal King: The Life and Times of James Michael Curley* 27–28 (Boston: Da Capo Press, 1992).

15. Eric A. Hanuskek and Ludger Woessmann, "The Economics of International Differences in Educational Achievement," in III *Handbook of the Economics of Education* 89, 168–69 (Eric A. Hanuskek, Stephen Machin and Ludger Woessmann, eds.) (San Diego: North-Holland, 2011).

16. Eric Hanushek, Paul E. Peterson, and Ludger Woessmann, *Endangering Prosperity: A Global View of the American School* Paperback 12, 61–63 (Brookings, 2013).

17. Lynne G. Zucker and Michael R. Darby, "Star Scientists, Innovation and Regional and National Immigration," in David B. Audretsch, Robert E. Litan, and Robert J. Strom (eds.), *Entrepreneurship and Openness: Theory and Evidence* 181 (2009).

18. Adler v. Ontario, [1996] 3 S.C.R. 609 at § 29 per Iacobucci J.

19. Josh Freedman, "The Farce of Meritocracy: Why Legacy Admissions Might Actually Be A Good Thing," *Forbes*, Nov. 11, 2013.

20. Daniel Golden, *The Price of Admission: How America's Ruling Class Buys Its Way into Elite Colleges—and Who Gets Left Outside the Gates* (New York: Three Rivers, 2006).

21. Even public universities play the legacy game, especially when it comes to the children of members of the state appropriations committee.

Reeve Hamilton, "Lawmakers' Role in UT Admissions Under the Microscope," *Texas Tribune*, Feb. 27, 2014.

22. Todd Balf, "The Story Behind the SAT Overhaul," *N.Y. Times Magazine*, March 6, 2014.

23. Suzanne Mettler, *Degrees of Inequality* (New York: Basic, 2014).

24. Richard Arum and Josipa Roksa, *Academically Adrift: Limited Learning on College Campuses* (U. Chicago P., 2010).

25. On how spending more money on schools does little to improve student performance, see Eric A. Hanushek and Alfred A. Lindseth, *Schoolhouses, Courthouses, and Statehouses: Solving the Funding-Achievement Puzzle in America's Public Schools* (Princeton U.P., 2009).

26. Eric A. Hanushek, Paul E. Peterson, and Ludger Woessmann, *Endangering Prosperity: A Global View of the American School* 96–98 (Washington: Brookings Institution, 2013).

27. Id. at 40–42.

28. http://www.stormfront.org/forum/t1009169/.

29. Ludger Woessmann, Elke Lüdemann, Gabriela Schütz, and Martin R. West, "School Accountability, Autonomy, Choice, and the Level of Student Achievement: International Evidence from PISA 2003," OECD Education Working Papers No. 13 at 20 (OECD Publishing, Nov. 14, 2008). See also Suzanne E. Cannon, Bartley R. Danielsen, and David M. Harrison, "School Vouchers and Home Prices: Premiums in School Districts Lacking Public Schools," ___ *Journal of Housing Research* ___ (2016).

30. "Caroline M. Hoxby, School Choice, and School Productivity. Could School Choice Be a Tide that Lifts All Boats?," in *The Economics of School Choice* (Caroline M. Hoxby, ed., U. Chicago P., 2003).

31. Emma Brown, "Stepped-up Competition for Students," *Washington Post*, July 2, 2014, at A1.

32. See Steven Brill, *Class Warfare: Inside the Fight to Fix America's Schools* (New York: Simon & Schuster, 2011). For inside (and not unbiased) accounts, see Chester E. Finn, *Troublemaker: A Personal History of School Reform since Sputnik* (Princeton U.P., 2008); Michelle Rhee, *Radical: Fighting to Put Students First* (New York: HarperCollins, 2013).

33. Open Secrets, Top All-Time Donors, 1989–2012, at http://www.opensecrets.org/orgs/list.php.

34. John J. Miller, "Why School Choice Lost," *Wall Street Journal*, Nov. 3, 1993.

CHAPTER 17

1. For the United States, see http://www.census.gov/prod/2010pubs/acs-11.pdf and http://www.cis.org/immigrants_profile_2007. For Canada, see http://www4.hrsdc.gc.ca/.3ndic.1t.4r@-eng.jsp?iid=38. For Australia, see http://www.immi.gov.au/media/fact-sheets/15population.htm. For Great Britain, see Office for National Statistics. http://www.statistics.gov.uk/downloads/theme_population/population-by-birthcountrynationality-apr09-mar10.zip (Great Britain).

2. Letter to Owen Lovejoy, August 11, 1855, *Lincoln: Speeches and Writings 1832–1858* 357, 358 (Library of America, 1974).

3. Speech at Chicago, July 10, 1858, id. at 439, 456.

4. Maldwyn Jones, *American Immigration* 224–38 (U. Chicago P., 1992). Restrictions on Chinese and Japanese immigration had previously been added, beginning in 1882 and renewed subsequently. Other legislation excluded undesirables, including paupers, convicts and anarchists.

5. 2012 Yearbook of Immigration Statistics: Office of Immigration Statistics (July 2013).

6. Bryan Baker and Nancy Rytina, Estimates of the Unauthorized Immigrant Population Residing in the United States: January 2012, Dept. of Homeland Security, Office of Immigration Statistic.

7. 8 The Social Contract Press (1998).

8. Ernest Renan, *Qu'est-ce qu'une nation?* (Paris: Presses-Pocket, 1992).

9. Samuel P. Huntington, *Who We Are: The Challenges to America's National Identity* (New York: Simon & Schuster, 2004); Arthur M. Schlesinger, *The Disuniting of America: Reflections on a Multicultural Society* (New York: W.W. Norton, 1998).

10. George J. Borjas, "The Slowdown in the Economic Assimilation of Immigrants: Aging and Cohort Effects Revisited Again," __ J.

Human Capital ___ (2015).

11. George J. Borjas, *Immigration Economics* 152–53 (Harvard U.P., 2014). For an argument that immigrants are a net benefit to native-born Americans, see Daniel T. Griswold, *Immigration and the Welfare State*, 32 Cato J. 159 (2012).

12. Id. at 94. See also Patricia Cortes, "The Effect of Low-Skilled Immigration on U.S. Prices: Evidence from CPI Data," 116 *J. Pol. Econ.* 381 (2008) (finding a two percent drop in low-skilled wages on a ten percent increase in immigration levels). For a dissenting view, see David Card, "Is the New Immigration Really So Bad?," 115 *Economic Journal* 300 (2005). Card looked at changes in the labor market in high immigration cities, and reported that he did not find that immigration harmed the low-skilled native-born. In response, Borjas argues that Card fails to take adequate account of native out-migration to other U.S. cities when faced with competition from immigrants.

13. George J. Borjas, Jeffrey Grogger, and Gordon H. Hanson, "Immigration and the Economic Status of African-American Men," 77 *Economica* 255 (2010) (using 1960–2000 data). See Edward S. Shihadeh and Raymond E. Barranco, "Latino Employment and Black Violence: the Unintended Consequence of U.S. Immigration Policy," 88 *Social Forces* 1393 (2010).

14. One economist estimates that up to 1.5 million skilled immigrants here on temporary visas are stuck in a queue awaiting a green card, and that most will return to their country of origin. Vivek Wadhwa, *The Immigrant Exodus: Why America Is Losing the Global Race to Capture Entrepreneurial Talent* (Wharton Press, 2012).

15. Alan J. Auerbach and Philip Oreopoulos, "The Fiscal Effect of U.S. Immigration: A Generational-Accounting Perspective," 14 *Tax Policy and the Economy* 123 (2000); Michael J. Greenwood and John M. McDowell, *Legal U.S. Immigration: Influences on Gender, Age, and Skill Composition* (Kalamazoo: W.E. Upjohn, 1999).

16. See, e.g., George J. Borjas, *Heaven's Door: Immigration Policy and the American Economy* 192–93 (Princeton U.P., 1999); Pia M. Orrenius and Madeline Zavodny, *Beside the Golden Door: U.S. Immigration Reform in a new*

Era of Globalization (Washington: AEI, 2010).

17. For Canada see http://www.cic.gc.ca/EnGLish/resources/statis-tics/facts2012/permanent/01.asp; for the U.S. see http://www.dhs.gov/sites/default/files/publications/ois_lpr_fr_2013.pdf.

18. Abdurrahman Aydemir and George J. Borjas, "Cross-Country Variation in the Impact of International Migration: Canada, Mexico, and the United States," 5 *Journal of the European Economic Association* 663 (2007).

19. George J. Borjas, "Making it in America: Social Mobility in the Immigrant Population," 16 *The Future of Children* 55 (2006).

20. Which is not to say that, on arrival, Canadian immigrants earn as much as native-born Canadians, particularly when they arrive from Third World countries. Foreign skills and education credentials don't translate into dollars as much as the skills and education natives acquire in Canada. However, immigrant earnings increase sharply after arrival. David A. Green and Christopher Worswick, "Entry Earnings of Immigrant Men in Canada: The Roles of Labour Market Entry Effects and Returns to Foreign Experience," in Ted McDonald, Elizabeth Ruddick, Arthur Sweetman, and Christopher Worswick (eds.), *Canadian Immigration: Economic Evidence for a Dynamic Policy Environment* 77 (Kingston, Ont.: McGill-Queen's U.P., 2010).

21. Abdurrhaman Aydemir, Wen-Hao Chen, and Miles Corak, "Intergenerational Earnings Mobility among the Children of Canadian Immigrants," IZA Discussion Papers 2085 (2006).

22. George J. Borjas, "Making it in America: Social Mobility in the Immigrant Population," 16 *The Future of Children* 55 (2006).

23. Mark Hugo Lopez and Paul Taylor, "Latino Voters in the 2012 Election," Pew Research Hispanic Trends Project (Nov. 7, 2012), at http://www.pewhispanic.org/2012/11/07/latino-voters-in-the-2012-election/.

24. Elise Foley, "Latino Voters in Election 2102 Help Sweep Obama to Reelection," *Huffington Post*, Nov. 7, 2012. See Peter S. Canellos, "Obama Victory Took Root in Kennedy-inspired Immigration Act," *Boston Globe*, Nov. 11, 2008.

25. At https://www.uschamber.com/immigration.

CHAPTER 18

1. See W. Kip Viscusi, "Regulation, Taxation and Litigation," in F.H. Buckley (ed.), *The American Illness: Essays on the Rule of Law* 270 (Yale U.P., 2013).

2. Sutirtha Bagchi and Jan Svejnar, "Does Wealth Inequality Matter for Growth? The Effect of Billionaire Wealth, Income Distribution, and Poverty," Institute for the Study of Labor Discussion Paper 7733, November 2013.

3. Gordon Tullock, "The Welfare Costs of Tariffs, Monopolies and Theft," 5 *Western Econ. J.* 224 (1967). See also Gordon Tullock, *Rent Seeking* (Brookfield, Vt.: Edward Elgar, 1993).

4. "Yoga in America Study 2012," *Yoga Journal*, at http://www.yoga-journal.com/press/yoga_in_america.

5. Chopra Centered Lifestyle, at http://www.chopra.com/ccl/exploring-the-seven-spiritual-laws-of-yoga.

6. Alex Grieg, "Obama Releasing 'Reformed' Guantanamo Prisoners for Reasons including Having Taken up Yoga and Showing a 'Positive Attitude'," *Daily Mail*, June 8, 2014.

7. A.G. Sulzberger, "Yoga Faces Regulation, and Firmly Pushes Back," *New York Times,* July 10, 2009.

8. Dick M. Carpenter and Lisa Knepper, "License to Work: A National Study—Burdens from Occupational Licensing, Institute for Justice" (2012). For an argument that licensing boards should be subject to antitrust review, see Aaron Edlin and Rebecca Haw, "Cartels by another Name: Should Licensed Occupations Face Antitrust Scrutiny," 162 *U. Pa. L. Rev.* 1093 (2014).

9. Edwards, v. District of Columbia, 755 F.3d 996 (2014).

10. St. Joseph Abbey v. Castille, 712 F.3d 215 (2013), cert. den. 134 S. Ct. 423 (2013).

11. Rosalind Helderman, "Uber's Aggressive Tactics Push Change," *Washington Post*, Dec. 14, 2014, at A1.

12. Christine Lagarde, "The Challenge Facing the Global Economy: New Momentum To Overcome a New Mediocre," at http://www.imf.org/external/np/speeches/2014/100214.htm.

13. "The Moment of Truth," The National Commission on Fiscal Responsibility and Reform, White House 2010 11 (Washington: White House). See also "Federal Debt and the Risk of a Fiscal Crisis," Congressional Budget Office, July 27, 2010.

14. Benjamin M. Blau, "Central Bank Intervention and the Role of Political Connections," Mercatus Center, George Mason University, October 2013.

15. Elizabeth Warren and Joe Manchin, "The Fed Needs Governors Who Aren't Wall Street Insiders," *Wall Street Journal*, Nov. 18, 2014, at A19.

16. George Stigler, "The Theory of Economic Regulation," 3 *Bell J. Econ.* 3 (1971).

17. Charles W. Calomiris and Stephen H. Haber, *Fragile by Design: The Political Origins of the Banking Crises and Scarce Credit* 208 (Princeton U.P., 2014).

18. See David Stockman, *The Great Deformation: The Corruption of Capitalism in America* 270–73 (New York: PublicAffairs, 2013).

19. Joseph E. Stiglitz, *The Price of Inequality: How Today's Divided Society Endangers Our Future* 244 (New York: W.W. Norton, 2012).

20. Carl Van Horn, Cliff Zukin and Allison Kopicki, *Left Behind: The Long-term Unemployed Struggle in an Improving Economy* (New Brunswick, N.J.: John J. Heldrich Center for Workforce Development, Sept. 2014).

21. Fareed Zakaria, "How to Restore the American Dream," *Time Magazine*, Oct. 21, 2010.

22. Mark P. Keightley and Molly F. Sherlock, "The Corporate Income Tax System: Overview and Options for Reform, Congressional Research Service" 7-5700 (Sept. 13, 2012).

23. See Corporate Income Tax: Effective Tax Rates Can Differ Significantly from the Statutory Rate, GAO-13-520, May 30, 2013. The GAO figures about the effective tax rate have been challenged. Andrew Lyon has argued that 2010 was an unrepresentative year, as it fell in the middle of the recession, and when he extended the analysis to a more representative period (2004–10) and counted foreign, federal, state,

and local taxes, he found that the effective tax rate was 36 percent. Andrew B. Lyon, "Another Look at Corporate Effective Tax Rates, 2004–2010," *Tax Notes* 313 (Oct. 21, 2013).

24. David Kocieniewski, "G.E.'s Strategies Let It Avoid Taxes Altogether," *New York Times*, March 24, 2011; John McCormack, "GE Filed 57,000-Page Tax Return, Paid No Taxes on $14 Billion in Profits," *Weekly Standard*, Nov. 17, 2011.

25. See Lucian A. Bebchuk and Jesse M. Fried, "Pay without Performance: The Unfulfilled Promise of Executive Compensation Overview of the Issues," 17 *Journal of Applied Corporate Finance* 8 (2005); Lucian A. Bebchuk and Jesse M. Fried, *Pay without Performance: The Unfulfilled Promise of Executive Compensation* (Harvard U.P., 2004).

26. Michael C. Jensen and Kevin J. Murphy, "Pay and Top-Management Incentives," 98 *J. Pol. Econ.* 225 (1990); Michael C. Jensen and Kevin J. Murphy, "CEO Incentives: It's Not How Much You Pay, But How," 3 *Harv. Bus. Rev.* (May-June, 1990).

27. Joseph Fuller and Michael C. Jensen, "Just Say No to Wall Street: Putting a Stop to the Earnings Game," 14 *J. App. Corp. Fin.* 41 (2002).

28. Harold Meyerson, "Workers Deserve to Benefit from their Productivity, too," *Washington Post*, September 18, 2014.

29. Currently, the fair market value of stock paid to executives is included in income at ordinary rates at the time the executive receives it. When compensated in stock options, only the value of the option is included in income on receipt. When the stock is sold, however, the gain is taxed at the lower capital gains rates. Executives also lower their taxes by moving their company stock into tax-preferred accounts such as 401(k)'s. It was reported that Mitt Romney's IRA was worth between 20 and 101 million dollars.

30. Marianne Bertrand and Sendhil Mullainathan, "Are CEOs Rewarded for Luck?," 116 *Q.J. Econ.* 901 (2001).

31. Managerial misbehavior theories also assume that firm managers of public firms overpay themselves because they aren't sufficiently policed by corporate boards, but their compensation has actually increased less

than that of managers in privately-held firms. Jon Bakija, Adam Cole, and Bradley T. Heim, "Jobs and Income Growth of Top Earners and the Causes of Changing Income Inequality: Evidence from U.S. Tax Return Data." Firms also discipline pooly performing managers. See also Kevin J. Murphy and Ján Zábojnik, "CEO Pay and Appointments: A Market-Based Explanation for Recent Trends," 94 *Am. Econ. Rev.* 192 (2004).

32. Steven N. Kaplan and Joshua Rauh, "Wall Street and Main Street: What Contributes to the Rise in the Highest Incomes?," 23 *Rev. Fin. Stud.* 1004 (2010).

33. Piscataway: Transaction, 1932.

34. See F.H. Buckley, "The Divestiture Decision," 16 *J. Corp. Law* 805 (1991).

35. Henry G. Manne, "Mergers and the Market for Corporate Control," 73 *J. Pol. Econ.* 110 (1965). If the offeree firm thought the offer price too low, it could always contest the bid through a buyback offer at a higher price.

36. Along with Congress, the courts also got into the act, by permitting offeree management to take defensive measures against takeover bids through "poison pills" that made the firm far less attractive to offerors. For example, the offeror's shares might be diluted after a successful bid, or incumbent management might be given the right to enormously lucrative severance agreements ("golden parachutes").

37. Henry G. Manne, "The Follies of Regulation," *Wall Street Journal*, Sept. 27, 2005. See also Jonathan R. Macey, *Corporate Governance: Promises Kept, Promises Broken* (Princeton U.P., 2008). Other corporate law reforms have served incumbent management well. The securities legislation passed in the 1930s by New Dealers who subscribed to the Berle-Means thesis protects large public firms and their managers from competition by upstarts, who find it much more costly to comply with burdensome prospectus requirements than did established businesses. See George J. Benston, "The Value of the SEC's Accounting Disclosure Requirements," 44 *Acc. Rev.* 515 (1969). In addition, populist-inspired legislation in America has made it more difficult for institutional investors such as pension plans and insurance companies, which own

large blocks of shares, to take the same kind of active role in supervising management that they do in European countries. See, e.g., Mark J. Roe, "Some Differences in Corporate Structure in Germany, Japan, and the United States," 102 *Yale L.J.* 1927 (1993); Mark J. Roe, *Strong Managers, Weak Owners* (Princeton U.P., 1996).

38. Richard Williams and Mark Adams, "Regulatory Overload" (Arlington VA: Mercatus Center, 2012).

CHAPTER 19

1. Reuven Brenner, *The Force of Finance: Triumph of the Capital Markets* 9 (New York: Texere, 2001).

2. Jesse Eisinger, "Why Only One Top Banker Went to Jail for the Financial Crisis," *N.Y. Times*, April 30, 2014.

3. See Jeffrey S. Parker, "Corporate Crime, Overcriminalization, and the Failure of American Public Morality," in F.H. Buckley, *The American Illness*, at 407, 408, 418.

4. Statement of Jim E. Lavine before the House Committee on the Judiciary Subcommittee on Crime, Terrorism, and Homeland Security, September 28, 2010, at http://judiciary.house.gov/hearings/pdf/Lavine100928.pdf. U.S. v. Evertson, 320 Fed. Appx. 509; 2009 U.S. App. LEXIS 5936 (9th Cir. 2009, cert. den., 130 Sup. Ct. 460 (2009).

5. Berry v. Leslie, 13-14092 (Eleventh Cir., Sept. 16, 2014). On the abuse of their authority by militarized American policemen, see Radley Balko, *The Rise of the Warrior Cop: The Militarization of America's Police Forces* (New York: Public Affairs, 2013).

6. Julie R. O'Sullivan, "The Federal Criminal 'Code' Is a Disgrace: Obstruction Statutes as a Case Study," 96 *J. Crim L & Criminology* 643, 643 (2006).

7. Id. at 652.

8. Abelard, "Intention and Sin," in *Freedom and Responsibility: Readings in Philosophy and Law* 170 (Herbert Morris, ed., 1964). See also Francis Sayre, "Mens Rea," 45 *Harv. L. Rev.* 974 (1932).

9. Oliver Wendell Holmes, *The Common Law* 38 (Boston: Little, Brown, 1881).

10. William Stuntz, "The Pathological Politics of Criminal Law," 100 *Mich. L. Rev.* 506, 511 (2001).

11. Quoted in Tom Wolfe, *Bonfire of the Vanities* 629 (New York: Bantam, 1988).

12. Edward B. Diskant, "Comparative Corporate Criminal Liability: Exploring the Uniquely American Doctrine through Comparative Criminal Procedure," 118 *Yale L.J.* 126 (2008).

13. Arthur Andersen LLP v. U.S., 544 U.S. 696 (2005).

14. United States Attorneys' Annual Statistical Report: Fiscal Year 2012, at http://www.justice.gov/usao/reading_room/reports/asr2012/12sstatrpt.pdf.

15. Statistics Canada, at http://www.statcan.gc.ca/pub/85-002-x/2010002/article/11293-eng.htm#a26.

16. See Ellen S. Pogdor, "The Challenge of White Collar Sentencing," 97 *J. of Criminal Law and Criminology* 731, 731–33 (2007).

17. On prosecutorial misbehavior, see Alex Kozinski, "Criminal Law 2.0," *Georgetown L.J. Ann. Rev. Crim. Proc.* I, xxii–xxvii (2015).

18. Harvey A. Silverglate, *Three Felonies a Day: How the Feds Target the Innocent* (New York: Encounter Books, 2009).

19. Id. at 114–22.

20. Felix G. Rohaytn, "The Blight on Wall Street," *New York Review of Books,* March 12, 1987; see also Michael M. Thomas, "Greed," *New York Review of Books*, March 29, 1990.

21. Daniel Fischel, *Payback: The Conspiracy To Destroy Michael Milken and his Financial Revolution* (Amazon Kindle, 2013). For a popular but not unsympathetic account of Milken's career, see Jesse Kornbluth, *Highly Confident: The Crime and Punishment of Michael Milken* (New York: William Morrow, 1992).

CHAPTER 20

1. Milton Friedman, "Economic Freedom behind the Scenes," Preface to Economic Freedom of the World Report: 2002 Annual Report (Washington: Cato, 2002).

2. "Where Is the Wealth of Nations? Measuring Capital for the 21st Century," (Washington: World Bank, 2006).

3. At http://data.worldjusticeproject.org/

4. At http://www.transparency.org/cpi2014/results.

5. Andrei Shleifer and Robert W. Vishny, "Corruption," 108 *Q.J. Econ.* 599 (1993); Stephen Knack and Philip Keefer, "Institutions and Economic Performance: Cross-country Tests Using Alternative Institutional Measures," 7 *Econ. & Politics* 207 (1995); Rafael L Porta, Florencio López-de-Silanes, Cristian Pop-Eleches, and Andrei Shleifer, "Judicial Checks and Balances," 112 *J. Pol. Econ.* 445 (2004). See generally Pranab Bardhan, "Corruption and Development: A Review of Issues," 35 *J. Econ. Lit.* 1320 (1997); Douglass North and Barry Weingast, "Constitutions and Commitment: The Evolutions of Institutions Governing Public Choice in Seventeenth Century England," 49 *J. Econ. Hist.* 803 (1989).

6. Sir Henry Maine, *Ancient Law* 165 (New York: Scribner, 1864).

7. See Michael Bridge, "An English Lawyer Looks at American Contract Law," in F.H. Buckley, *The American Illness*, at 291; Richard Epstein, "Contracts Small and Contract Large: Contract Law through the Lens of Laissez-Faire," in F.H. Buckley (ed.), *The Fall and Rise of Freedom of Contract* 25 (Duke U.P., 1999).

8. 847 F.2d 564 (9th Cir., 1988).

9. Erin O'Hara, O'Connor, and Larry E. Ribstein, "Exit and the American Illness," in F.H. Buckley, *The American Illness*, at 336.

10. J. Mark Ramseyer and Eric B. Rasmusen, "Are Americans More Litigious," in Buckley, *The American Illness*, at 69.

11. W. Kip Viscusi, "Does Product Liability Law Make Us Safer?," in F.H. Buckley, *The American Illness*, at 137.

12. See Michael Trebilcock and Paul-Erik Veel, "A Tamer Tort Law: The Canada-US Divide," and Daniel Jutras, "The American Illness and Comparative Civil Procedure," in F.H. Buckley, *The American Illness*, at 229, 159.

13. The extent to which the Supreme Court decision in Daimler AG v. Bauman, 571 U.S. ___ (2014) will prevent forum shopping of this kind remains an open question.

14. For a summary of the facts, see the decision of the NAFTA tribunal, which was shocked by the Mississippi decision but which

nevertheless decided that it lacked jurisdiction to overturn the award, see Loewen Group v. U.S., at http://www.state.gov/s/l/c3755.htm.

15. See Alexander Tabarrok and Eric Helland, "Court Politics: The Political Economy of Tort Awards," 42 *J. Law & Econ.* 157 (1999).

16. Richard Neely, *The Product Liability Mess: How Business Can Be Rescued from the Politics of State Courts* 4 (New York: Free Press, 1988).

17. See J. Mark Ramseyer and Eric B. Rasmusen, in F.H. Buckley, *The American Illness*, at 69.

CHAPTER 21

1. For an example of such a reform, see Elizabeth Nolan Brown, "Ohio Just Made It a Little Harder to Accidentally Commit a Crime," *Reason*, December 23, 2014.

2. This would close loopholes left open by the 2005 Class Action Fairness Act, and also address the problems of bias in interstate cases that are not class or mass tort actions.

3. Hegel's *Phenomenology of Spirit* §§ 178–96 (trans. A.V. Miller (Oxford U.P., 1977).

4. Alexandre Kojève, *Introduction to the Reading of Hegel: Lectures on the Phenomenology of Spirit* (trans. J.H. Nichols) (Cornell U.P., 1969).

5. Francis Fukuyama, *The End of History and the Last Man* 204 (New York; Avon, 1992).

6. Francis Fukuyama, *The Origins of Political Order: From Prehuman Times to the French Revolution* (New York: Farrar, Straus and Giroux, 2011); *Political Order and Political Decay: From the Industrial Revolution to the Globalization of Democracy* (New York: Farrar, Straus and Giroux, 2014).

7. Joseph A. Schumpeter, *Imperialism and Social Classes* 156 (New York: Augustus M. Kelly, 1951).

8. Mancur Olson's *The Rise and Decline of Nations: Economic Growth, Stagflation, and Social Rigidities* (Yale U.P., 1982).

9. Farrand I.133.

10. Montesquieu, *The Spirit of the Laws* 124 at VIII.16 (Cambridge U.P., 1989); Jean-Jacques Rousseau, *Social Contract* III.2 (Cambridge U.P., 1997).

11. David Hume, "Idea of a Perfect Commonwealth," in *Hume, Political Essays* 221 (Cambridge U.P., 1994).

12. Farrand I.136.

13. See George Tsebelis, *Veto Players: How Political Institutions Work* ch. I (Princeton U.P., 2002).

14. Friedrich Hayek, *The Fatal Conceit: The Errors of Socialism* (U. Chicago P., 1991).

15. Mancur Olson, *Power and Prosperity: Outgrowing Communist and Capitalist Dictatorships* 19–23 (New York: Basic Books, 2000).

16. *Bolingbroke: Political Writings* 257–58 (David Armitage ed., Cambridge U.P., 1997).

17. On how stronger political parties reduce minoritarian misbehavior costs, see Philip Keefer and Stuti Khemani, When Do Legislators Pass on Pork? "The Role of Political Parties in Determining Legislator Effort," 103 *Am. Pol. Sc. Rev.* 99 (2009).

APPENDIX A

1. Richard V. Burkhauser, Jeff Larrimore, and Kosali I. Simon, A "Second Opinion" on the Economic Health of the American Middle Class, 65 *National Tax Journal* 7 (2012).

2. Unlike Piketty-Saez and the CBO, Burkhart and his colleagues based their calculations on household earnings and not on separate tax filings or tax units within household. (A tax unit is every person who files a tax return, and there are more of them than there are households, since a household may be composed of the number of unmarried people who file separately.) To complicate things further, the authors divided the household income by the square root of the number of people in the family. Why the square root, and not simply by the number of family members? To take account of economies of scale in household finance. Two can't live as cheaply as one, in other words, but they are 1.41 (or 21/2) times better off than two people living separately. See Burkhauser on the Middle Class, Library of Economics and Liberty, at http://www.econtalk.org/archives/2012/04/burkhauser_on_t.html (interview with Russ Roberts).

3. "The Distribution of Household Income and Federal Taxes," Table 7, Congressional Budget Office, July 10, 2012.

4. Philip Armour, Richard V. Burkhauser and Jeff Larrimore, "Levels and Trends in U.S. Income and its Distribution: A Crosswalk from Market Income towards a Comprehensive Haig-Simons Income Approach," 81 *Southern Econ. J.* 271 (2014); Philip Armour, Richard V. Burkhauser, and Jeff Larrimore, "Deconstructing Income and Income Inequality Measures: A Crosswalk from Market Income to Comprehensive Income," 103 *Am. Econ. Rev.* 173 (2013).

5. Quoted in Thomas B. Edall, "What if We're Looking at Inequality the Wrong Way?," *New York Times*, June 26, 2013, at http://opinionator.blogs.nytimes.com/2013/06/26/what-if-were-looking-at-inequality-the-wrong-way/.

APPENDIX B

1. Harvard U.P., 2014.

2. Jonah Goldberg, Mr. Piketty's Big Book of Marxiness, *Commentary*, June 2014.

3. Piketty, at 93.

4. Robert J. Gordon, "Is U.S. Economic Growth Over? Faltering Innovation Confronts the Six Headwinds," NBER Working Paper 18315 (August 2012). For a response to his critics, see Robert J. Gordon, The Demise of U.S. Economic Growth: Restatement, Rebuttal, and Reflections (Jan. 20, 2014), at http://www.scribd.com/doc/208017699/The-Demise-of-U-S-Economic-Growth-Restatement-Rebuttal-and-Reflections.

5. Chris Giles, "Piketty's Findings Undercut by Errors," *Financial Times*, May 23, 2014. For Piketty's not unpersuasive response on the limitations of the data, see http://blogs.ft.com/money-supply/2014/05/23/piketty-response-to-ft-data-concerns/. See also Alan Reynolds, "Why Piketty's Wealth Data Are Worthless," *Wall Street J.*, July 10, 2011, at A11.

6. Edward N. Wolff and Maury Gittleman, "Inheritances and the Distribution of Wealth, Or Whatever Happened to the Great

Inheritance Boom?," BLS Working Paper 445 (January 2011).

7. Thomas Piketty, "About *Capital in the Twenty-First Century*," 105 *Am. Econ. Rev.: Papers and Proceedings* 1 (2015).

8. Daron Acemoğlu and James A. Robinson, "The Rise and Fall of General Laws of Capitalism" (August 2014), at http://economics.mit.edu/files/9834.

APPENDIX C

1. Strictly speaking, polynomial regressions (using both x and x^2 as explanatory variables) can be considered as multiple regressions, although this more generally refers to two explanatory variables that are not perfectly related according to a simple mathematical formula.

APPENDIX D

1. W.D. Hamilton, I *Narrow Roads of Geneland*, at 172–73.

2. For simplicity we're assuming that the character of altruism does not change between generations: either one is altruistic or one is not. We're also eliding over the difference between phenotypes (the observable characteristics of altruism) and genes.

3. Does that mean that parents should sacrifice everything for their children? Because they don't, even if it may seem like that on occasion. Instead we apply what economists call a "social discount rate" when it comes to future generations. We front-end load our pleasures and discount those of our descendants—even if this might happen to be inconsistent with selfish gene theories. What we might end up with is something like Lawrence Kotlikoff's 80-20 ratio that we saw in the last chapter. With an additional $100, we'd save $80 for our children and spend only $20 on ourselves.

4. I *Narrow Roads of Geneland*, at 173–74.

5. Price found a superb biographer in Oren Harman, *The Price of Altruism: George Price and the Search for the Origins of Kindness* (New York: W.W. Norton, 2010).

Index